CONTEMPORARY APPROACHES TO BEHAVIOUR AND MENTAL HEALTH IN THE CLASSROOM

Based on latest research in the field, this book links theory and practice with key agendas and policies on behaviour, children's mental health and well-being. It considers how policy and research influence each other and provides a range of whole-school and individual-teacher actions to support all children, but particularly for those whose behaviour is seen as challenging.

Emma Clarke provides guidance on how practitioners can most effectively support children and manage pupils' behaviour and tracks how theory and policy has had a meaningful impact on what we do in the classroom. The book is divided into three distinct parts, each with its own set of reflective activities and thinking points as well as suggestions for further reading. Chapters in Part I include a focus on what informs the actions taken to support and manage behaviour in the classroom. In Part II, the chapters move on to consider specific approaches and delve into the theories and research which underpin them. Part III shares ethos-focused approaches to supporting behaviour, including the use of philosophical inquiry by Dr Aimee Quickfall, a timely and highly important review of the 'eternal' verities' by Professor John Visser, and an overview of Finnish perspectives on behaviour in schools, as Finland is often, and rightly, held up as a beacon on good practice.

The book presents a range of research, policy and practice and, as such, aims to be of use to a range of readers. It can support and develop practitioners in the classroom, from early career teachers to those with a wealth of experience, as well as senior leaders and those working in wider contexts with children. It will also be useful for students and researchers due to the balance of theory and practice presented.

Dr Emma Clarke is a lecturer in Education at Bishop Grosseteste University, UK, after teaching in primary schools for almost 18 years. Her interests include approaches to managing behaviour and challenging behaviour in schools. She has presented her research nationally and internationally, as well as publishing both in books and peer-reviewed journals.

Connecting Research with Practice in Special and Inclusive Education
Series edited by Philip Garner

This new series represents a commitment to supporting the emergence of applied research in Special and Inclusive Education. It comprises an authoritative collection of books which examine in depth the key issues being experienced in the field, both currently and into the future. These have been selected to illustrate both national and international dimensions of a chosen theme in Special and Inclusive Education. Each book has been commissioned from leading writers each of whom has substantial experience in their topic and who is also recognised for their capacity to connect a body of systematic evidence to the needs of a practitioner audience. Authors contributing to the series are often practitioners or practitioner-researchers themselves.

On Educational Inclusion
An Exploration of Meanings, History, and Issues
Edited by James M Kauffman

Establishing Pathways to Inclusion
Investigating the Experiences and Outcomes for Students with Special Educational Needs
Richard Rose and Michael Shevlin

Contemporary Approaches to Behaviour and Mental Health in the Classroom
Weaving Together Theory, Practice, Policy and Educational Discourse
Emma Clarke

For more information about this series, please visit: https://www.routledge.com/Connecting-Research-with-Practice-in-Special-and-Inclusive-Education/book-series/CRPSIE

CONTEMPORARY APPROACHES TO BEHAVIOUR AND MENTAL HEALTH IN THE CLASSROOM

Weaving Together Theory, Practice, Policy and Educational Discourse

Emma Clarke

LONDON AND NEW YORK

First published 2022
by Routledge
2 Park Square, Milton Park, Abingdon, Oxon OX14 4RN

and by Routledge
605 Third Avenue, New York, NY 10158

Routledge is an imprint of the Taylor & Francis Group, an informa business

© 2022 Emma Clarke

The right of Emma Clarke to be identified as author of this work has been asserted by her in accordance with sections 77 and 78 of the Copyright, Designs and Patents Act 1988.

All rights reserved. No part of this book may be reprinted or reproduced or utilised in any form or by any electronic, mechanical, or other means, now known or hereafter invented, including photocopying and recording, or in any information storage or retrieval system, without permission in writing from the publishers.

Trademark notice: Product or corporate names may be trademarks or registered trademarks, and are used only for identification and explanation without intent to infringe.

British Library Cataloguing-in-Publication Data
A catalogue record for this book is available from the British Library

Library of Congress Cataloging-in-Publication Data
A catalog record has been requested for this book

ISBN: 978-0-367-47426-3 (hbk)
ISBN: 978-0-367-47427-0 (pbk)
ISBN: 978-1-003-03552-7 (ebk)

DOI: 10.4324/9781003035527

Typeset in Bembo
by SPi Technologies India Pvt Ltd (Straive)

CONTENTS

Introduction: new perspectives on classroom behaviour?   1

PART I
Framing the actions we take   15

1   Behaviour, well-being and mental health   17

2   Acronyms and attitudes   35

3   School policies: possibilities and problems   52

Framing the actions we take: conclusion   71

PART II
Introduction: Attitudes, beliefs and perspectives   73

4   Theory and the classroom   75

5   Restorative practice: reconciliation and restitution   105

6   Solution focused working: celebrating success   124

Attitudes, beliefs and perspectives: conclusion   142

PART III
Beyond strategies to embedded ethos 145

7 Philosophical inquiry as a tool for well-being 147
   Aimee Quickfall

8 Verities revisited: keeping behaviour in perspective 161
   John Visser

9 International perspectives: behaviour management in Finland 176
   *Erkko Sointu, Katariina Waltzer, Juuso Pursiainen,
   Aino Äikäs and Kristiina Lappalainen*

Beyond strategies to embedded ethos: conclusion 202

Final thoughts 209

Index 212

INTRODUCTION

New perspectives on classroom behaviour?

It may seem unusual to begin a book on 'new perspectives' by questioning whether any perspectives actually are new! The aim of this book is not to claim knowledge of a host of radical new perspectives that mean you are never challenged by behaviour in the classroom again, but to review, re-introduce, refresh and possibly reinvigorate your perspectives on the behaviours that you encounter. In this sense then, the 'new perspectives' relate to providing an opportunity to consider and reflect on practice in schools and how (or if and when) research and policy influence the work with children whose behaviours challenge. These 'new perspectives' might indeed be entirely 'new' for you as a reader. You might be familiar with the approach or strategy, but the 'new' perspective could be understanding how policy has influenced actions in schools, or how research underpins or even contradicts approaches with children. You may also be an experienced practitioner or have a wealth of experience in an allied field and are simply engaged in life-long learning – after all, can we ever really know enough about a topic? Whatever stage you are at and for whatever reasons you are engaging with this book, I hope that by providing you with information – but also, critically, the opportunity to reflect on what this might mean for you, in your own setting, with your own pupils or within your own philosophy of teaching – that the 'perspectives' in this book will provide an opportunity to understand practice in a 'new' or different way.

In a research paper evaluating the impact of a specific approach to supporting behaviour (discussed in Chapter 5), the author highlighted one of the biggest advantages for those involved in the project was the opportunity to engage in a what she described as

> [a] fundamental reassessment of teaching and relationships with students ... it ... challenged them but also offered them a more fulfilling way of being a teacher, perhaps reminding some why they had first come in to the profession.
>
> (McCluskey, 2016, p. 23)

DOI: 10.4324/9781003035527-1

While an impossible aim for this book, I do hope that it provides a pause for you to sit back and assess the many strengths you already have and the good practice you understand and/or use daily when managing behaviour. It may also provide an opportunity to review a range of different approaches you may not regularly use and to consider if, how, or when, these might be helpful to support your practice and your work with the children in your care or to develop and broaden your understanding.

Throughout this book I use the terms 'you' and 'we' – 'you' refers to the reader, and I am often making the assumption that this is someone who has direct experience of working in the classroom with children, for example a teacher, support worker or allied profession, or someone who understands day-to-day practice in school. The term 'we' is used in the broadest sense, including all those who have an interest (either directly as a practitioner or indirectly as a student/researcher, etc.) in supporting children's behaviour in schools.

Who the book is for?

The chapters in the book present a range of research, policy and practice and as such, aim to be of use to a range of readers. If you are an *early career or trainee teacher*, you may find the book helpful to introduce you to new concepts and develop knowledge you have gained from your training and experience in schools so far. You may also be able to gain a deeper understanding of the chronology of policy in relation to behaviour and how (or not!) it has impacted on classroom practice in many schools. You may also find the further reading at the end of the chapters handy to follow up on any new areas or aspects with which you are not as familiar.

The book can also be used by *experienced teachers and senior leaders* in schools. The research focus in the chapters could be helpful to develop your understanding of the theoretical and empirical aspects that underpin practice, or to contribute to developing further research-informed strategies to support behaviour in schools.

Students and researchers more broadly can also use the chapters in this book to support their understanding of how research, policy and practice have interacted in schools as well as the range of approaches and strategies to support children's behaviour in schools. The appendix of further reading may also provide a useful starting point for those wishing to follow up the chapters with more in-depth academic reading and links to policy.

How to use this book

The book is structured in a series of sections. Like a good meal you might find it most satisfying to progress from the starter, to the main course and then on to desert – or in this case from Part I to Part II, and then on to Part III. However, you might be short on time, have a particular interest in learning more about a certain approach or idea, or find a chapter that particularly captures your attention. So, like a good meal, it is also possible to dip in and out of this book. You might (like me) have a dangerously sweet tooth or a rebellious streak and want to start with Part III. You might not have time for a starter and want to get straight to the main course – the book is written in such a way that each Part and chapter also stand alone.

To help you navigate through the book, all of the chapters will have common features. Each chapter will begin with a set of keywords and aims, so you are clear about what to expect, and end with a review and suggested further reading, to enable you to follow up in greater detail on the themes discussed, if you wish. The chapters are also subdivided into:

- *Foundations* – these sections will examine a combination of research evidence, policy and theory that will provide background to the theme and help to deepen your knowledge and understanding of the key issues the chapter focusses on.
- *Building Blocks* – these sections will consider the practical implications for schools, pupils, teachers and others who work with children in schools, for example, teaching assistants.
- *Review* – these sections will provide you with a summary of the key points of the chapter. This will lead onto a consideration of implications for *whole school actions* as well as specific *individual teacher actions*. The review section will also highlight any *possible mental health and well-being implications* linked with the theme of the chapter or specific interventions discussed.
- *Practice-Related Take-Away* – this will follow on from the review and give a very concise idea of how the focus of the chapter could be embedded in practice.
- *Practitioner Reading* – these sections provide a suggestion of more focussed reading to follow up on should you wish.
- *Further Reading* – this appendix at the end of the book contains a list of extended reading for each chapter should you wish to delve deeper into the issues discussed.

Each chapter will also include *Thinking Stops*, where you will be asked to reflect on key ideas or issues. There will also be *Activity Stops* where you can use what you have read and your own experience to consider what the practical, classroom-based implications of the chapter might be. The aim of these, in whatever way you choose to complete them – in full in the book, in your head, in discussion with others – is to allow you to reflect on what you have read and how it might have changed or developed your understanding or view, and in turn, how this might affect what actions you take in the classroom. In addition, the chapters will feature a 'storyboard' reflection activity where you will be asked to draw (stick-people are more than acceptable!) how an incident of behaviour from your own experience might have been enacted differently and have different outcomes for the child(ren) and teacher(s).

This book aims to strike a balance between practical, classroom-based suggestions for developing strategies to support children with their behaviour, alongside theoretical, philosophical, research and policy-based discussions to underpin these

4 Introduction

strategies. This means that you, as the reader, will be armed with not only (possibly new) ideas on supporting children but also a clear understanding of why they might work and how they fit in a wider theoretical understanding of behaviour. Within all of this, though, it is key to remember that it is *who* you are as a teacher and the relationships you are able to form, rather than *what* you do that makes a difference. Visser (2006) highlighted from his extensive work and research with children that the 'approaches in and of themselves do not make the difference. ... pedagogues make the difference; the approaches support or hinder the process'.

? ACTIVITY STOP 1

Before the chapter progresses any further, let's consider Sproson's (2004) idea of a behaviour suitcase. He suggested that teachers should have a full 'suitcase' of mixed and varied strategies to manage behaviour. The idea was that children can be helped to fill their own 'suitcase' and develop their own strategies from the teacher's modelling. Pause here and think about the array of different strategies you may already have in your suitcase. Is there anything else at this stage you would like to add, or feel is missing? Make a note of it in the suitcase (Figure 0.1). Each section will end with the same 'suitcase', so it will provide a simple way to track any changes or development in your views and skills as you read this book.

FIGURE 0.1 The strategies that are already in your behaviour suitcase.

The chapters in Part I focus on 'Framing the Actions We Take' and consider the broader background on perspectives on behaviour. Chapter 1 considers how the language used to talk about children and the behaviours they exhibit also influences the ways in which we relate to them and frame their behaviours. Chapter 2 offers a discussion on why challenging behaviour is so difficult to definitively define, and how our experiences as teachers and practitioners means that what we view as 'challenging behaviour' varies. Chapter 3 discusses how policy, both school-based and nationally, informs the actions we take (or not) in the classroom, and how the range of tensions schools currently face have resulted in problematic practices such as 'zero tolerance' policies and 'off-rolling'. Although the focus here is on the developments within the British education system, there are clear parallels in many other countries, and as a result, these chapters will be useful and pertinent if you are reading this outside of the English context. Chapters in this section include:

- Behaviour and Mental Health
- Acronyms and Attitudes
- Policy, Possibilities and Problems

Part II, 'Beliefs and Perspectives', examines how our own beliefs and values impact on our work with children. This part of the book considers a range of strategies that could be used in school to support children managing their behaviour, and moves away from a consideration of using rewards and sanctions to mould behaviours. Chapter 4 examines the array of beliefs that underpin the strategies that might be used in the classroom to manage or support behaviour. It considers how different theoretical positions and beliefs lead us as teachers to view behaviour in different ways, and it discusses the tensions between some of the research on behaviour and classroom practice. The book then looks at two different approaches in more detail; this begins with Chapter 5 on restorative practices, followed by Chapter 6 on solution-focused approaches, both of which are supported by different beliefs and actions than the more well-known behaviourist approach and its associated used of sanctions and rewards. These chapters ask you as a reader to consider specific incidents and how they might have played out differently if either a solution-focused or restorative approach had been used. The chapters in Part II include:

- Theory and the Classroom
- Restorative Practices – Reconciliation and Restitution
- Solution-Focused Approaches– Celebrating Successes

The chapters in Part III, 'Beyond Strategies to Embedded Ethos', to examine how behaviour can be supported – not only by discrete approaches, but through the everyday life of the classroom. These chapters draw on a number of different authors, all of whom are specific experts in their fields. It begins with Chapter 7, a consideration by Dr Aimee Quickfall of the benefits of using philosophy in the classroom to support children's behaviour and the inclusion of 'Philosophy for Children (P4C)'. Much of Aimee's work as a teacher in schools – and latterly as a researcher – has focused on the wider benefits of using a P4C approach with children as well as a specific consideration of how this influenced both teachers' and children's behaviours. With Chapter 8, we move on to a (re)consideration of eternal verities. Here, Professor John Visser sets out his rationale of the core guiding values or 'eternal verities' that should be evident in all teachers' work, and particularly when supporting children whose behaviour challenges us. John's work on these 'verities' is the distillation of an extensive career working with children as a teacher and an academic, and is built on his experiences, particularly with children whose behaviours challenge. His hugely popular academic paper on 'eternal verities' has been read by thousands of practitioners and academics, but the reconsideration of his verities here is both timely and exclusive! Part III concludes with Chapter 9, an overview of the Finnish perspectives on supporting behaviour. The team of writers are all Finnish and work in teacher education at the University of Eastern Finland, either in the classroom supporting trainee-teachers, teachers and children, or as researchers and lecturers at the university. Finland is often regarded as the gold standard of education, and in this chapter, the team of writers share not only a range of strategies but also the guiding cultural and educational philosophies that shape their work with children in schools. The chapters in Part III include:

- Philosophical Inquiry as a Tool for Well-Being
- Verities Revisited
- International Perspectives – Managing Behaviour in Finland

The book concludes with a series of reflections and 'Thinking Stops'. These aim to support you, in drawing together what you have learnt and to consider how you might want incorporate some of the aspects you have read about into your own practice or school.

My own experiences

My own interest in supporting children's behaviour began (rather more suddenly than I was ready for) on my first day in the classroom. I was a very nervous, newly qualified teacher taking over a 36-strong Year 6 class mid-way through the academic year after the sudden departure of the previous class teacher and a very cursory interview for the post. Retrospectively, perhaps this should have warranted more caution than I exhibited.

After managing to coax the children into the classroom and through the register, I then launched full-tilt into a maths lesson on fractions. A child who, up until this point had been relatively quiet, announced, whilst I was furiously scribbling on the

Introduction 7

💭 THINKING STOP 1

Briefly review the titles of the chapters and sections in the overview. Using the diagram (Figure 0.2), which chapters sound like they might develop and further your existing knowledge and understanding, and which (if any) might introduce you to something new and unknown?

FIGURE 0.2 Chapters developing new and existing knowledge.

blackboard, that he found my lesson boring, my clothing rubbish and my personal hygiene poor (I am paraphrasing, as his vocabulary was much more expressive, articulate and varied than I can possibly hope to recreate here). He then managed – or at least, it seemed so to me – to push, shove or kick every one of the 35 remaining children on his way to the door. Unsure of what to do, I stood motionless and sweating, watching him stroll down the pavement outside the classroom window before exchanging what I could only assume were pleasantries with the deputy head. Back in the classroom, I simply carried on while a child near the front told me reassuringly that, 'he always does that 'cos he doesn't like maths'. As the morning wore on, I assumed I was over the worst. Sadly, this was not the case, as the boy returned after lunch with an inflatable hammer and proceeded to spend half of the afternoon running into the classroom and hitting whoever he could with it before I could catch him. The other half he spent evading the deputy head.

Once the children left for the end of the day, I burst into tears, walked home and swore I would never return. I did, however, and I grew incredibly fond of the young man that had given me such an unusual first day. We had many more such incidents as the year went on and I continued to have many more experiences of behaviours that challenged me in that school – some funny, some frightening but most utterly heart-breaking. As my career in the classroom developed I was privileged enough to spend it with a range of children in mainstream and alternative provision (pupil referral units and nurture groups) whose behaviour I regularly found challenging. These classroom-based experiences fed my interest in supporting children's behaviour more widely, and I completed a master's degree with a focus on challenging behaviour before undertaking my PhD, which again studied behaviour in the classroom. I have since left the classroom and now work in a university teaching on undergraduate and postgraduate Initial Teacher Education courses and supervising master's and doctoral students. This has given me the opportunity to continue to develop my understanding of a range of strategies and theoretical perspectives on managing behaviour, both in England and in the wider European context.

❓ ACTIVITY STOP 2

Reflect for a moment on your own experiences working with children, particularly those times when you have dealt with behaviours that you have considered challenging. Using the diagram (Figure 0.3), begin to think about what skills you already possess and what aspects of your personality (for example, empathy, sense of humour, calmness) have helped you to develop your own specific skills for supporting children with their behaviour.

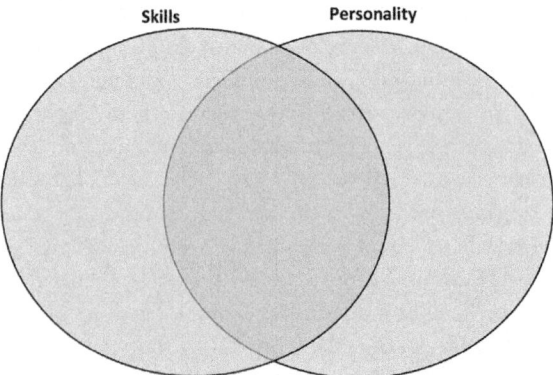

FIGURE 0.3 My own experiences and personal characteristics that help me to support behaviour.

Introduction 9

Where are we now?

One of the key current agendas that impacts on behaviour and how it is managed is that of developing children's mental health and well-being. In their 2014 publication (updated in 2018 [DfE, 2014, 2018]) the DfE explicitly acknowledged for the first time that the behaviours some children exhibit in the classroom are linked to wider mental health issues, suggesting that schools need 'to support pupils whose mental health problems manifest themselves in behaviour' (p. 3, DfE, 2018). This, and wider societal changes, have encouraged a clearer focus on developing children's well-being and have raised questions about how this can be done in schools – particularly whether well-being is at odds with, or supported by the ways in which schools manage behaviour. The House of Commons Health and Education Committees (2017) raised criticisms of what had been suggested to be 'a false dichotomy' between the concurrent focus on both 'achievement and on well-being' in schools.

❓ ACTIVITY STOP 3

Use the diagram (Figure 0.4) to help you think about the (possibly) competing aims of schools to raise children's achievement and to develop their well-being. Imagine for a moment two schools – one focusing entirely on pupils' achievement and the other prioritising well-being:

- How might the teacher's role be described or viewed in these two schools?
- What might the classroom layout/environment look like?

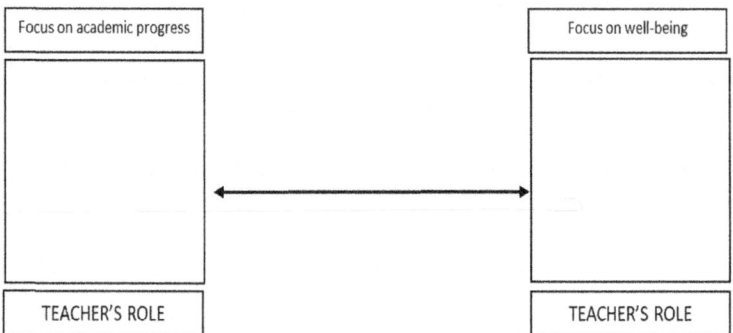

FIGURE 0.4 Diagram to consider differences on a focus on well-being and on achievement.

- What would relationships between teachers and pupils look like?
- What are the advantages, and for whom?
- What are the disadvantages, and for whom?

(You may want to revisit your ideas here when reading chapter "*Final thoughts*" on approaches in Finland.)

Imagine schools existing on a spectrum between these two foci (achievement and well-being):

- Where would you place your current setting or school (or one known to you)?
- Why?
- How do you know?
- Who does this work well for? Why?
- Who does this not work as well for? Why?

❓ ACTIVITY STOP 4

Throughout the chapters in this book, you will be invited and encouraged to record your thoughts using a storyboard format (regardless of your artistic skills). In this, the first activity of this kind, I would like you to pick an incident of poor behaviour in a school or setting known to you, it can be recent or historical, major or minor. Can you draw images – stick people are fine, or words if that is easier – using the storyboard (Figure 0.5) to show:

- How this incident might have been managed and what the outcomes for a range of stakeholders might have been had the school prioritised achievement?
- How this incident might have been managed and what the outcomes for a range of stakeholders might have been had the school prioritised well-being?

THE INCIDENT AS IT HAPPENED AND MAY BE ACTED ON BY A SETTING WHOLLY CONCERNED WITH ACADEMIC PROGRESS			
Antecedence (what happened just before the incident)	The incident (what happened)	Outcomes (what happened after the incident)	Impact on the teacher, child, class, school community

THE INCIDENT AS IT HAPPENED AND MAY BE ACTED ON BY A SETTING WHOLLY CONCERNED WITH WELL-BEING			
Antecedence (what happened just before the incident)	The incident (what happened)	Outcomes (what happened after the incident)	Impact on the teacher, child, class, school community

FIGURE 0.5 Storyboard comparing and contrasting achievement and well-being.

This activity has asked you to consider extremes; in reality, very few schools are focused *only* on pupils' achievement or on their well-being. Most are working to fulfil a range of needs and aims under a range of internal and external pressures. However, this activity demonstrates that the aims, values and purposes of an organisation or individual will influence how they manage incidents of behaviour – either consciously or subconsciously – depending on what they are trying to achieve. The Derrington Report (Derrington, 2008) which was at the time, the largest review of teachers' perceptions of behaviour, acknowledged that many of the teachers surveyed did not recognise the effect of their own behaviour on that of their pupils. It is key, therefore, to consider what we think is the fundamental role of the teacher – multifaceted and polyvalent as that may be – and what we are trying to achieve with the children in our care.

💭 THINKING STOP 2

Teaching has been described as an 'intensely human' and emotional profession (Gray, Miller and Noakes, 1994).

- Do you agree or disagree with this description?
- Why?
- What might be the advantages of acknowledging its human and emotional aspects?
- What might be the disadvantages of acknowledging its human and emotional aspects?

Before this introductory chapter ends and the book begins in earnest, I invite you to begin this activity. Using Figure 0.6, begin to collate your thoughts on the chapters as you progress through this book, reflecting on how they support or challenge your own views and practice.

Chapter	I think....	What I like...	What doesn't fit with my views...	What I would like to find out more about...
Introduction: behaviour and mental health				
Acronyms and Attitudes				
Policy: Possibilities and Problems				
Theory and the Classroom				
Restorative Practices: Reconciliation and Restitution				
Solution Focused Approaches: Celebrating Success				
Philosophical Inquiry as a Tool for Well-being				
Verities Revisited				
International Perspectives: Managing Behaviour in Finland				

FIGURE 0.6 Table to reflect on chapter content.

Review

This chapter has introduced some of the aspects the book will cover and some of the ways in which you might want to engage with the content. It has outlined the structure and features of the chapters and some of the types of activities you will be invited to do. The current educational climate in England and the growing importance of considering mental health and well-being linked to behaviour has also been introduced.

Practice-related take-away:

- Explicit links are now being made in policy between behaviour and mental health. This should also be evident in some way in practice in schools.

Practitioner reading:

Glazzard, J. & Bostwick, R. (2018). *Positive Mental Health: A Whole School Approach.* St. Albans: Critical Publishing.

References

Department for Education. (2018). *Mental Health and Behaviour in Schools.* London: DfE.
Department for Education. (2014). *Mental Health and Behaviour in Schools: Departmental Advice.* London: DfE.
Derrington, C. (2008). *Behaviour in Primary Schools Final Report.* London: True Vision Productions.

Gray, P., Miller, A., & Noakes, J. (1994). Challenging behaviour in schools: An introduction. In Gray, P., Miller, A. and Noakes, J. (Eds.), *Challenging Behaviour in Schools* (pp. 1–4). London: Routledge.

House of Commons Health and Education Committee. (2017). *Children and Young People's Mental Health - The Role of Education*. London: DfE.

McCluskey, G. (2016). Restoring the possibility of change? A restorative approach with troubled and troublesome young people. *International Journal on School Disaffection*, **7**(1), pp. 19–25.

Sproson, B. (2004). Some do and don't: Teacher effectiveness in managing behaviour. In Wearmouth, J., Glynn, T., Richmond, R., & Berryman, M. (Eds.), *Inclusion and Behaviour Management in Schools: Issues and Challenges* (pp. 311–321). London: David Fulton Publishers.

Visser, J. (2006). Keeping violence in perspective. *International Journal on Violence and Schools*, **1**, pp. 57–64.

PART I
Framing the actions we take

As already discussed, this book is divided into three distinct yet related sections, each dealing with a specific set of elements, or 'pieces'. Together, these sections begin to build an understanding of the 'jigsaw' of behaviours that challenge and show how many different pieces need to be joined together to see the 'whole picture'. This perspective of arranging pieces together, of a multiplicative and multifaceted understanding of behaviours, moves from the reductive narrative often heard focusing on teacher control and discipline which can give the impression working with children to support behaviour is simply a matter of being authoritative enough or strict enough, and so on. This simplifies supporting behaviours to a unidirectional, consistent approach that could work with any child at any time and in any context, whereas the reality – at least in my experience – was anything but. For me and for the children I worked with, managing behaviour was a two-way street, a reciprocal relationship, with the children influencing what I did and my actions influencing them (although not always positively!).

These parts in the book mirror my own positionality and are a commentary from my perspective, with the chapters in each part leaning towards a relational focus. For me, relationships were, and remain, the cornerstone of my personal and professional development in this area. The relationships that have shaped my own understanding include those with the children I taught, my fellow teachers and peers in schools, my academic colleagues within and beyond my own institution and leading researchers in the field. The chapters in Part I centre on how external influences, including language, policy and current drives such as developing well-being in schools, influence the understanding of the causes of behaviours that challenge and, as a result, guide the formation of relationships with children and the actions taken with them.

1
BEHAVIOUR, WELL-BEING AND MENTAL HEALTH

This chapter follows on from some of the issues discussed in the Introduction and examines in greater depth the issues surrounding mental health, well-being and behaviours that challenge. Throughout this book, I will use the term 'behaviour that challenges', because there is no clear definition of the more commonly used term 'challenging behaviour'. The use of the term 'challenging behaviour' seems to imply a globally accepted and agreed meaning – yet this is not the case. We all have behaviours we find challenging that other staff seem to be able to take in their stride. For example, despite a fairly long and happy career in the classroom, I never identified strategies that successfully managed the 'anonymous hummer', that child who is unidentifiable yet audibly humming. This for me was a behaviour that challenged, as I did not have any successful strategies for dealing with it. Behaviours that are challenging for a newly or recently qualified teacher, someone with a broader experience, might be able to deal with quickly and straightforwardly and so on. As a result, I am using the term 'behaviours that challenge' to acknowledge that we all actually – no matter our experience or confidence – have a range of behaviours we find difficult to manage positively, if at all, and that these might vary depending on experience, training and confidence, or even the day of the week, or the weather.

The language used when talking about behaviour is a recurring theme in this part of the book, and it has been shown to have a powerful impact on the actions we take, as will be discussed in Chapters 2 and 3. The new Code of Practice for Special Educational Needs and Disabilities (SEND) revised the terminology used in reference to behaviour difficulties, from the previous 'Behavioural, Social and Emotional Needs' to that of 'Social, Emotional and Mental Health Difficulties' (DfE & DoH, 2015). The ambiguity, specifically in these general terms related to behaviours that challenge, have been noted as a site of difficulty. Norwich and Eaton (2015) argued that the DfE/DoH reclassification in the Code of Practice did nothing to improve the vagueness inherent in the previous term, an issue highlighted when 'specifying thresholds for identifying difficulties', for example in multi-agency working. In fact, it was even suggested that the revision in language used in the Code in reference to behaviour was simply to cut the numbers of pupils identified as having SEND, which 'Ofsted happened to endorse' (Norwich & Eaton, 2015), rather than to support greater understanding. Following on from this, the chapter aims to:

- Examine the links between behaviour and mental health and well-being
- Investigate what well-being is and why it is a key focus
- Consider policy in England in relation to this
- Discuss how considering some behaviours as a mental health need might influence the way in which we engage with children

Foundations

The term 'well-being' is now common currency in many professions as well as in the popular psyche. In education, developing well-being has been a big policy drive for children and teachers, specifically in primary schools in England (Pollard & Lee, 2003). The Department for Education in England recently highlighted their focus on ensuring schools 'have a clear offer to promote pupils' mental health and wellbeing' (DfE, 2018), and from 2020 that teaching children to look after their mental health and well-being is mandatory (DfE and the Rt. Hon. Damien Hinds MP, 2019). A range of research has pointed to either a rise in the number of cases of – or possibly a greater readiness to share and talk about – mental health problems (Danby & Hamilton, 2016; House of Commons Education and Health Committees, 2017; Roffey, 2016). It has been noted that between 10% and 20% of children and young people suffer from mental health problems (McPherson et al., 2014) and that 1 in 10 have a 'diagnosable mental disorder' (Glazzard & Bostwick, 2018; Marshall, Wishart, Allison & Smith, 2017). These statistics equate to around three children in each class throughout the school struggling with mental health and well-being-related issues at some level. Mental health and well-being issues have also been highlighted in relation to behaviour, where it has been noted that schools 'need to be alert to how mental health problems can underpin behaviour issues' (DfE & DoH, 2015). Glazzard and Bostwick (2018) have also shown a range of research that identifies the increased risk for children identified having a SEND in developing mental health issues. This can ultimately result in the removal of these children from full-time education, impacting on their attainment. A vicious cycle can then occur for children whose behaviour challenges, with the DfE (2012) highlighting the link between pupils identified as having a SEND with 'higher levels of self-reported or observed misbehaviour' and significantly higher rates of both fixed-term (nine times more likely) and permanent (eight times more likely) exclusions. This suggests, then, that schools are experiencing a range of issues in relation to children's mental health and well-being, and that children whose behaviour challenges are more likely to experience problems with their well-being puts them at risk of being taken out of mainstream schooling and compounding their problems even further.

The impact of schools and schooling on mental health and well-being cannot be underestimated. However, data collected from the 'Good Childhood' reports conducted by the Children's Society (2015, 2019) showed that only children in South Korea rated 'life satisfaction' lower than children in England, and that English children's ratings for 'liking going to school' were in the bottom third of all countries participating. Even worse, children in England ranked 14th out of 15 for positive relationships with their teachers (Roffey, 2016).

THINKING STOP 1

Reflect on the children in your class or your school more widely and use the table (Figure 1.1) to collate your ideas:

- Do these statistics reflect what you have seen?
- Are there any other issues you would add on here?
- How many of the 'in-school' factors related to the issues can you change of amend?

Issue	Does it fit with your experiences?	What might be the causes of this?	
		In school	Out of school
10% of children with diagnosable mental health issue			
Children rate 'life-satisfaction' as low			
Children rate 'liking going to school' as low			
Children rate 'positive relationships with teachers' as low			
Any other issues?			

FIGURE 1.1 Table to collect ideas of factors related to children's disaffection.

When this is considered in the context of the total time children spend at school – approximately 7,800 hours (Cowburn & Blow, 2017) – the role of the school in supporting children becomes clear. Indeed, schools have been described as having a 'front line role in promoting and protecting children's mental health and well-being' (House of Commons Education and Health Committees, 2017).

The World Health Organisation (2001, p. 1, in UNICEF, 2009) defined a 'child friendly school' as one which was

> a supportive and nurturing environment, providing education which responds to the reality of the children's lives ... promotes self-esteem and self-confidence.

This definition from the WHO mirrors the recent focus in policy, as well as in a range of research (Cowburn & Blow, 2017; DfES, 2001; Hornby & Atkinson, 2003; Roffey, 2016) on children's well-being in school. The message from all of these is that there is 'overwhelming evidence that pupils learn more effectively if they are happy in their work, believe in themselves, like their teachers and feel school is supporting them' (Weare, 2000).

Despite being regularly used, the term 'well-being' is not always clearly defined, yet the prevalence of the term can sometimes lead to the assumption that it is easily defined and systematically understood by all who use it. However, as will be discussed in Chapter 2, semantics and the language used when discussing these aspects is key in understanding how we frame our actions. As Weare (2000), in line with others, has noted, summing up well-being or mental health in a single sentence is often simplistic and inappropriate, and that reducing this multifaceted and complex concept to a simple definition is impossible. It has also been argued that in trying to do so, our own 'values, preconceptions and assumptions' are side-lined (Weare, 2000), despite the fact that concepts such as mental health and well-being are influenced by our own personal views of what is usual or desirable, what behaviours are 'normal' and so on. Carr (2000, in Gott, 2003) asserted that concepts such as self-esteem(s) and well-being were not 'value neutral' but were always influenced by a range of factors and contexts, and as a result, any definitions provided are usually influenced by the 'professions, communities, societies and cultures' that devise them. This means that definitions of well-being used in other contexts might not automatically transfer to schools, and what constitutes a definition of well-being or mental health for one group might not be the same for another group. Weare (2000) noted that the term 'mental health' was often not associated with research in education, or in teachers' own understandings where the terms 'emotional, social or personal education' were usually more well-known and used. This reflects the concerns of Norwich and Eaton (2015), noted in the Introduction, that there is a range of language used to talk about 'behaviour' and 'well-being' that are not easily defined and rely, at least in part, on context and personal views.

THINKING STOP 2

How might you define well-being for the children in your care? Will one definition fit all children, or does it need to be flexible and/or personalised?

Mental health as a concept has also shifted and changed from medical and deficit models where it was once considered as the absence of a mental illness, to a state or condition in its own right – a 'strength perspective' (Spratt, Shucksmith, Philip & Watson, 2006). However as noted, it would be naïve to suggest that mental health or well-being can be simply and easily defined, or that they are a fixed state. One of the key hurdles in explicitly defining the 'elusive' (Ortega-Alcázar & Dyck, 2012) concept of well-being is that it is not a discrete entity, but rather multi-factorial and multi-dimensional (Dodge, Daly, Huyton & Sanders, 2012; Masters, 2004). It has been suggested to be 'commonly used but inconsistently defined' in a systemic review of the literature (Pollard & Lee, 2003) nevertheless, a helpful definition of well-being is the one outlined here by Dodge et al. (2012, pp. 229–230):

> Maintaining the balance between resources and challenges ... which may be internal or external, and operate in a dynamic flux over time.

As part of their academic research, Dodge et al. (2012) also provided an illustration of well-being using this definition (Figure 1.2). My colleagues and I (Thompson, Clarke, Quickfall & Glazzard, 2020) have used this model as part of our research on well-being and have found it has helped our participants share their understanding of this complex issue, and it has become known to us as the 'see-saw'. Conceptualising it in this way can be helpful for staff and children, and I will return to this later in the chapter.

This concept of well-being as shifting and dynamic, rather than an 'achieved' or fixed state echoes Glazzard and Bostwick's (2018) view. Drawing on a range of research, they conceptualise mental health as existing on a continuum with 'good mental health' and 'mental illness' at either end, with a child (or adult's) movement along this continuum influenced by a range of aspects including 'social, biological and psychological factors' (Glazzard & Bostwick, 2018).

Given the statistics and research discussed here, it is clear that schools have the ability to play a vital role in supporting and developing children's mental health and well-being, and indeed, that it is important they do so. If the evidence of the essential role schools can play is clear, then it may be questioned why more is not done and why schools are not devoting time in their day to doing so, particularly when the links between mental health issues and externalised (or internalised) displays of behaviour have been made. It has been argued that the 'school environment has the potential to either enhance or damage the mental well-being of both staff and

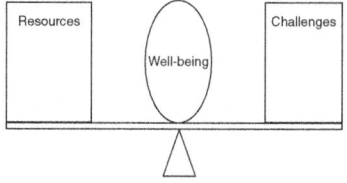

FIGURE 1.2 The well-being 'see-saw' adapted from Dodge et al. (2012, p. 230).

pupils' (Spratt *et al.*, 2006, p. 15) and that unmet needs 'inevitably impact on children's learning' (Hornby & Atkinson, 2003, p. 8).

Why then, when addressing behaviour, are issues of mental health and well-being not core? Here, echoes of the activities and discussion in the previous chapter can be heard regarding the core role of the school. There have been a range of suggested reasons for this – some research has cautioned that teachers are concerned about the associations once held with the medical model of mental health and semantic associations with mental illness (Spratt *et al.*, 2006). The DfE (2018, p. 5) highlighted that school staff were not 'mental health experts and should not try to diagnose conditions', possibly cementing concerns related to the medical model. This is in spite of previous findings commissioned by the DfE that 82% of schools relied on 'ad hoc identification' of children's mental health difficulties by staff whilst recognising 36% of staff lacked the knowledge and understanding to do so (Marshall *et al.*, 2017). This same study also acknowledged that 74% of schools cited 'commissioning local services' such as the Child and Adolescent Mental Health Services (CAHMS) and funding (71%) as barriers to mental health provision, rather than in-school factors. Hornby and Atkinson (2003) found in their study that some teachers felt that addressing the mental health needs of their pupils did not 'fall within their remit'. This contrasts with research suggesting that parents saw school staff as a source of support, and were more likely to go to a teacher for support with children's mental health difficulties than 'any other professional or service' (Cowburn & Blow, 2017). As Glazzard and Bostwick (2018) noted, although teachers are not mental health experts, they do spend much more time with children than other professionals and therefore can be in a position to offer a range of support.

Forty years ago, Tutt (1985, cited in Gott, 2003, p. 9) noted that the 1891 Education Act, with its focus on greater inclusion, resulted in 'unintended consequences' which set up a vicious cycle. He suggested that once pupils with additional or non-standard needs had been identified, unless there were processes and systems to then address these needs, 'a system would be created where anxieties about unmet needs increase, rather than decrease, leading to an exposure of more and more layers on concern'. Gott (2003) suggested that these 'unintended consequences' were being repeated in relation to mental health and well-being issues whereby once children were identified the subsequent 'flood of referrals to CAHMS' could cause school staff to feel they were 'unable to intervene in areas where they have very little expertise'. This reflects issues with considering behaviour from a medical model (discussed further in Chapter 4) which often significantly limits the actions staff in school can take. Although this paradigm shift from the deficit medical model to more current views of mental health as a stigma-free, positive state may be linked to issues in its promotion in school, research suggests this is not straightforward. It has been argued that developing well-being and mental health are seen as contrary to pupil attainment and that there is an either/or dichotomy at play.

> Emotional health and well-being is a swing away from Ofsted and diverts attention into making schools a more humane place, better for pupils and

staff, a school where pupils (and staff) feel happy, are encouraged and are developing self-confidence surely has a greater long-term effect than a school focusing purely on achievement.

(Gott, 2003, p. 10)

This idea that achievement, attainment and mental health cannot be achieved hand-in-hand has been attributed to externalised pressures on English schools. Cowburn and Blow (2017) cited what they saw as an 'imbalance' with schools focused on academic outcomes rather than social and emotional aspects such as well-being and mental health. This pressure on academic attainment, external league tables and reporting may mean that teachers are actually 'less likely to have the time or patience to establish positive relationships with challenging pupils' (Roffey, 2016, p. 38). This can then set up a downward spiral where behaviour worsens and teacher stress increases even further. Weare (2000) noted that the relationship between well-being and achievement was reciprocal, and that:

It is vital that those who seek to promote high academic standards and those who seek to promote mental, emotional and social health realise that they are on the same side, and that social and affective education can support academic learning, not simply take time away time from it.

(p. 5)

? ACTIVITY STOP 1

Pause here and think about your own setting, or one known to you. You can complete this activity either focusing on the whole school, or on your own classroom or setting if that is easier. Using the diagram (Figure 1.3), fill in under each heading the activities, routines, learning and so on that are linked to it. In the intersection, place any of these that you think fulfil both criteria.

Look at the completed diagram:

- Which part is the fullest?
- Is that what you expected?
- Does that fit with your view/philosophy of teaching?
- Does it match the needs of the children in your care?
- If you could/wanted to shift the balance of activities, what could you/are you able to do?

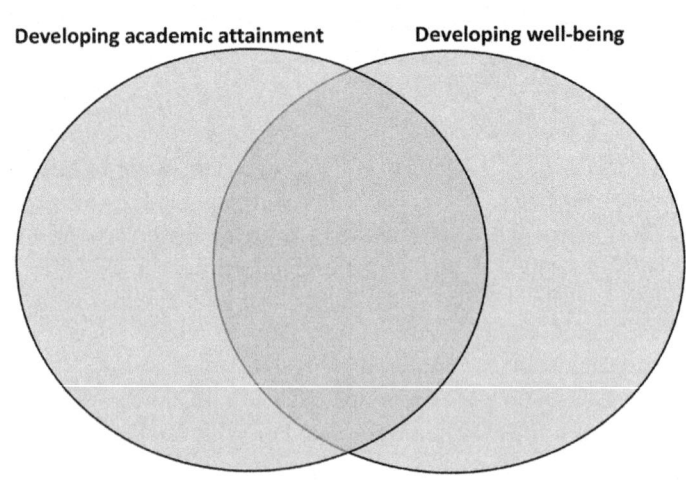

FIGURE 1.3 Diagram considering the balance between academic attainment and well-being.

Gray, Miller and Noakes (1994), as noted in the Introduction to this book, classified teaching as an 'intensely human' profession and an 'emotional endeavour'. From this perspective, it was suggested that misbehaviour can be felt as a direct and personal threat to teachers' authority and as a personal failure by individual teachers (Maguire, Ball & Braun, 2010). Studies (Postholm, 2013; Poulou & Norwich, 2002, cited in Wearmouth, Glynn & Berryman, 2005) have highlighted the links between teachers' and children's well-being, noting how classes can act as 'receivers of teachers' messages'. It was suggested that this process of sending and receiving emotional messages between teachers and children is a circular and interactive process developing 'complex, causal relationships'. It is essential, then, that the messages the teacher sends and that the children receive are positive, that teacher well-being is protected in these exchanges and a virtuous, and not a vicious, cycle of emotional 'messages' is perpetuated. This reciprocal aspect of well-being is one which has received relatively little attention in practice. Conditions in schools (and specifically related to the closure of schools in England) during the Covid-19 pandemic have highlighted the needs of children's mental health, and some organisations, such as the charity Education Support (McGuinness, 2021) are making explicit links between the impact of teachers' well-being and mental health and those of their pupils.

The drive in many schools to support staff well-being and pupil well-being appears, at times, to be done in isolation from each other as opposed to doing so with an understanding that improved staff well-being is key to supporting children's well-being. It could be suggested from the research considered already in this chapter that behaviours that challenge have the possibility of challenging staff emotionally and impacting more significantly on their well-being. A range of strategies to support all staff and children with well-being would be beneficial but specifically with some consideration of how these strategies can work in tandem with each other, rather than being run separately, may well have a significant benefit for staff and children and further develop a virtuous, rather than a vicious, cycle of depleted well-being for the school community as a whole.

Working with behaviours that challenge can be a source of specific stress for staff. As such, even greater consideration needs to be given to how to develop and protect the well-being of staff to ensure that it does not impact on the children in their care who may be exposed to a number of factors which put them at greater risk of developing well-being issues.

The sources considered up to this point have shown that supporting children's mental health and well-being has far-reaching advantages, for the children themselves as well as for the teachers working with these pupils. However, the discussion so far has been fairly generic and abstract, and we will now move on to consider the specific links between behaviour and mental health, and why a focus on developing mental health and self-esteem(s) may be more beneficial than simply addressing behaviour. The way in which behaviour is addressed in schools can either support or constrain (or even harm) the well-being and mental health of children, particularly those whose behaviours mean they may regularly be experiencing strategies aimed at managing their behaviour. Roffey (2016) notes how, for example, zero-tolerance policies (discussed in greater detail in Chapter 4), which are currently experiencing something of a resurgence, have been described as a 'school to prison pipeline' that undermines children's ability – particularly disadvantaged children – to form trusting relationships with teachers.

Building blocks

The policy and research reviewed here shows a range of shifts and tensions, all of which impact on what we do with children in schools and how we support behaviour, particularly those whose behaviour challenges. However, a range of steps can be taken in schools to support both children and staff. Weare (2000) suggested that schools can find it 'hard to see the relevance of mental health to their central concern with learning'. It could be suggested that the first step any school needs to take is to make this relevance clear and explicit. This can be done through a range of formal and informal strategies and through both the taught and the 'hidden' curriculum (DfE, 2018).

The research discussed in the previous section has highlighted the importance of relationships with teachers as supportive in developing well-being and positive mental health. It has also shown that surveys have ranked English schools as poor in this. It is clear, then, that this area needs focus in schools, requiring strategies to support the development of these relationships, both holistically as a school and for individual teachers (a range of strategies to do this will be discussed in Part II of this book). Hornby and Atkinson (2003) supported this, arguing that schools and teachers in particular were 'uniquely placed' in their ability to influence children's mental well-being. Findings have also shown (Spratt *et al.*, 2006) that the ability for teachers to form positive relationships is key for 'hard to reach' children and those at risk of exclusion. Roffey (2016, p. 37) also noted that practices which included:

> a focus on positive relationships within schools appear to be not only effective in improving behaviour, but also provide more protective factors for vulnerable and challenging pupils.

This supports other research (Marzano, Marzano & Pickering, 2003) which suggested that, in their study, the better the relationship between teacher and pupil, the fewer the behaviour issues, recording a 31% decrease in discipline issues in some classrooms. Hornby and Atkinson (2003) also highlighted the importance of the 'rapport' teachers were able to develop with their pupils as a key factor in developing children's mental health and well-being. In other research (Postholm, 2013), the relationships teachers formed with their pupils and the teacher's own personal qualities were highlighted as the most important aspect of pupils' learning. The relationships between teachers and pupils are so important for children's mental well-being, as they can determine how behaviour issues are supported and/or addressed. Spratt *et al.* (2006) found that it was usually the class teacher who decided whether a behaviour incident would be addressed 'as a disciplinary matter or pastoral care issue', and that the outcome of these two options was likely to result in very different forms of either support or sanctions being issued for the child.

In spite of research showing that addressing unmet mental health needs has a significant impact on behaviour, particularly for those children with behaviours that challenge, moves to support well-being in schools often result in what has been described as 'fragile and patchy provision' (Spratt *et al.*, 2006). Historically, research on well-being has been focused on pupils whose were seen as 'troubled or troublesome' as well as those with a range of additional learning needs rather than all pupils (Weare, 2000). Glazzard and Bostwick (2018) have highlighted that meeting the mental health and well-being needs of children cannot be an isolated endeavour. In their research, Spratt and her colleagues (2006) found in their study of Scottish schools that approaches to developing well-being and positive mental health were often not embedded due to perceived conflicts between the existing school ethos and the promotion of mental well-being. They observed school approaches to developing mental health as discrete rather than embedded – for example, anti-bullying weeks or peer-to-peer mentoring. This rather tick box approach or 'tinkering around the edges' resulted from external pressures:

> in spite of recent policy shifts (in Scotland) away from over emphasis on attainment in its narrower sense, school management … continued to feel under pressure to concentrate on the measurable attainment of pupils.
> (Spratt *et al.*, 2006, p. 16)

Brown (2018) noted in her review of published policies and information on mental health and well-being provision in schools for the DfE that schools had a 'range of duties' including developing 'a range of whole-school approaches and activities' to support the development of children's mental health and well-being. One way in which this can be done, to ensure a whole-school as opposed to a piecemeal approach, is through key policies documents. The school behaviour policy can be seen as integral to this. The DfE's (2018) non-statutory guidance highlights the importance of a close fit between the behaviour policy and mental health, noting the importance of consistency between the two, despite no requirement to have a 'stand-alone mental health policy'.

There are a range of ways in which a whole-school behaviour policy can either contribute to or restrict children's mental well-being. It has been found that policies which were supportive in promoting well-being and mental health had a proactive focus on developing children's self-esteem(s) and their own strategies for self-discipline rather than a reliance on sanctions. Allied to this, polices that enabled an understanding of behaviour as resulting from unmet emotional, social or mental health needs, and therefore to support children through 'pastoral support', were also key (Brown, 2018). It has been suggested that support from the school's senior leadership team (SLT) is essential as well as the possibility of having a school governor who is able to 'champion' whole-school approaches (Glazzard & Bostwick, 2018; Public Health England, 2015).

❓ ACTIVITY STOP 2

The diagram (Figure 1.4), taken from Hornby and Atkinson (2003, p. 4) shows a range of strategies at can be implemented at different levels of the school. Reflect on:

- How many are possible within the current educational climate and context?
- Which of these does your school or setting currently do well?
- Are there are any aspects suggested in the diagram that could be either be improved or initiated in your school or setting?
- How many of the areas in the diagram can be developed by individual teachers within their classroom, and how many rely on whole-school strategic planning?
- What implications might this have?

28 Framing the actions we take

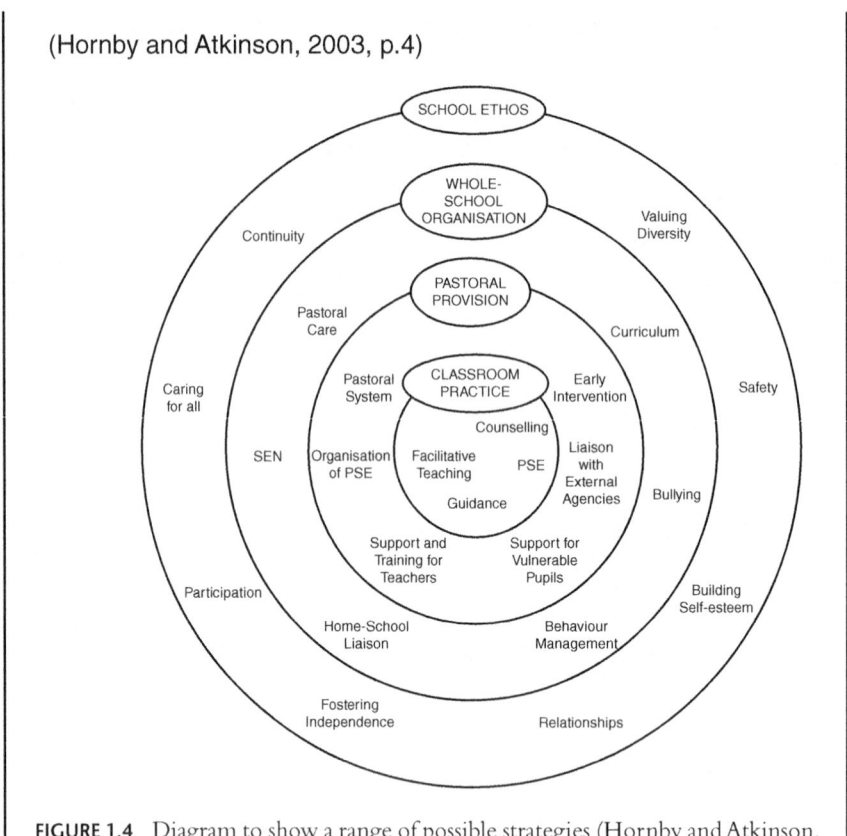

FIGURE 1.4 Diagram to show a range of possible strategies (Hornby and Atkinson, 2003, p. 4).

Approaches that are not rooted in developing mental well-being can exacerbate issues for children whose behaviour is challenging – both for the child or children and for their teachers. Spratt *et al.* (2006) noted teachers' frequent reference to the 'tensions' they felt in reconciling the necessary individual behaviour approaches for some children who did not 'easily fit into a system' with the expectations of a typical school – which were often suggested to be 'in opposition to prioritising welfare'. They argued that often, for children who did experience some form of 'pastoral interventions' to support their behaviour, the key driver for this was not the child but rather to 'teach them to conform' to the system 'rather than examining the system to see how it could better meet the needs of the child' (Spratt *et al.*, 2006, p. 16). It has been argued that this approach and the need for children to 'fit' the system:

> locate the [child's] difference, in the eyes of teachers, firmly in the child and relieved teachers from any responsibility to examine their own responses to children.
>
> (Spratt *et al.*, 2006, p. 16)

The lack of flexibility in some school's behaviour systems might then have a dehumanising effect on both children and teachers. It has also been noted that this is counterintuitive to developing and supporting mental well-being.

> Schools are traditionally concerned with the management of medium to large groups of people. The emphasis is on discipline and control using behaviour management strategies. Consequently, the influencing factors are external control as school staff shape the pupil's immediate environment to influence their inner self. Mental health interventions ... rely much more on analysis of the inner self, encouraging individual reflection. The focus is on the individual and the development of personal regulation rather than external regulatory restrictions.
>
> (Finney, 2006, p. 24)

This 'change the system vs change the child' dichotomy echoes the tension felt by schools in relation to the 'achievement vs well-being debate'. Although this polarisation exists in research, in real life the divide is probably not so clear or inflexible. However, it is important to question whether children need to meet the needs of the system or vice versa, and what happens to those children who cannot – for whatever reason – currently meet the needs of the system. This can be exemplified in the vignette about Billie.

? ACTIVITY STOP 3

Vignette: Billie

After an incident at her home, Billie is dropped off at school by a police car. This is not the first time this has happened, but she has arrived late to school and has been seen by her classmates emerging from the police car in the school's drive. When she gets into the classroom, a supply teacher is there instead of her usual teacher with whom she often has a good relationship. As the class are crowding around the supply teacher collecting the worksheets for the lesson, Billie is knocked on the hand by the new teacher. She immediately struggles to control her reactions; swearing at the teacher and knocking over a table before running from the school site.

Using the storyboards (Figure 1.5 and 1.6) reflect on an incident of misbehaviour you have experienced or observed in a school or setting – you could also use the vignette. Consider how the incident might have played out if was managed as a pastoral issue – draw if you are feeling artistic, or write notes if you are not.

30 Framing the actions we take

BEHAVIOURAL INCIDENT MANAGED AS A PASTORAL ISSUE			
The incident (what happened)	Outcomes (what happened after the incident)	Impact on the child	Impact on the teacher

FIGURE 1.5 Storyboard to record the outcomes of a behaviour incident as a pastoral issue.

Now, using the same incident, and in the next storyboard (Figure 1.6), think about what might have been different had it been managed as a disciplinary issue.

BEHAVIOURAL INCIDENT MANAGED AS A DISCIPLINARY ISSUE			
The incident (what happened)	Outcomes (what happened after the incident)	Impact on the child	Impact on the teacher

FIGURE 1.6 Storyboard to record the outcomes of a behaviour incident as a disciplinary issue.

When you have completed (in whichever way) the storyboards, consider for the child(ren) in your example, and Billie in the vignette. Reflect on Billie's incident and underline the observable behaviour in one colour and then the possible causes of it in a different colour. Firstly, consider the answers to the following questions if the issue had been dealt with taking into account only the observable behaviour and then if the issue had been dealt with accounting for behaviour and the possible drivers for the behaviour:

- Who has the better outcome in the two scenarios?
- How have the child and teacher been affected?
- What could be the impact of each of these on the class as a whole (whether they witnessed it or not) and on the wider school community?

Review

This chapter has reviewed policy and research linking unmet mental health issues with behaviour, particularly behaviours that challenge, and what schools can do to support these (and all) children. It has examined the key role of schools in supporting and developing children's mental health and well-being as well as the barriers that might prevent this from being done effectively. It has highlighted the importance of developing positive relationships between staff and pupils and considered how managing behaviour as a behavioural or pastoral issue can impact on the outcomes for the child and the teacher. We have also considered the difficulties in defining well-being and how different professionals' understandings of the term is influenced by their own views as well as the context they work in, meaning that different people may have a different understanding of the same term.

Whole-school actions might include some or all of the following:

- Ensure there is a common understanding for staff and children of terms such as 'well-being'.
- Make it clear through policy, the curriculum and the 'hidden curriculum' why developing mental health and well-being is important for pupils and staff.
- Consider how key policies, such as the behaviour policy, as well as every-day practices help to develop positive relationships between teachers and pupils.
- Although discrete, 'add-on' activities such as anti-bullying weeks can be helpful, these in themselves do not sufficiently develop children's mental well-being.
- Consider how to align the required individualised approaches some children need with whole-school policies.
- Ensure whole-school practices support and safeguard the well-being of staff who can be challenged by the additional stress of behaviours that challenge.

Individual teacher actions might include some or all of the following:

- Ensure there is a clear understanding of how the school can support individual teachers who raise concerns about children's mental health and behaviour. This may be making referrals or sharing concerns more informally with a designated mental health lead or understanding the processes and polices the school has to support specific children.
- Develop strategies to ensure positive relationships with children, particularly those who are 'hard to reach'.
- Reflect on how activities to support and develop mental well-being can be incorporated into the school day, either through discrete teaching such as PSHE or through cross-curricular work.
- Seek support (if necessary) in strategies to develop individual well-being as research shows teachers' well-being affects children's own mental well-being.

Possible mental health and well-being implications:

- Developing positive well-being, mental health and schooling are sometimes seen as contradictory aims. Specific consideration needs to be given to how all children are supported, but particularly those with behaviours that challenge to develop their self-esteem(s) and well-being.
- Developing and maintaining positive relationships are often the foundation of well-being and mental health. Schools and teachers may need to consider how policy, routines and specific strategies either support or undermine these relationships – for both pupils and teachers.

Practitioner-related take-away:

- There is a reciprocity between children's well-being and teachers' well-being. Children's well-being cannot be supported in school if staff well-being is not an equal priority.

Practitioner reading:

Cowburn, A., and Blow, M. (2017). *Wise Up - Prioritising Wellbeing in Schools*. https://youngminds.org.uk/media/1428/wise-up-prioritising-wellbeing-in-schools.pdf.

References

Brown, R. (2018). *Mental Health and Wellbeing Provision in Schools*. London: DfE.
The Children's Society. (2015). *The Good Childhood Report*. https://www.basw.co.uk/system/files/resources/basw_14829-10_0.pdf
The Children's Society. (2019). *The Good Childhood Report*. https://saphna.co/wp-content/uploads/2019/11/the_good_childhood_report_2019.pdf
Cowburn, A., and Blow, M. (2017). *Wise Up – Prioritising Wellbeing in Schools*. https://www.readkong.com/page/wise-up-prioritising-wellbeing-in-schools-7256446
Danby, G., and Hamilton, P. (2016). Addressing the 'elephant in the room'. The role of the primary school practitioner in supporting children's mental well-being. *Pastoral Care in Education*, **34**(2), pp. 90–103.
Department for Education and Skills. (2001). *Schools Achieving Success*. London: DfES
Department for Education. (2018). *Mental Health and Behaviour in Schools*. London: DfE.
Department for Education and the Rt. Hon. Damien Hinds MP. (2019). *All Pupils will be Taught about Mental and Physical Wellbeing*. London: DfE.
Department of Health and the Department for Education (2015). *Special Educational Needs and Disability Code of Practice: 0 to 25 Years Statutory Guidance for Organisations which Work with and Support Children and Young People Who Have Special Educational Needs or Disabilities*. London: DfE.
Dodge, R., Daly, A., Huyton, J., and Sanders, L. (2012). The challenge of defining wellbeing. *International Journal of Wellbeing*, **2**(3), pp. 222–235.

Finney, D. (2006). Stretching the boundaries: Schools as therapeutic agents in mental health. Is it a realistic proposition? *Pastoral Care in Education*, **24**(3), pp. 22–27.

Gott, J. (2003). The school: The front line of mental health development? *Pastoral Care in Education*, **21**(4), pp. 5–13.

Glazzard, J., and Bostwick, R. (2018). *Positive Mental Health: A Whole School Approach*. St. Albans: Critical Publishing.

Gray, P., Miller, A., and Noakes, J. (1994). Challenging behaviour in schools: An introduction. In Gray, P., Miller, A., & Noakes, J. (Eds.), *Challenging Behaviour In Schools* (pp. 1–4). London: Routledge.

Hornby, G., and Atkinson, M. (2003). A framework for promoting mental health in school. *Pastoral Care in Education*, **21**(2), pp. 3–9.

House of Commons Health and Education Committee. (2017). *Children and Young People's Mental Health – The Role of Education*. London: DfE.

Maguire, M., Ball, S., and Braun, A. (2010). Behaviour, classroom management and student 'control': Enacting policy in the English secondary school. *International Studies in Sociology of Education*, **20**(2), pp. 153–170.

Marshall, L., Wishart, R., Allison, D., and Smith, N. (2017). *Supporting Mental Health in Schools and Colleges: Quantitative Survey*. London: DfE.

Marzano, R., Marzano, J., and Pickering, D. (2003). *Classroom Management that Works: Research-Based Strategies for Increasing Student Achievement*. Alexandria, VA: Association for Supervision and Curriculum Development.

Masters, G. (2004). Conceptualising and researching student wellbeing. *Australian Council for Educational Research*, 1–6. http://research.acer.edu.au/research_conference_2004

McGuinness, F. (2021). *Teacher Wellbeing: The Benefits for Children's Mental Health | Education Support*. Teacher Wellbeing: The Benefits for Children's Mental Health. https://www.educationsupport.org.uk/blogs/teacher-wellbeing-benefits-childrens-mental-health

McPherson, K., Kerr, S., McGee, E., Morgan, A., Cheater, F., McLean, J., and Egan, J. (2014). The association between social capital and mental health and behavioural problems in children and adolescents: An integrative systematic review. *BMC Psychology*, **2**(1), pp. 1–16.

Norwich, B., and Eaton, A. (2015). The new special educational needs (SEN) legislation in England and implications for services for children and young people with social, emotional and behavioural difficulties. *Emotional and Behavioural Difficulties*, **20**(2), pp. 117–132.

Ortega-Alcázar, I., and Dyck, I. (2012). Migrant narratives of health and well-being: Challenging 'othering' processes through photo-elicitation interviews. *Critical Social Policy*, **32**(1), pp. 106–125.

Pollard, E., and Lee, P. (2003). Child well-being: A systematic review of the literature. *Social Indicators Research*, 61(1), pp. 59–78.

Postholm, M. (2013). Classroom management: What does research tell us? *European Educational Research Journal*, **12**(3), pp. 389–402.

Public Health England. (2015). *Promoting Children and Young People's Emotional Health and Wellbeing*. London: PHE.

Roffey, S. (2016). Building a case for whole-child, whole-school wellbeing in challenging contexts. *Educational and Child Psychology*, **33**(2), pp. 30–42.

Spratt, J., Shucksmith, J., Philip, K., and Watson, C. (2006). "Part of who we are as a school should include a responsibility for well-being": Links between the school environment, mental health and behaviour. *Pastoral Care in Education*, **24**(3), pp. 14–21.

Thompson, S., Clarke, E., Quickfall, A., and Glazzard, J. (2020). Averting the crisis in trainee teacher well-being – learning lessons across European contexts: A comparative study. *Journal of Comparative & International Higher Education* **12**, pp. 38–56.

UNICEF. (2009). *Child Friendly Schools Manual.* https://www.unicef.org/publications/files/Child_Friendly_Schools_Manual_EN_040809.pdf

Weare, K. (2000). *Promoting Mental, Emotional and Social Health: A Whole School Approach.* London: Routledge.

Wearmouth, J., Glynn, T., and Berryman, M. (2005). *Perspectives on Student Behaviour in Schools.* London: Routledge.

2
ACRONYMS AND ATTITUDES

This chapter will consider how the language used to describe children with behaviours that challenge influences and affects the actions taken to manage and support these individuals or groups. It will also discuss how the language used in schools, and in policy more broadly, has framed and changed attitudes to children's behaviour and shaped the responses from staff in schools. This chapter aims to:

- Share the range of current and historical acronyms and labels used to describe children whose social behaviour is perceived as challenging
- Consider how changes in the terms used has reflected changing attitudes
- Reflect on attitudes framing children as 'mad' 'bad' or 'sad'

Foundations

The language used to discuss and talk about most things changes over time and often either reflects or precipitates a change in attitudes and actions related to its subject – for example, the terms used to describe an individual's gender, race or sexuality. The language used in education and in schools is no different. However, a key factor when considering the language used to describe children's behaviours – and often as a result the children themselves – is the impact it has on those working with them, and ultimately how children are perceived and what actions are deemed suitable to manage them. Chan, Arnold, Webber, Riches, Parmenter and Roger (2012) stated that the language used shapes the 'thoughts, beliefs and emotions' experienced, and this highlights the importance of careful consideration of the language and terms associated with children and their behaviours. The language used in schools, or labels for children's behaviour, can sometimes lead to an initial and erroneous assumption that all children who are organised under a label or heading, whatever that may be, are a distinct and homogeneous group. As this chapter will discuss, there has been and continues to be a myriad of terminology – official and unofficial – to describe this often-disparate group of children. O'Brien and Guiney (2005) argued it was the label that was used that 'conferred similarities' rather than the traits of the children under that label. Others too have highlighted the pressures in the education system that 'encourage schools to treat diverse students alike in response to teaching strategies' (Wearmouth, Glynn & Berryman, 2005, p. 7). However, there are significant issues in providing support for children whose needs are different and who are grouped together using terms such as 'emotion' and 'behaviour' difficulties, which 'are amongst the most difficult concepts in the educational lexicon' (Garner & Gains, 1996).

? ACTIVITY STOP 1

Labels in education and schools are a fact of life; however, their use is not always advantageous. Reflect for a moment, before we move forward, on Garner and Gains's (1996) argument about grouping children under headings or labels and how this often automatically assumes children have the same issues, challenges, etc.:

- Do you agree with their statement?
- Is this something you have seen in a school or setting?
- If not, how was this, or how could this be avoided?

Using the diagram (Figure 2.1), begin to jot some thoughts down:

- Are there any advantages to 'labelling' children?
- If so, what might they be, and what might this help to achieve?
- Are there any disadvantages to 'labelling' children?
- If so, what might they be, and what issues might this cause?

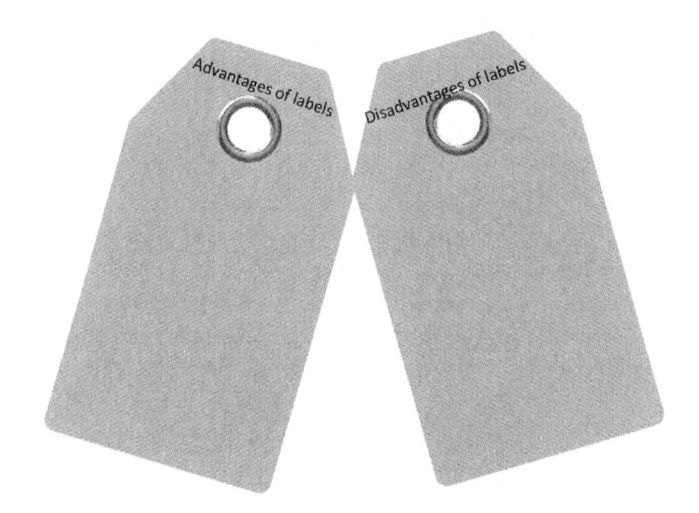

FIGURE 2.1 Diagram to consider the advantages and disadvantages of 'labelling' children.

Behaviours that challenge have existed as far back as records extend, and they are not in any way a recent phenomenon. There are examples in Roman poetry detailing the beating of school boys who had infringed rules, and records of armed English pupils taking part in violent mutinies and 'destroying all of the most famous public schools at least once' (Wearmouth *et al.*, 2005, p. 36). Wearmouth *et al.* (2005) noted an example they came across of a teacher in the 1800s enquiring about money for shin pads because the children in his class kicked him each day! So, although the range of behaviours children exhibit does not seem to have changed since Roman times, the language used in association with them certainly has, and there has (as expected) been a radical shift from historic terms used to describe children with a range of behaviours that challenge. These terms included 'deviations' from behavioural norms in the late 19th century which were categorised under the medical terms of 'idiot, imbecile or fatuous' (Cooper, 1999). Despite the unacceptability of these terms in today's society, studies by Sully in 1895 into the experiences of these 'physiologically defective' children led to the insight – which is still relevant today, even over 100 years later – that:

> the normal child is one who is in adequate adjustment with his environment; the so-called abnormal child is, in the vast majority of cases, merely a maladjusted child, not a child suffering from gross pathological defect.
>
> (cited in Cooper, 1999, p. 15)

Early in the 20th century, terms of reference such as 'moral imbeciles' were common, with 'disturbed' – although some argued for 'disturbing' (Daniels & Cole, 2002) in regular use – descriptions that would rightly never be considered appropriate or accurate in current thinking. It is easy to imagine how teachers and others might relate to a child who had been labelled 'disturbing', and how this would have influenced the relationship between the two. These terms saw a significant shift in 1945 when the 'Handicapped Pupils and Health Service Regulations' was introduced; this was followed by the 1944 Education Act, commonly referred to as the 'Butler Act' (Cooper, 1999). These post-Second World War acts marked what Cooper (1999) described as a shift towards therapeutic approaches which saw 'exponential growth' of provision for children whose behaviours challenged. This move towards a therapeutic approach was, at least in part, a response to the devastating and destructive impact the war had on many families and on children in particular. Despite this, the shift in terminology used to describe and define children at this time had been suggested to be vague and confusing, an issue which has been argued to persist even in the most recent definitions of behaviour (Norwich & Eaton, 2015). The term 'maladjusted' was first used in these post-war legislations and was used to describe pupils who:

> show evidence of psychological disturbance or emotional instability and who require special educational treatment in order to affect their personal, social or emotional readjustment.
>
> (Cooper, 1999, p. 21)

In English documents in the 1960s and 1970s (DES, 1967, 1978), the term 'behavioural deviance' emerged, and 'maladjusted' continued to be used. Although these are significantly less pejorative than those very early terms, they clearly still relate to the issues being within the child. They also suggest a (possibly purposeful) mismatch between the overarching system – i.e. the school or society – and the child, where the child is unable to fit into the expectations of the system, rather than reconsidering how fit for purpose the expectations of the system might be. However, in the 1980s the Warnock Report and the 1981 Education Act (DES, 1978, 1981) saw a distinct movement away from the medicalised language associated with earlier descriptions of behaviour such as 'maladjusted' and 'deviant'. These publications introduced terms still familiar to many, such as 'special educational needs' and 'learning difficulties' to replace the previous term of 'handicapped', and recommended the removal of the previously pathologising system (Cooper, 1999). At this time children previously defined as 'maladjusted' also began to be described – by the preferred term of educational psychologists – as having 'emotional and behavioural difficulties'. This change in terminology represented a shift in ideas, from behaviour issues being a deficit or problem within the individual child, to a recognition that issues in behaviour may also stem from the environment in which the child operated, which included the classroom.

Following on from this, in the late 1980s the Children's Act (DES, 1989) and 'Discipline in Schools', or the 'Elton Report', were published (DES, 1989). The Children Act (DES, 1989), in line with changing terminology, cemented the legal basis of the relationships between children and adults, marking the shift between adults having rights over children to one where adults 'had responsibilities of care towards children (Cooper, 1999; Cooper and Jacobs, 2011). The Elton Report (DES, 1989), commissioned by the government, was at the time, the biggest survey of attitudes towards classroom behaviour and again reinforced the importance of considering the environmental and external influences on children's behaviour. More recent terms show a development of this view, with the use of terms such as EBD – 'Emotional and behavioural difficulties' (DfE, 1994) and its augmentation to include the term 'social' – SEBD/BESD. These labels show the impact of emotional and social factors on a child's behaviour and enable the possibility that factors which affect the child and their behaviour may, at times at least, lay outside their own control. This is illustrative of a movement to see behaviour as not always caused by a deficit within the child – as something they are 'missing' – but as indicative of issues within the systems in which they operate. The current term of reference in England of SEMH – 'Social, Emotional Mental Health' (DoH & DfE, 2015), for the first time makes explicit the impact of mental health on a child's behaviour, and clearly states that behaviours may be a result of unmet mental health needs.

The use of the acronym SEMH has developed from the published guidance setting out school's legal responsibilities for working with children with a range of non-standard or 'special' needs. The Code of Practice which governs the processes schools must use to provide support for these pupils has changed surprisingly little since its inception after the Warnock report (DES, 1978). Indeed, Tutt and Williams (2015, p. 7) noted that the review of the Code in 2014 (DoH & DfE, 2015) was its most 'comprehensive overhaul for 30 years'. The Code has undergone changes previously but these had not been as significant; for example, in 2001 (DfES, 2001) the terminology shifted to include 'disabilities', broadening the acronym to become SEND. However, as the overlap between the terms SEN and SEND was never made clear or explicit, both became commonly used in school, again adding to – rather than resolving – the lack of clarity around terminology. The Code separated the range of additional needs into the categories: communication and interaction, cognition and learning, behaviour, emotional and social difficulties (changed to SEMH in the 2014 Code) and physical/sensory impairment. The Code's most recent iteration includes a number of key changes, and specifically the need for schools to make a 'local offer' to parents and children detailing their provisions for children with additional needs, including those with an Education and Health Care plan (EHCP) which replaced the previous Individual Education plans and Statements (DfES, 2001).

This concept of a 'local offer' signals perhaps the most dramatic shift so far for those with non-standard needs whereby schools are now compelled to make explicit 'offers' to pupils and parents detailing what services can be provided and accessed through the school, enabling much greater choice (and perhaps echoing the marketised provision long since available to mainstream learners). This shift from a requirement to 'include', to the expectation of schools to 'offer' a package of support to children, positions them much more as active consumers of the services schools give with the associated expectations and aspirations, as opposed to simply passive receivers of provision with relatively little choice over its implementation or range.

However, despite official government publications, there remain a number of terms used to describe this frequently disparate group of children whose needs can be significantly different to others often defined under the same term – as Garner and Gains (1996) argued almost 25 years ago. For example, 'challenging behaviour' is commonly used in the UK in fields such as education, health and social care, whilst the term 'emotional and behavioural disorders' is used by the World Health Organisation (Cooper & Jacobs, 2011). The *Diagnostic and Statistical Manual of Mental Disorders* (DSM) (APA, 2020) is also commonly used in other countries (although much less frequently in education in the UK) and the number of categories, and thus the terminology it includes, has vastly increased with each version (it is now in its fifth edition). It could be questioned whether the changing (and increasing) terminology and varying definitions between groups and countries is because of the way in which knowledge about childhood has increased, or rather whether the notions of what is okay or 'normal' behaviour has narrowed. It may also be due to the systems in which children are placed; for example, in the United States (US), funding is associated with a given diagnosis. As a result, both those holding and seeking this funding need to refine the diagnosis criteria in order to 'prudently' allocate funds.

However, no terms are value free and, as noted, there are always cultural aspects involved in the diagnosis or label children are given. For example, China uses the DSM criteria for diagnosis, as do a number of western cultures, as though the criteria have no cultural bases, despite significant differences in norms and expectations of children's behaviours in the Chinese and American education systems. This may result in little parity between behaviours under certain diagnoses across cultures and countries and can be illustrated in the number of diagnoses for attention deficit hyperactivity disorder (ADHD) and attention deficit disorder (ADD). It has been reported (Russell, Rodgers, Ukoumunne & Ford, 2014) that 6.3% of children aged between 5 and 9 has been diagnosed with ADHD or ADD in the US, whilst only 2.4% of children in the UK aged between 5 and 15 had the same diagnosis (despite more children falling within the wider age range in the UK). This is despite a large-scale systematic review which suggested there were no differences in the prevalance of ADHD and ADD between Europe and the US. This suggests, then, that it is instead a range of cultural and contetxual biases and norms that result in either a greater or lesser likelihood of a diagnosis. If this is the case for ADHD and ADD, it could also be assumed to follow for a range of other diagnosable conditions and labels.

Diller (2006) noted what he perceived as a shift from nurture to nature in relation to explaining behaviours (i.e. social and/or environmental to medical), which he tracked back to the early 1950s. He also asserted that issues with behaviours that challenge were 'dimensional' rather than 'categorical' (Diller, 2006, p. 8) which is still reflected in the current ambiguity and variety of terms. This imprecision is the direct result of the 'dimensions' and range of socially and culturally appropriate (and inappropriate) behaviours which makes a 'categorically' accepted and understood definition between practitioners, other professionals and other contexts almost impossible.

Chan *et al.* (2012) argued that 'challenging behaviour' as a label can be disempowering, and rather than highlighting the 'challenge', reconceptualising the term as 'behaviours that concern' may be more appropriate. This shows that, despite significant evolution in the terms used to consider behaviours that challenge, we are still a long way from a shared, multidisciplinary and commonly understood language to talk about children's behaviours.

> ### 💭 THINKING STOP 1
>
> How does the language we use affect our actions? Consider what acronyms (both whole-school and 'staffroom only') are used within your setting or that you have experienced working in schools.
>
> - How many can you list?
> - What do these acronyms and labels suggest about the practitioners' perspective on children's behaviour?
> - How might it influence the strategies they use to manage behaviour?
> - Use these ideas to make a brief list in Figure 2.2 of what you consider to be 'non-negotiables' in relation to terminology used in your school/setting/practice to describe children whose behaviour can present a challenge.
>
> **BEHAVIOUR NON-NEGOTIABLES**
>
> **FIGURE 2.2** Figure of non-negotiable terminology to discuss behaviour.

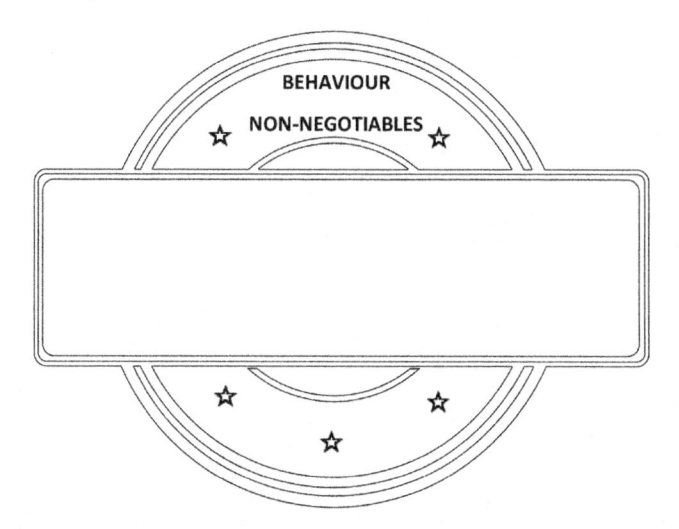

Carefully considering the language we use when supporting children is important. Macleod (2006), in her research on approaches to support children in Scotland with a range of behavioural needs, highlighted that the 'views held by adults on the causes of troubling behaviour have a direct impact on the experience of young people' (p. 55). She found that professionals' views on the causes of behaviours that challenge fell into three board categories;

> Young people … can be seen as passive victims of circumstance who are in need of help; as individuals responsible for their own behaviour who need to be punished; or as sufferers from a medical condition that require treatment.
>
> (Macleod, 2006, p. 55)

These were distilled into categories of understanding behaviours as a result of children being either 'mad', 'bad' or 'sad' (Macleod, 2006). From the 'mad' perspective, behaviours are viewed by staff as the cause of some 'disorder', where the child is ill in some way and may require medication. If the child is seen as having some sort of deficit, they were classed as 'bad', whilst victimhood or issues related to, for example, social inequalities, resulted in children perceived as 'sad'. Whilst these distinctions are very broad, it can be seen that each of these different understandings and views would result in different ways of supporting children and/or managing their behaviour and legitimise the use of very different strategies within the classroom. All of the views Macleod (2006) collated from her participants were based on some form of understanding of behaviour as caused by either an individual child's 'failing' or broader structural inequalities. These ideas of the causes of behaviour being a child or systemic deficit will be explored in greater detail in Chapter 4.

❓ ACTIVITY STOP 2

Vignette: Steven

Steven had a history of behaviours that challenged. He was care-experienced and had attended a number of schools before his current placement. He had struggled to form relationships with his peers in Year 5 and the decision had been made by the SLT to move him to the Year 6 class where he had some friendships. Steven had recently attended a multi-disciplinary meeting about spending more time with his mum, but she had been unwilling to make the necessary changes to her routines and Steven was told visits with his mum would not be as frequent as he had hoped. The following day at school he had struggled with his behaviour and at playtime, after a seemingly minor altercation with a pupil, he retrieved a scaffolding bar from underneath a mobile classroom and tried to attack pupils and staff with it. This (in culmination with a range of previous incidents and associated plans and paperwork) resulted in his permanent exclusion from the school.

Record (in pictures or in words) your ideas on a 'storyboard' format (Figure 2.3) tracking the antecedence and outcomes of the same incident of challenging behaviour. How might these look different from the 'mad', 'bad' and sad' conceptualisations (Macleod, 2006)? You can use an incident from your own experience or the example in the vignette to do this.

BEHAVIOURAL INCIDENT MANAGED FROM THE 'MAD' PERSPECTIVE			
The incident (what happened)	Outcomes (what happened after the incident)	Impact on the child	Impact on the teacher
BEHAVIOURAL INCIDENT MANAGED FROM THE 'BAD' PERSPECTIVE			
The incident (what happened)	Outcomes (what happened after the incident)	Impact on the child	Impact on the teacher
BEHAVIOURAL INCIDENT MANAGED FROM THE 'SAD' PERSPECTIVE			
The incident (what happened)	Outcomes (what happened after the incident)	Impact on the child	Impact on the teacher

FIGURE 2.3 Storyboards to consider how outcomes may differ depending on the perspectives used to frame behaviours.

Reflect on what the outcomes may be for the child, the teacher and the school community from these different perspectives:

- What are the key advantages for each group when behaviour is managed from these different understandings?
- What are the key limitations for each group?

The language used to frame children's behaviour and structure school's responses is also influenced by societal attitudes, government policy and the personal and professional experiences of whoever is assessing the behaviour. It was argued (Forness, 1996, cited in Kavale, Forness & Mostert, 2005) that:

> definitional problems are compounded by the different social contexts where they are used ... [a] label is assigned through cultural rules that demonstrate considerable variability across contexts and make the process inherently subjective.
>
> (p. 45)

This suggests that any definition used is influenced by who uses it and the place where it is used. For example, as noted earlier, there are differing understandings and definitions between psychological, educational and medical professionals which can exacerbate difficulties in essential inter-agency and multi-disciplinary working. Wearmouth *et al.* (2005) noted that descriptions that are used to share and talk about behaviours that challenge have no 'absolute meaning' and are meaningful only in the context of the incident. There may also be variation across contexts – behaviours that can be managed and supported in an alternative provision setting may be considered unmanageable by a new teacher in a mainstream setting, and so on. This again asserts the challenges in understanding each other's perceptions of behaviour without knowing how and where it happened and how that fits with what is usual or accepted for that child. Wearmouth *et al.* (2005) suggested that understandings of behaviour are influenced at a number of levels, including the individual child, the teacher and the whole school, and as a result are not easy to define, or as simple as they might initially sound.

To make discussions around behaviour even more complex, it can be conceptualised as existing along a 'continuum of tolerance' effect' (McCall, 2004), which changes with political and social pressures. For example, with greater pressure from the government, there may be less (or even zero) tolerance of misbehaviour in schools, and with less pressure, there may be greater acceptance of, or support for, misbehaviour. It could then be argued that it is society's values and norms that have changed to be currently less accepting of behaviour, as opposed to any specific change in the type, frequency or severity of behaviours experienced in schools. Over the last forty years there has been an increased focus on 'retributive and punitive' punishments and a reduction of 'tolerance and therapy' (Gray, Miller & Noakes, 1994). These external pressures on schools are increasingly addressed by a focus on teacher and school *control* of children and their behaviours – a sustained theme in government publications (Bennett, 2017; DfE, 2013, 2016). Armstrong (2014) argued that this demonstrated government policies on behaviour were retrogressive and 'against and away' from modernising discussions around behaviour. He stated this was evident in policies that focused on 'discipline', 'authority' and 'respect', rather than any consideration of the causes of behaviours that challenge (Armstrong, 2014). Indeed, the current (and long-standing) prevalence of language such as 'discipline' and 'control' in English government documents related to behaviour in schools (DfES, 1989; DfE, 1994, 2013, 2016) encourages specific approaches and can at times close down alternatives.

> **THINKING STOP 2**
>
> As we have discussed in this chapter, the language used to talk about behaviour affects our understanding of the causes of behaviour and, as a result, how we manage it or support children. Can you highlight any language you think is used in these two excerpts – both from English government publications – to talk about behaviour?
>
> The two basic assumptions are that children respond in kind to courteous and considerate treatment by adults and that they will work with concentration and diligence at tasks which are suited to their abilities.
> (DES, 1967, p. 267)
>
> And: Teachers can discipline pupils whose conduct falls below the standard which could reasonably be expected of them. This means that if a pupil misbehaves, breaks a school rule or fails to follow a reasonable instruction the teacher can impose a punishment on that pupil.
> (DfE, 2016, p. 7)
>
> - What do you notice?
> - Do the dates of these excerpts surprise you?
> - How might each statement legitimise behavioural interactions with children?

Building blocks

Clearly, the language used by professionals matters in schools, and the research examined in this chapter suggests it can also mediate the way in which children are supported in schools and settings. One of the key formalised sources of language for teachers and practitioners is their school's behaviour policy, which is often (but not always) a distillation of key government policies or documents. In England, the DfE's requirements for schools to publish their behaviour policies on their websites and to include how they use rewards and sanctions limits the range of approaches most schools are able to take. The DfE themselves have acknowledged that:

> Schools have become skilled at meeting government targets, but too often have had their ability to do what they think is right for their pupils constrained by government directions or improvement initiatives.
> (DfE, 2010, p. 8)

It has been argued that in England, government policy has resulted in schools' 'compulsory adoption' of a policy centred on rewards and sanctions, despite this behaviourist focus (see Chapter 4 for more details on behaviourism) being 'all but lost' in wider aspects of education (Payne, 2015). Indeed, Payne (2015) proposed that the 'behaviourist ideas' which were required to form the foundation of schools' policies represented 'a potentially confused set of aims and theoretical principles'. For example, in much teaching, a child-led, questioning approach is advocated, where pupils are encouraged to take responsibility for developing and assessing their own progress and to become independent learners who persevere through a carefully differentiated or scaffolded approach. However, the way in which behaviour is managed does not always mirror this approach to learning, causing issues for some children and staff. This can lead to a perceived and artificial separation of 'behaviour' from other facets of school life such as learning and teaching, and a view that behaviour is something that occurs in a vacuum rather than being influenced by a myriad of other school- and non-school-based factors. This dichotomy can be evident in a whole-school behaviour policy that does not link with other key policies in school because behaviour is seen as a self-contained issue.

The separation between learning, teaching and behaviour is sometimes reinforced by the 'off the shelf' nature of interventions some schools use, such as for example Assertive Discipline (this will be discussed in greater detail in Chapter 4), which can sometimes be seen to make behaviour a standalone issue, rather an integrated, holistic whole-school feature. This 'add-on' aspect – where behavioural interventions, policies, support and so on are bolted onto other aspects of school life – follows a 'machine system' view of the school. From this perspective, things can be added on to 'fix' behaviour, as opposed to a 'social system' view which takes account of the school as a whole (Watkins and Wagner, 2000). The language used in polices that relate to behaviour, therefore, needs to be reinforced and replicated in other polices such as teaching and learning, well-being and so on. This will ensure that the language used to support children's behaviour is consistent with the ethos of the school as a whole. A carefully worded, whole-school, cross-referenced behaviour policy will also provide a firm foundation for a consistent use of language when working with children, and as a result begin to develop a consistent framework for understanding and working with children who have behaviours that challenge.

As discussed in this chapter, the language used impacts on thoughts and actions. It might be beneficial to provide an opportunity for staff, for example through an INSET day or staff meetings, to talk about the language used by staff, other professionals and the children themselves in relation to behaviour and examine the assumptions that underpin the vocabulary. Although it may not be possible, or even desirable, for all staff to have the same philosophical understandings of the causes of behaviour, the opportunity to consider their own implicit views and perceptions may be helpful to work towards a whole-school understanding, reinforced by careful use of language. In line with this, a consideration of government policy and the language cascaded into schools from those documents would be valuable. Much of the language used in government policy on behaviour currently implies the school and teacher's role as one of being 'in control'. The language associated with control in relation to behaviour can limit the range of strategies to support children and can also make it adversarial to some degree and even more 'high-stakes' for both children and teachers. Many teachers, particularly early in their careers, or during a transition (for example, to a new year group or new school) can be concerned with the idea of losing control of a class or group in the classroom. It has been suggested that some teachers have reported:

> feeling completely isolated when faced with challenging behaviour, and reluctant to seek support due to their fears of loss of credibility with other staff ... It seems as if the discipline, or the behaviour management aspect is how you are judged as a good teacher.
>
> (Spratt, Shucksmith, Philip & Watson, 2006, p. 18)

As a result, considering whether, or how, the language of control and discipline is enacted in your school or setting, and its impact on children and staff, is useful. It might be much more difficult for a teacher to 'control' children than it is, for example, to form positive relationships with them.

THINKING STOP 3

Reflect on the importance of 'discipline' and 'control' in the classroom.

- What might you see if a teacher was 'in control'?
- What might the advantages be?
- What might the limitations be?
- What strategies would they be likely to use to maintain 'control'?

If we consider an approach that might lie at the opposite end of the spectrum to control – that of empathy and relationships – how might your answers to these questions be different?

- Does a relational and/or empathetic approach broaden or reduce the strategies and approaches to manage and support children's behaviours?

Although it is too simplistic to consider the strategies we use to work with, and support children as an either/or, or a control vs relationships dichotomy, it might be helpful to consider whether the strategies we use in schools are providing children with 'behaviour for learning' – for example, 'control' and 'managing behaviour' – or 'behaviour for life' – such as 'democracy' and 'respect' (Maguire, Ball & Braun, 2010).

> ### ☁ THINKING STOP 4
>
> Following on from what you have read and the points we have discussed in this chapter about the importance of language, think about the following statement:
>
> > policy such as DfE (2010) conceptualises challenging behaviour by children as a pragmatic 'problem' which can be intuitively 'solved' by a focus on discipline, attendance and sanctions.
> >
> > (Armstrong, 2014, p. 741)
>
> - Is thinking of children's behaviours as a 'problem' helpful?
> - When?
> - Why?
> - If behaviour is a 'problem', who has the 'solution'?
> - What are the advantages of this group 'solving' the 'problem'?
> - What are the limitations of this group 'solving' the 'problem'?
> - If you were to re-word this statement for your school, setting, a specific group of children or even an individual child, what might it say, and what difference might this make to the chid(ren) and the adults?

Review

This chapter has focused on the impact of language on our understanding of the causes of, and the actions we chose to take related to behaviour. We have tracked the evolution of the language used to describe children and their behaviours from early definitions of 'disturbed' to the most recent term of 'social, emotional, mental health difficulties'. There has also been a consideration of how language has changed in line with changing social views and tolerances, and how ways of talking about behaviour and understating its causes legitimises different ways of working with children.

Whole school actions might include some or all of the following:

- Examine carefully the language in school policies – specifically the behaviour policy – and whether it reflects the school's ethos and principles.
- Provide time for staff to work together to examine the language they, and others, use when talking about behaviour; for example, a whole school INSET.
- Consider whether consistency in language and/or terminology to discuss behaviour is advantageous for the school or setting. If so, could a whole school set of non-negotiables related to language be drawn up?

Individual teacher actions might include some or all of the following:

- Think about how the language used inside and outside the classroom affects how behaviour is managed.
- Consider how the way in which language is used frames behaviour, and the understandings of the causes of behaviour.
- Review whether the vocabulary used links with the behaviour policies, and associated whole-school polices.

Possible mental health and well-being implications:

- The term 'mental health' is now explicit in the most recent terminology for children whose behaviour challenges.
- It is essential that issues of behaviour are considered from the perspective of possible unmet mental health needs.
- When taking the explicit connections now made in policy between mental health and behaviour, it could be argued that a behaviour policy and range of interventions that only deploy rewards and sanctions may not support all children, specifically those who are suggested to have a range of unmet mental health needs.
- Schools will need to consider how they can support children with a range of needs and what whole-school, group and individual strategies and interventions can support those who specifically struggle with mental health as well as what training staff will need to feel confident in doing so.

Practitioner-related take-away:

- The language used to talk about children and their behaviours will often – consciously or subconsciously – guide the actions and interventions that are taken by practitioners.

Practitioner Reading:

Armstrong, D., and Squires, G. (2012) *Contemporary Issues in Special Educational Needs: Considering the Whole Child*. Maidenhead: McGraw-Hill/Open University Press.

References

American Psychological Association. (2020). *Diagnostic and Statistical Manual of Mental Disorders* (5th ed.). Arlington: APA.

Armstrong, D. (2014). Educator perceptions of children who present with social, emotional and behavioural difficulties: A literature review with implications for recent educational policy in England and internationally. *International Journal of Inclusive Education*, **18**(7), pp. 731–745.

Bennett, T. (2017). *Creating a Culture: How School Leaders Can Optimise Behaviour*. London: DfE.
Chan, J., Arnold, S., Webber, L., Riches, V., Parmenter, T., and Roger, S. (2012). Is it time to drop the term "challenging behaviour"? *Learning Disability Practice*, **15**(5), pp. 36–39.
Cooper, P. (1999). Educating children with emotional and behavioural difficulties: The evolution of current thinking and provision. In Cooper, P. (Ed.), *Understanding and Supporting Children with Emotional and Behavioural Difficulties* (pp. 13–42). London: Jessica Kingsley Publishers.
Cooper, P., and Jacobs, B. (2011). *Evidence of Best Practice Models and Outcomes in the Education of Children with Emotional Disturbance/Behavioural Difficulties: An International Review*. Co. Meath: University of Leicster and NCSE.
Daniels, H., and Cole, T. (2002). The development of provision for young people with emotional and behavioural difficulties: An activity theory analysis. *Oxford Review of Education*, **28**(2), pp. 311–329.
Department for Education. (1994). *The Education of Children with Emotional and Behavioural Difficulties Circular 9/94*. London: DfE.
Department for Education. (2010). *The Importance of Teaching: The School's White Paper 2010*. London: DfE.
Department for Education. (2013). *Behaviour and Discipline in Schools: Guidance for Governing Bodies*. London: DfE.
Department for Education. (2016). *Behaviour and Discipline in Schools: Advice for Headteachers and School Staff*. London: DfE.
Department for Education and Skills (DES). (2001). *Special Educational Needs Code of Practice*. London: DfES.
Department of Education and Science (DES). (1967). *Children and Their Primary Schools: A Report of the Central Advisory Council for Education (England)*. London: DES.
Department of Education and Science (DES). (1978). *Special Educational Needs Report of the Committee of Enquiry into the Education of Handicapped Children and Young People*. London: DES.
Department of Education and Science (DES). (1981). *Education Act 1981 (Repealed 1.11.1996)*. London: DES.
Department of Education and Science. (1989). *Discipline in Schools. Report of the Committee of Enquiry. (Chairman: Lord Elton)*. London: DES.
Department of Health and the Department for Education. (2015). *Special Educational Needs and Disability Code of Practice: 0 to 25 years Statutory Guidance for Organisations which Work with and Support Children and Young People Who Have Special Educational Needs or Disabilities*. London: DoH/DfE.
Diller, L. (2006) *The Last Normal Child: Essays on the Intersection of Kids, Culture and Psychiatric Drugs*. Westport: Prager Publishers.
Garner, P., and Gains, C. (1996). Models of intervention for children with emotional and behavioural difficulties. *Support for Learning*, **11**(4), pp. 141–145.
Gray, P., Miller, A., and Noakes, J. (1994). Challenging behaviour in schools: An introduction. In Gray, P., Miller, A., and Noakes, J. (Eds.), *Challenging Behaviour In Schools* (pp. 1–4). Abingdon: Routledge.
Kavale, K., Forness, S., and Mostert, M. (2005). Defining emotional or behavioural disorders: The quest for affirmation. In Clough, P., Garner, P. Yuen, P., and Yuen, F. (Eds.), *Handbook of Emotional and Behavioural Difficulties* (pp. 45–58). London: SAGE Publications Ltd.
Macleod, G. (2006). Bad, mad or sad: Constructions of young people in trouble and implications for interventions. *Emotional and Behavioural Difficulties*, **11**(3), pp. 155–167.

Maguire, M., Ball, S., and Braun, A. (2010). Behaviour, classroom management and student 'control': Enacting policy in the English secondary school. *International Studies in Sociology of Education*, **20**(2), pp. 153–170.

McCall, C. (2004). Perspectives on behaviour. In Wearmouth, J., Richmond, R., Glynn, T., and Berryman, M. (Eds.), *Understanding Pupil Behaviour In Schools: A Diversity of Approaches* (pp. 16–24). London: David Fulton Publishers.

Norwich, B., and Eaton, A. (2015). The new special educational needs (SEN) legislation in England and implications for services for children and young people with social, emotional and behavioural difficulties. *Emotional and Behavioural Difficulties*, **20**(2), pp. 117–132.

O'Brien, T., and Guiney, D. (2005). The problem is not the problem: Hard cases in modernist systems. In Clough, P., Garner, P., Pardeck, J., and Yuen, F. (Eds.), *Hanbook of Emotional and Behavioural Difficulties* (pp. 141–154). London: SAGE Publications Ltd.

Payne, R. (2015). Using rewards and sanctions in the classroom: Pupils' perceptions of their own responses to current behaviour management strategies. *Educational Review*, **67**(4), pp. 483–504.

Russell, G., Rodgers, L., Ukoumunne, O., and Ford, T. (2014). Prevalence of parent-reported ASD and ADHD in the UK: Findings from the millennium cohort study. *Journal of Autism and Developmental Disorders*, *44*(1), pp 31–40.

Spratt, J., Shucksmith, J., Philip, K., and Watson, C. (2006). "Part of who we are as a school should include responsibility for well-being": Links between the school environment, mental health and behaviour. *Pastoral Care in Education*, **24**(3), pp. 14–21.

Tutt, R., and Williams, P. (2015). How the SEN framework changed. In *The SEND Code of Practice: Policy, Provision and Practice.* (pp. 7–13). London: SAGE Publications.

Watkins, C., and Wagner, P. (2000). *Improving School Behaviour*. London: Paul Chapman Publishing Ltd.

Wearmouth, J., Glynn, T., and Berryman, M. (2005). *Perspectives on Student Behaviour in Schools*. London: Routledge.

3
SCHOOL POLICIES
Possibilities and problems

This final chapter in Part I of this book considers what influences how behaviour is supported and managed in the classroom. The aim of this chapter is to consider how school policy mediates (or doesn't) how behaviour is managed. It will examine the impact of the wider political policy that informs the management of behaviour in schools, and specifically the policies schools develop themselves to manage behaviour. Schools face a wide range of tensions: increased academic pressures, a competitive climate resulting from greater parental choice and a growing number of children identified as having unmet social, emotional and mental health needs. It has been suggested that these have led to a reassurance in 'zero-tolerance' policies and increased exclusion rates, or 'off-rolling', as schools attempt to maintain their competitive image (Bradbury, 2018; Parliamentary Select Committee for Education, 2018; Watkins & Wagner, 2000).

This chapter aims to:

- Share what is expected from a school behaviour policy
- Examine responses to applying behaviour policies
- Discuss how the broader political and educational context influences behaviour policies
- Consider how these all interact and influence how behaviour is actually managed in the classroom

Foundations

Policy has been defined as 'normative guidelines for action' which govern 'how things should be done' (Thomas & Loxley, 2001). From this definition, it could be assumed that policies and applying them are straightforward and essentially for the greater good. Despite much of the research in this area typifying policy implementation as messy, with inconsistent approaches and variability from implementer to implementer and from school to school (Coburn & Stein, 2006; Datnow & Stringfield, 2000), Ball (1997) believed policy makers saw the 'problems' to be fixed as residing in the school or in the teacher, but never in the policy. Ball, Hoskins, Maguire and Braun (2011) argued that behaviour policies 'presented particular and unusual challenge to schools' – specifically in how they are applied, or not applied. Approaches to implementing policies are suggested to exist on a continuum between strict conformity at one end and complete modification at the other, with 'acquiescence, compromise and avoidance' somewhere in between these two extremes (Datnow & Stringfield, 2000; Thomas & Loxley, 2001). In their research, Datnow and Stringfield (2000) found that variable responses to policy were 'ubiquitous' and the norm rather than the exception. Spillane, Reiser and Reimer (2002) highlighted the impact of the different ways in which people could understand the same policy, and therefore, the range of different ways that they might (or might not) act on it. Datnow and Stringfield (2000) warned against the view that policy could be implemented identically anywhere, at any time, and suggested that this view flew in the face of both research and common sense. As Thomas and Loxley (2001) stated in regard to policy, 'we can ignore it, extend it, subvert it and rewrite it, but we cannot escape it'!

Levin (1998) suggested that the aim of policy had changed dramatically and that fear – as opposed to a sense of possibility – was at that time the primary focus of educational policy, with standards, accountability and testing featuring heavily in the educational reforms of many countries. Research (Thomas & Loxley, 2001) found that over twenty years, there had been a dramatic increase in policies throughout education 'on almost every aspect of schooling'. This is still seen in many schools and countries, and particularly in England; indeed, Ball *et al.* (2011) argued that policies were a particularly English preoccupation, which were 'composites' and 'unstable, synthetic entities'.

THINKING STOP 1

What do you think about Levin's (1998) suggestion that fear drives (or did at the time of his writing) policy in education? If we consider behaviour in schools specifically:

- Do any fears guide the writing of school behaviour policies (i.e. fear of being inspected, being 'competitive')?
- What fears impact on the way in which we chose to manage behaviour (i.e. fear of losing control, fear of parental/SLT reactions)?
- What might school policies or strategies in the classroom look like if they were undertaken with a 'sense of possibility'?

Despite his assertion, Levin (1998) suggested education policies have at their centre a focus on the 'preparation of a workforce' and developing the ability of children to compete internationally. An aspect of this can be seen in the UK's comparison with other countries' educational outcomes in league tables such as the Programme for International Student Assessment (PISA), which are increasingly referred to in government publications (DfE, 2012). Levin (1998) argued that the changes in the emphasis of policies encouraged an increased marketisation of schooling, partly as a result of external testing and published league tables, and that hand-in-hand with this was a change in parental agency, specifically greater parental choice. It was suggested that regardless of a 'rhetoric of inclusion' in many school policies (and in those of the government), this marketisation, parental choice and the resulting competition between schools made them less accepting of certain students and behaviours than they previously may have been (Wearmouth, Glynn & Berryman, 2005). Nevertheless, Levin (1998, p. 133) questioned how much choice parents had in reality:

> they (the government) have also been taking steps that may result in schools being more similar and the choice therefore being less meaningful.

This is particularly pertinent in England, where the requirements of the National Curriculum, as well as national testing and a common Ofsted inspection framework for schools, realistically make any differences schools may wish to exert almost impossible to exercise.

A key whole-school policy, and one that must be published on the school's website, is the behaviour policy. Goodman (2006) stated that great importance is laid at the door of a school's behaviour policy, and it has been seen by some as a 'conduit for moral instruction'. Visser and Stokes (2010) suggested that there are three different types of rights – legal, civil and human – and that all three required addressing within a framework for managing behaviour again, placing great importance on the school's behaviour policy. However, when considering policy governing specific issues such as behaviour, which often 'ignore the systemic and interconnected conditions that influence classroom practice' (McLaughlin, 1991), additional problems can abound. The Elton Report (DfES, 1989) had earlier suggested that on a larger scale, the behaviour policy itself ensured that 'a whole range of processes are consistent with one another'. It warned that without this consistency across policies, schools could become a mere collection of classrooms with 'contrasting disciplinary regimes' that resulted in 'fragmentation' and 'demoralisation' for teachers and pupils alike.

McLaughlin (1991) believed these 'episodic' or separate and discrete interventions, such as the ones often related to behaviour, were only likely to be implemented in the interim as they were short-term priorities which quickly become replaced with another short-term priority. A continuous wave of new and at times conflicting demands, as well as government policies being in what McLaughlin (1991) had described as 'a constant state of flux', compound difficulties. Datnow and Stringfield (2000) defined schools as being 'awash' with new policies and suggested that they were often balancing 'multiple issues'.

> Schools and teachers are expected to be familiar with, and be able to implement multiple (and sometimes contradictory) policies that are planned for them by others and they are held accountable for this task.
>
> (Maguire *et al.*, 2010, p. 156)

Datnow's (2000) previous research highlighted the difficulties of achieving commitment to any externally mandated policy and confirmed findings from Odden's (1991) earlier research that proposed these polices 'were doomed to failure on the beaches of local policy implementation resistance'. If behaviour policies, rather than supporting a consistent and cohesive approach to managing behaviour, are considered, as some research suggested, as 'episodic interventions' with consistent implication defying 'common sense' they may be 'doomed' to resistance from staff. This view supports Thomas and Loxley's (2001) earlier assertion that without revision of the 'odd collection of rules and practices', children's misbehaviour was 'almost an inevitable consequence'. Wearmouth *et al.* (2005, p. 23) also pointed out that the 'real dilemma for schools is how to *act* in a situation which is beset by often irreconcilable tensions' – something that is specifically pertinent around discussions on behaviour.

? ACTIVITY STOP 1

Reflect on some of the challenges that policies are said to encounter in schools. Using the diagram (Figure 3.1), consider the behaviour policy in your school or setting:

- What problems might staff have implementing it?
- How do you know?
- How might this impact on behaviour?
- What could be done about it?

56 Framing the actions we take

- What problems might staff have implementing the policy?
- How do you know?
- How might this impact on behaviour?
- What could be done about it?

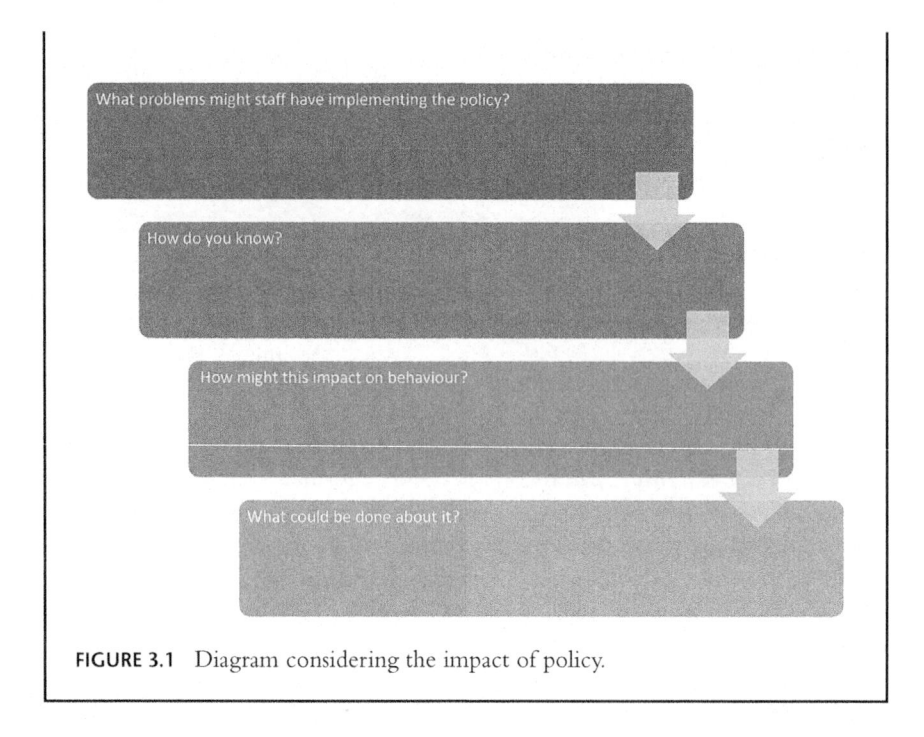

FIGURE 3.1 Diagram considering the impact of policy.

As the chapter progresses, you might find that some of these questions are answered. But considering your own context at this point will be useful in guiding your thinking about your own behaviour policy.

In order to ensure that the behaviour policy is implemented, it has been suggested that the policy should aim to be part of the 'oral tradition' of the school and be 'enmeshed within the organisational culture' (Thomas & Loxley, 2001), as opposed to a stand-alone bureaucratic procedure. This mirrored Rowe's (2006) views about the importance of internalising the values inherent within a behaviour policy rather than simply complying with it, and echoed O'Brien's (1998) statement that 'a policy cannot be allowed to decay on a shelf – it should be alive in practice'. These views supported a wide range of research which showed that the behaviour policy must be integral to the school (including: DfE, 2013; Visser, 2007; Watkins & Wagner, 2000). However, this is particularly problematic when coupled with descriptions of whole-school behaviour policies that have included 'unhelpful', 'complex' and 'inconsistently applied', with little staff 'buy in' (Canter, 2010; Ofsted, 2005, 2014).

Despite the assertion that behaviour policies should be 'integral' to, rather than isolated from, the school's life, research showed there is often a lack of 'collective responsibility', with few staff aware of key influential government documents on behaviour, or even their own school's policy (DfE, 2014b; Maguire *et al.*, 2010; Turner, 2003). Ofsted (2014) found that a sixth of the teachers they surveyed suggested their school's behaviour policy was 'unhelpful', and only around 50 percent of them agreed that they applied it consistently. Fifty-three percent of the respondents who participated in a Teacher Voice survey (DfE, 2014c) were reportedly unaware of the government's updated publications on behaviour, and this large-scale study of senior leaders and classroom teachers ($n = 2425$) was, the authors suggested, 'largely representative of schools nationally'. This, then, suggests that there are a range of issues with policies governing behaviour, that they may be isolated from other school polices, not applied consistently or valued by staff, and may not meet expected government guidelines or updates.

Moving on from factors related to implementation to the contents of a policy also highlights a number of possibly problematic or contentious issues. A behaviour policy is usually framed either as reactive or proactive; where reactive approaches usually take the form of corrective, post-incident responses such as sanctions, which have been shown to lead to negative teacher reactions. Despite this, they remain commonly used and actively promoted in English government documentation, which explicitly encourages schools to state how rewards and sanctions will be used (DfE, 2016) in spite of evidential research on 'the effectiveness of proactive strategies' (Clunies-Ross, Little & Kienhuis, 2008). A reactive policy can be exemplified by a 'tariff approach', where the main purpose is to 'codify a set of responses to particular student misdemeanours' (Watkins & Wagner, 2000). In practice this is often seen as a list of behaviours escalating by seriousness, or by further transgression of school rules, which is linked to a hierarchy of sanctions which themselves also grow in severity. This tariff approach has been implicated – historically and currently – in the increasing number of school exclusions, as reactive approaches have been shown to 'encourage rule-laden inflexibility' which, in turn, can lead to various forms of 'disaffection' (Watkins & Wagner, 2000) and increase, rather than decrease, behaviour issues.

Wearmouth *et al.* (2005) highlighted the incompatible drives for schools to be inclusive and also to be competitive, and drew links between the introduction of the National Curriculum and testing in England in the 1990s, and the rise in the number of exclusions. Permanent exclusions grew fourfold, from 3000 in 1990 to 12,000 in 1997–1998, and Parsons (1999, cited in Wearmouth *et al.*, 2005) argued at the time that national testing conflicted with the 'acceptance and involvement of all children' in schools, something which has been reiterated in recent documentation.

> An unfortunate and unintended consequence of the Government's strong focus on school standards has led to school environments and practices that have resulted in disadvantaged children being disproportionately excluded, which includes a curriculum with a lack of focus on developing pupils' social and economic capital. There appears to be a lack of moral accountability on the part of many schools and no incentive to, or deterrent to not, retain pupils who could be classed as difficult or challenging.
> (House of Commons Education Select Committee, 2018, Para. 36)

It has been suggested that a key political and continued message to schools, along with increased control, was what the English government observed as an ineluctable link between 'fixing' behaviour and 'fixing' learning (Maguire et al., 2010). It could be argued this has only increased pressure on schools and has contributed to a narrowing of their curricula and an increase in the implementation of tariff-related polices – with zero-tolerance policies at the extreme end of this spectrum. This continues to lead to an increase in the number of both formal and informal exclusions in schools and to typically to remove those pupils who are the least academically able (House of Commons Education Select Committee, 2018).

The number of school exclusions – both permanent and fixed-term (language which the DfE has suggested should revert to the previous terms of expulsion and suspension to avoid confusion [DfE, 2019]) is often overshadowed in the media and wider public discussions by 'off-rolling'. The term itself, as with a range of others in education (discussed in Chapter 2) is not one which is definitively understood (Rowe, 2019). It has been described by the DfE (2019) as:

> the practice of removing a pupil from the school roll without a formal, permanent exclusion or by encouraging a parent to remove their child from the school roll, when the removal is primarily in the interests of the school rather than in the best interests of the pupil.

This is not a new phenomenon, and off-rolling in one form or another has been evidenced for many years. Cooper (1999) noted from a 1992 study in Scotland that in one authority – which was not considered exceptional – for every two pupils that were recorded by their schools as permanently excluded, another 30 had been off-rolled in some form.

The findings from studies have noted that vulnerable children, such as those with a SEND or other non-standard needs were currently most at risk of off-rolling, and that schools with Ofsted judgements of 'requires improvement' or those in special measures were the most likely to off-roll pupils (Graham, White & Potter, 2019; Rowe, 2019). Graham et al. (2019) highlighted, in their review for the DfE on factors contributing to exclusion, that although children with a SEND account for only 14% of the school population, they represent 50% of all permanent exclusions. A YouGov survey (Rowe, 2019) also reported that half of the teachers (1018 in total) suggested the key reason schools off-rolled pupils was in order to 'manipulate league tables' (Rowe, 2019, p. 12), which mirrored wider concerns (House of Commons Education Select Committee, 2018) and reflects the tensions between being competitive and being inclusive. Graham et al. (2019, p. 36) cite a report by the children's commissioner which showed some stark findings related to attainment on off-rolling:

> In its 2017 briefing for MPs, the Children's Commissioner presented analysis based on data from earlier years indicating that 89% of mainstream schools would have worse GCSE pass rate if the exam results of the pupils who had been sent to AP [alternative provision] or otherwise off-rolled at any time over the Years 7 to 11, were included in their annual results.

Findings (Rowe, 2019) also showed that schools with above-average numbers on roll, academies and struggling schools in disadvantaged areas had higher-than-average numbers of pupils off-rolled, with behaviour issues the most commonly cited reason to justify a child's off-rolling. However, although this is the most widely reported named reason, teachers in this survey believed most off-rolling was underpinned by concerns over the child's academic achievement rather than their behaviour (Rowe, 2019). There is agreement among many educational professionals that issues with behaviour can be associated with low academic achievement, supporting these teachers' concerns that academic results, rather than behaviour issues, were a key factor in off-rolling for many schools.

As discussed, the myriad of pressures on schools have been linked to off-rolling and a rise in zero-tolerance polices (DfE, 2019). Despite the increase, the consequences of zero-tolerance policies have been highlighted in a range of research, with an American review (APA, 2006, cited in Roffey, 2010) drawing attention to the negative impacts of these approaches, not only for the children directly involved and sanctioned, but also for other children in the class. The study noted the detrimental effect of this approach on relationships and trust between children and teachers and also the negative impact on children's academic progress. This would contradict, at least to some degree, the English government's assumed and simplistic link to 'fixing' behaviour to 'fix' learning. Another key finding of this study (APA, 2006, cited in Roffey, 2010) was the impact on the life chances of the children these policies excluded, the so-called 'school to prison pipeline'. This was something that resonated in England on GSCE results day in 2018, when students pasted mock-up 'school to prison' maps over tube maps on the London Underground (shown in Figure 3.2).

FIGURE 3.2 The 'school to prison pipeline' maps posted on the London Underground trains by GCSE students.

Source: Aaamall/Twitter in Smith, 2018.

A key facet of zero-tolerance policies is their consistent implementation with no allowances made to account for individual circumstances. The issue of consistency in applying behaviour policies is one of the most challenging issues, with arguments found in research supporting both consistency and flexibility. Much research has espoused whole-school consistency as essential (Bennett, 2017; Canter, 2010; DfE, 2014, Ofsted 2008, 2014; Taylor, 2011; Visser, 2007), whilst others have seen consistency as impossible and undesirable (DES, 1989; Goodman, 2006; Watkins & Wagner, 2000). Watkins and Wagner (2000) believed that consistency in itself was not valuable, advising that it could lead to a reduction in 'staff coherence' and suggested that perpetuating the belief that consistency was necessary for children was 'not only inaccurate' but 'likely to be damaging'. They argued, rather, that part of children's development process was learning to how respond in various situations (Watkins & Wagner, 2000). Nonetheless, it was noted that the consequences of inconsistency meant that pupils need a 'great degree of sophistication' to deal with conflicting teacher expectations (Wright, Weekes & McGlaughlin, 2004). The Elton Report (DES, 1989) also found that 'complete uniformity' was both 'impossible and undesirable', and the later White Paper (DfE, 2010) focused on the significance of 'professional judgement' for teachers, in addition to knowledge of the child when 'unacceptably poor behaviour' was dealt with.

There are also arguments that a consensus-based message which comes from 'the school as an institution rather than the teacher as an individual' is important (Galvin & Costa, 1995). Visser (2007) found that a critical mass of professionals within the organisation, either in number or influence, were required for consistent policy application, without which children reported that the management of behaviour was unfair and without coherence. Research also showed that unless pupils were involved in the consultation process and were able to voice their opinions regarding the policy, they could reject it out of hand (2CVResearch, 2010). Ofsted (2005) suggested that a lack of consistency was linked to increased behaviour problems and cautioned that unclear boundaries and inconsistent application caused 'resentment' in children who recognised the importance of rules and sanctions being consistently applied. These findings were replicated in an Ofsted report (2014) almost ten years later, showing the entrenched nature of the problem.

Building blocks

The research considered in relation to policy, and school behaviour policies specifically, has some clear implications for schools. A range of published work suggests that the very best policies changed the focus from misbehaviour to good behaviour, where an emphasis on positive behaviour management strategies within the policy benefited all pupils (DfE, 2014, 2014a, 2014b; Hallam, 2007; Visser, 2003). Lund (1996) also stated that policies should ensure the development of high self-esteem(s) and 'value', not only for pupils but for all members of the school community, and that 'behaviour management' and a focus on 'discipline' should form only a small part of the school's overall policy. This was also seen in the government's concerns over pupil resilience, where they pointed to a school's importance in being a safe and affirming place in which children developed a 'sense of belonging and feel able to trust and talk openly', and one where resilience was promoted (DfE, 2014a). This can be seen to be linked with the WHO's definition of a child friendly school, as noted in the previous chapter.

? ACTIVITY STOP 2

Behaviour policies have a central role to play in schools, but Kohn (1996) suggested that we need to ask '*Cui bono*' – who benefits – from the actions we take to manage behaviour? Before you read any further, make a list (it could be short and sweet, or more detailed) using the table (Figure 3.3) of attributes you would like the children in your school to have in ten years' time.

As you read through this chapter, reflect on how behaviour is managed in your school, setting or experience and whether it sets the foundations for the attributes you have listed, supports children in achieving them or works against them.

10 years from now I would like the children in my class/care to be...
•
•
•
•
•
•
•
•

FIGURE 3.3 Table considering key attributes children should have ten years from now.

Schools have been strongly encouraged in publications by the English government, both historically and recently (DfEE, 1997; DfE, 2016) to ensure their behaviour polices include the use of rewards and sanctions. It has been claimed that this has resulted in schools' 'compulsory adoption' of a policy centred on rewards and sanctions, despite this focus being 'all but lost' in wider aspects of education (Payne, 2015). Indeed, Payne (2015) proposed that the 'behaviourist ideas' (see more on behaviourism in Part II of this book) which were required to form the foundation of schools' policies represented 'a potentially confused set of aims and theoretical principles'. However, others argued the behaviourist framework of rewards and sanctions was seen by staff as 'emotionally safe', whereas less structured policies which required teachers and other staff to consider their own views and feelings about behaviour were seen as 'emotionally loaded' (Radford, 2000). It is interesting to compare the pervading focus on rewards and sanctions with earlier perspectives:

> rewards and punishments in the ordinary sense may seem to have little or no place, there is in fact a substitute in the form of approval and disapproval. The more sympathetic a teacher is, the more successfully he or she establishes with the children a relationship of affection and respect, the more clearly will approval be a reward, and withdrawal in some sense a punishment. Such a system is preferable to arbitrary authoritarianism, but if it involves the abrogation of one kind of power, it bestows another and must be used with understanding and scrupulousness.
>
> (DES, 1967, p. 268)

❓ ACTIVITY STOP 3

A lot of perspectives have been covered in the previous paragraph alone, and they might benefit from reflection. Payne (2015) essentially argued that the ways schools manage behaviour is out of step with the broader strategies used in school around learning. For example, much teaching and learning in school now focuses on independence, being child-led and suited to the individual. Even at a simplistic level, it would be considered poor practice by many not to address in some way the range of different learning needs, and it is very rare to provide the whole class with the same work, in the same way, and have the same expectations in regard to outcome for them all.

Consider your school or setting's behaviour policy and teaching and learning policy (if you have one – use an example from a school's website if not), and use the diagram (Figure 3.4) to think about:

- What expectations of children do they set out that are similar?
- Where do their expectations of children differ?
- Does this matter?
- What would the school be like if the behaviour policy was more in line with the teaching and learning policy?

School policies **63**

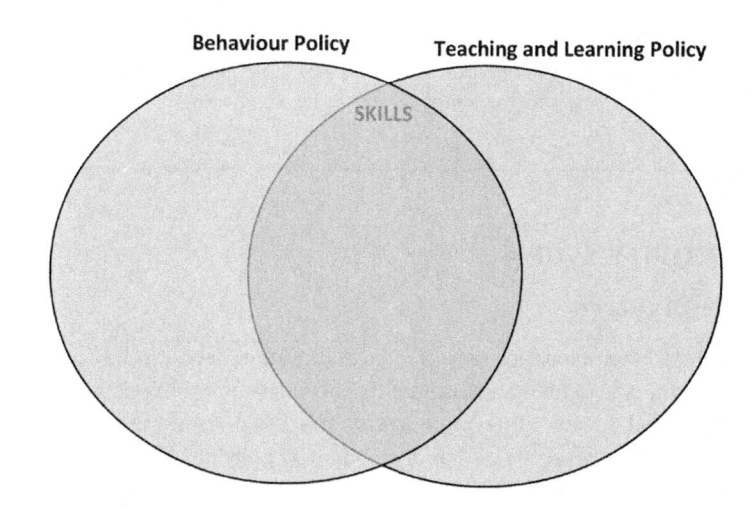

FIGURE 3.4 Diagram to consider similarities and differences between behaviour and teaching and learning policies.

One of the key issues with policies that use rewards and sanctions, also called reactive or tariff policies, is that behaviour is addressed retrospectively after an incident. This necessarily advocates a hierarchy of sanctions and punishments where many 'punishments' often fall outside the remit of the class teacher. This can result in members of the senior leadership team being seen as 'someone to send naughty children to', as opposed to most of the routine discipline being handled in the classroom by teachers (Watkins & Wagner, 2000). This reflected Lund's (1996) earlier research which found that autonomy from a rigid hierarchy of rewards and sanctions was important for teachers and pupils, and that it was the teacher's 'belief and confidence in the approach' that made it 'effective'. Goodman (2006) too argued for much greater autonomy in respect to discipline, stating that staff were the ones who knew and understood best both the child and the context.

This discussion on behaviour polices and policy implementation may have raised more questions than it has answered. Debate on policy content and how it should be implemented can appear to present polarised views with an either/or course of action. In schools and classrooms, this dichotomy is often more pragmatically enacted, with teachers and schools personalising their approaches. Nevertheless, it is important to consider what the whole-school aims are, both for policy and the way it is used in the school for the range of stakeholders. If the aim is for all staff to apply the behaviour policy consistently, then training needs to be undertaken and staff need to be involved in writing the policy. This sense of ownership will help all staff to have a shared understanding of what managing behaviour looks like in practice, and to have a school-wide understanding of approaches. Conversely, if autonomy and individual decision making is encouraged for staff when managing behaviour, training needs to be available for all staff to support them in developing a range

64 Framing the actions we take

of approaches to meet the diverse needs of children. There also needs to be clear overarching principles or a 'mission statement' to guide staff to ensure coherence – rather than consistency – in the range of strategies used.

> ### ❓ ACTIVITY STOP 4
>
> **Vignette: Aaron**
>
> Aaron had been experiencing aggressive and intimidating behaviour from some of the girls in his class. His parents had made a number of visits to see the headteacher and other members of the STL, and some of the girls' behaviours were being treated as an incident of bullying. Aaron's behaviour in the classroom was usually good, although he was often observed off task and engaged in a number of low-level disruptive activities. He had never received a formal school sanction but was commonly on the end of the 'teacher look' from members of staff. During that lunchtime, Aaron had been to see a staff member about 'threats' he had received from the girls, and on his return to class the group of girls teased him when he answered a question from the teacher incorrectly. Aaron pushed over his table and swore at the girls, as well as his class teacher when he tried to calm the situation. Aaron absconded from the school premises, and both his parents and the police were called.
>
> The discussion on policy has highlighted some of the advantages and limitations of consistent whole-school strategies for managing behaviour and those allowing individual teachers flexibility and autonomy. Use the storyboards (Figures 3.5 and 3.6) to help you consider the best and worst possible outcomes for managing an incident of behaviour (or behaviours) with consistency across the whole school, and then with a range of individual teacher approaches. You might like to use your own experiences or the one described in this vignette (or the previous vignettes).
>
> | BEHAVIOURAL INCIDENT MANAGED WITH WHOLE-SCHOOL CONSISTENCY |||
> |---|---|---|
> | | | |
> | The incident (what happened) | Best possible outcome(s) for child, teacher (and class) | Worst possible outcome(s) for child, teacher (and class) |
>
> **FIGURE 3.5** Storyboard to consider outcomes when behaviour is managed consistently.

BEHAVIOURAL INCIDENT MANAGED WITH A RANGE OF INDIVIDUAL APPROACHES		
The incident (what happened)	Best possible outcome(s) for child, teacher (and class)	Worst possible outcome(s) for child, teacher (and class)

FIGURE 3.6 Storyboard to consider outcomes when behaviour is managed with individual approaches.

Review

This chapter has considered what should form part of a school's behaviour policy, how it should be implemented and how this can impact on staff and pupils. We have discussed the issues – both advantages and limitations – of policies based on rewards and sanctions and how the marketisation of schools has increased the use of zero-tolerance policies and their impact in off-rolling pupils.

It was suggested that behaviour policies should be 'assertive, appropriate, watchful, supportive and conflict avoiding' (Sproson, 2004). Cole (2004) argued that in relation to behaviour, there had been little consistent guidance about whether policies should achieve the qualities Sproson (2004) cited through 'control, therapy, welfare or education', all of which have been proposed.

THINKING STOP 2

As this chapter has shown, there are a range of approaches to writing policies, and a range of actions (or not) these can lead to. Cole (2004) questioned whether behaviour policies should achieve their outcomes through 'control, therapy, welfare or education'. Think about these options:

- Which aligns most closely with current government policy?
- Which matches the ethos of your school?
- What might be the advantages of these different approaches?
- What might be the limitations of these approaches?
- What would be the implications of these different approaches for staff (training, consistency across the school etc.), and children?

Whole-school actions might include some or all of the following:

- Ensure there are clear links between the behaviour policy and other key policies in school and that these complement each other.
- Consider specifically whether the aims (either implicit or explicit) in the behaviour policy are reflected in the teaching and learning policy.
- Review when the last whole-school staff meeting/INSET/training was provided on using the behaviour policy. Have all staff had the opportunity to access training or support in using the behaviour policy?
- Is sufficient time set aside for new members of staff to develop a clear understanding of what is included in the school's behaviour policy and how to use it in the classroom? Could this form part of the induction for new staff?
- Consideration needs to be given to ensure a close match between the ethos of the school and the behaviour policy. For example, are they in synergy with each other, or are their aims competing?
- If a key facet of the behaviour policy is consistent application, what support is offered for individual staff/children who may find this difficult?
- If the behaviour policy allows teachers autonomy in the way they manage behaviour, what are the training needs of individual staff and how can these be addressed?
- Are an individual teacher's strategies for managing behaviour complementary? Are they consistent with the ethos and aims of the school, and is there a 'golden thread' of expectations that runs throughout the school for staff and pupils?
- If a policy with a hierarchy of punishments or sanctions is used, to what degree is behaviour unnecessarily passed up to senior staff, and what effect does this have on the pupil's and the teacher's perceptions?

Individual teacher actions might include some or all of the following:

- Ensure you are familiar with the school behaviour policy and seek guidance or training if necessary.
- Consider the impact of 'passing up' issues of behaviour to senior staff (if this is part of the school policy). What messages might this send to the pupils in your care?
- Do you have different expectations in relation to how you support children's learning and how you support their behaviour? Are these complementary or opposing?

Possible mental health and well-being implications:

- If behaviour that challenges is considered as an unmet mental health need, care needs to be taken in how this is supported or addressed in the school behaviour policy.

- Research suggests that children with SEMH are most at risk of permanent exclusion and that this significantly negatively affects their overall life changes. Protective measures need to be in place to support those most at risk of mental health difficulties.
- Research (Graham *et al.*, 2019) found that in schools with low exclusion rates, relationships between staff and pupils and valuing children were key. These factors have also been supportive factors to protect children's mental health.
- Policies shown to be particularly supportive of children with a range of SEMH are those that focus on developing a sense of 'belonging' for pupils. Being part of a positive community is also key in supporting positive mental health for children.

Practitioner-related take-away:

- Consistent expectations for behaviour from pupils is often at odds with the range of accepted expectations for attainment from pupils.

Practitioner reading:

Department for Education (2019). *The Timpson Review of School Exclusion: Government Response*. London: DfE.

References

Ball, S. (1997). Policy, sociology and critical social research: A personal review of recent education policy and policy research. *British Educational Research Journal*, **23**(3), pp. 257–274.

Ball, S., Hoskins, K., Maguire, M., and Braun, A. (2011). Disciplinary texts: A policy analysis of national and local behaviour policies. *Critical Studies in Education*, **52**(1), pp. 1–14.

Bennett, T. (2017). *Creating a Culture: How School Leaders can Optimise Behaviour*. London: DfE.

Bradbury, J. (2018, June). *Off-Rolling: Using Data to See a Fuller Picture*. Ofsted Blog, London: Schools, Early Years, Further Education and Skills. https://educationinspection.blog.gov.uk/2018/06/26/off-rolling-using-data-to-see-a-fuller-picture/

Canter, L. (2010). *Assertive Discipline* (4th ed.). Bloomington: Solution Tree Press.

Clunies-Ross, P., Little, E. and Kienhuis, M. (2008). Self-reported and actual use of proactive and reactive classroom management strategies and their relationship with teacher stress and student behaviour. *Educational Psychology*, **28**(6), pp. 693–710.

Coburn, C., and Stein, M. (2006). Communities of practice theory and the role of teacher professional community in policy implementation. In Honig, M. (Ed.), *New Directions in Education Policy Implementation: Confronting Complexity* (pp. 25–47). New York: State University of New York Press.

Cole, T. (2004). The development of provision for children and young people "with EBD": Past, present and future. In Wearmouth, J., Glynn, T., Richmond, R. and Berryman, M. (Eds.), *Inclusion and Behaviour Management in Schools: Issues and Challenges*. London: David Fulton Publishers.

Cooper, P. (1999). Educating children with emotional and behavioural difficulties: The evolution of current thinking and provision. In Cooper, P. (Ed.), *Understanding and Supporting Children with Emotional and Behavioural Difficulties*. London: Jessica Kingsley Publishers.

Datnow, A. (2000). Power and politics in the adoption of school reform models. *Educational Evaluation and Policy Analysis*, **22**(4), pp. 357–374.

Datnow, A., and Stringfield, S. (2000). Working together for reliable school reform. *Journal of Education for Students Placed at Risk (JESPAR)*, **5**(1–2), pp. 183–204.

Department for Education. (2010). *The Importance of Teaching: The School's White Paper 2010*. London: DfE.

Department for Education. (2012). *Review of the National Curriculum in England: What can We Learn from the English, Mathematics and Science Curricula of High-performing Jurisdictions?* London: DfE.

Department for Education. (2013). *Behaviour and Discipline in Schools: Guidance for Headteachers and Staff*. London: DfE.

Department for Education. (2014). *Mental Health and Behaviour in Schools*. London: DfE.

Department for Education. (2014a). *Behaviour and Discipline in Schools*. London: DfE.

Department for Education. (2014b). *Mental Health and Behaviour in Schools: Departmental Advice*. London: DfE.

Department for Education. (2014c). *School Behaviour and Attendance Research Priorities and Questions*. London: DfE.

Department for Education. (2016). *Behaviour and Discipline in Schools: Advice for Headteachers and School Staff*. London: DfE.

Department for Education. (2019). *The Timpson Review of School Exclusion: Government Response*. London: DfE.

Department for Education and Employment. (1997). *Excellence in Schools. White Paper*. London: DfEE.

Department of Education and Science (DES). (1967). *Children and their Primary Schools A Report of the Central Advisory Council for Education (England)*. London: DES.

Department of Education and Science (DES). (1989). *Discipline in Schools. Report of the Committee of Enquiry. (Chairman: Lord Elton.)*. London: DES.

Galvin, P., and Costa, P. (1995). Building better behaved schools: Effective support at the whole school level. In Gray, P., Miller, A., and Noakes, J. (Eds.), *Challenging Behaviour in Schools* (pp. 145–163). London: Routledge.

Goodman, J. (2006). School discipline in moral disarray. *Journal of Moral Education*, **35**(2), pp. 213–230.

Graham, B., White, C., and Potter, S. (2019). *School Exclusion: A Literature Review on the Continued Disproportionate Exclusion of Certain Children*. London: DfE.

Hallam, S. (2007). Evaluation of behavioural management in schools: A review of the behaviour improvement programme and the role of behaviour and education support teams. *Child and Adolescent Mental Health*, **12**(3), pp. 106–112.

House of Commons Education Select Committee. (2018). *Forgotten Children: Alternative Provision and the Scandal of Ever Increasing Exclusions*. London: House of Commons.

Kohn, A. (1996). *Beyond Discipline: From Compliance to Community*. Alexandria: Association for Supervision & Curriculum Development.

Levin, B. (1998). An epidemic of education policy: (What) Can we learn from each other? *Comparative Education*, **34**(2), pp. 131–141.

Lund, R. (1996). *A Whole-School Behaviour Policy: A Practical Guide*. London: Kogan Page Limited.

Maguire, M., Ball, S., and Braun, A. (2010). Behaviour, classroom management and student 'control': Enacting policy in the English secondary school. *International Studies in Sociology of Education*, **20**(2), pp. 153–170.

McLaughlin, M. (1991). Learning lessons from experience: Lessons from policy implementation. In Odden, A. (Ed.), *Educational Policy Implementation* (pp. 185–195). New York: State University of New York Press.

O'Brien, T. (1998). *Promoting Positive Behaviour*. London: David Fulton Publishers.

Odden, A. (1991). The evolution of educational policy implementation. In Odden, A. (Ed.), *Educational Policy Implementation* (pp. 1–12). New York: State University of New York Press.

Ofsted. (2005). *Managing Challenging Behaviour*. London: Ofsted.

Ofsted. (2008). *The Deployment, Training and Development of the Wider School Workforce*. London: Ofsted.

Ofsted. (2014). *Below the Radar: Low-Level Disruption in the Country's Classrooms*. London: Ofsted.

Payne, R. (2015). Using rewards and sanctions in the classroom: Pupil's perceptions of their own responses to current behaviour management strategies. *Educational Review*, **67**(4), pp. 483–504.

Radford, J. (2000). Values into practice: Developing whole school behaviour policies. *Support for Learning*, **15**(2), pp. 86–89.

Roffey, S. (2010). Classroom support for including students with challenging behaviour. In Rose, R. (Ed.), *Confronting Obstacles to Inclusion: International Responses to Developing Inclusive Education* (pp. 279–292). London: Routledge.

Rowe, D. (2006). Taking responsibility: School behaviour policies in England, moral development and implications for citizenship education. *Journal of Moral Education*, **35**(4), pp. 519–531.

Rowe, J. (2019). *Exploring the Issue of Off-Rolling*. London: DfE.

Smith, A. (2018, August 23). "School to prison line" tube posters highlight school exclusions. *Metro News*. https://metro.co.uk/2018/08/23/school-to-prison-line-tube-posters-highlight-school-exclusions-on-gcse-results-day-7874710/

Spillane, J., Reiser, B., and Reimer, T. (2002). Policy implementation and cognition: Reframing and refocusing implementation research. *Review of Educational Research*, **72**(3), pp. 387–431.

Sproson, B. (2004). Some do and don't: Teacher effectiveness in managing behaviour. In Wearmouth, J., Glynn, T. Richmond, R., and Berryman, M. (Eds.), *Inclusion and Behaviour Management in Schools: Issues and Challenges* (pp. 311–321). London: David Fulton Publishers.

Taylor, C. (2011). *Good Behaviour in Schools: Checklist for Teachers*. London: DfE.

Thomas, G., and Loxley, A. (2001). *Deconstructing Special Education and Constructing Inclusion*. Buckingham: Open University Press.

Turner, C. (2003). How effective and inclusive is the school's behaviour policy? *Emotional and Behavioural Difficulties*, **8**(1), pp. 7–18.

2CV Research. (2010). *Customer Voice – Behaviour and Discipline Powers in Schools*. London: DfE.

Visser, J., and Stokes, S. (2010). Is education ready for the inclusion of pupils with emotional and behavioural difficulties: A rights perspective? *Educational Review*, **55**(1), pp. 65–75.

Visser, J. (2003). *A Study of Children and Young People Who Present Challenging Behaviour – Literature Review*. London: Ofsted.

Visser, J. (2007). *Social, emotional and behavioural difficulties: can mainstream schools meet these pupils needs? SEBCD 1st European Conference*, Malta.

Watkins, C., and Wagner, P. (2000). *Improving School Behaviour*. London: Paul Chapman Publishing Ltd.

Wearmouth, J., Glynn, T., and Berryman, M. (2005). Understanding inclusion and behaviour management. In Wearmouth, J., Glynn, T., and Berryman, M. (Eds.), *Perspectives on Student Behaviour in Schools* (pp. 1–24). London: Routledge.

Wright, C., Weekes, D., and McGlaughlin, A. (2004). Teachers and pupils – Relationships of power and resistance. In Wearmouth, J., Richmond, R., Glynn, T., and Berryman, M. (Eds.), *Understanding Pupil Behaviour In Schools: A Diversity of Approaches* (pp. 67–88). London: David Fulton Publishers.

FRAMING THE ACTIONS WE TAKE

Conclusion

The first three chapters have covered a wide range of topics, including the interlinks between mental health and behaviour, and the importance of addressing and supporting children who have issues with both in the classroom. They have considered how the language used to think and talk about children's behaviour influences the actions taken and how the language used in government publications has changed over the years in line with, or at times driving, public narratives in education and with children. Finally, policy was examined including what the purpose of school behaviour policies are and how people work with them. Issues of consistency were discussed, and how staff may need support and/or training to effectively implement the behaviour policy, regardless of its content.

The foci of the chapters were about how the actions to support children with their behaviour are influenced or 'bounded' by external factors, such as policy, the language of the government/school or setting and the challenge of concurrently supporting behaviour and meeting external academic targets. This may all seem slightly removed from your own classroom practice; however, it is important to understand the implicit and unspoken influences that affect views about children and their behaviour, and as a result, the actions taken. As Part I of the book draws to a close, it is important to jot down your thoughts:

☁THINKING STOP 1

- Have you read anything that has surprised you?
- Have you learnt anything new?
- Have you read anything that has made you reflect on the way in which you work with children in the classroom?
- Will anything change for you as a result of reading these chapters?

Returning to the idea of a 'behaviour suitcase' (Sproson, 2004), what have you have read in this section that you can add to your 'suitcase' of ideas to support children and their behaviour? Make a note of it in Figure C1.1.

FIGURE C1.1 Sproson's 'behaviour suitcase' to add ideas to.

References

Sproson, B. (2004). Some do and don't: Teacher effectiveness in managing behaviour. In Wearmouth, J., Glynn, T., Richmond, R., and Berryman, M. (Eds.), *Inclusion and Behaviour Management in Schools: Issues and Challenges* (pp. 311–321). London: David Fulton Publishers.

PART II
Introduction

Attitudes, beliefs and perspectives

Part II of this book builds on the previous chapters by deepening the focus on understanding what our personal views are and considering how these could be enacted in the classroom. It again focuses on relationships by considering how personal lenses for understanding behaviours reveal different beliefs for its causes and, as a result, different beliefs on how to work with children.

These chapters move beyond simple linear cause-and-effect models and again focus sharply on relationships; specifically, how teachers relate to the children in their care, how children relate to each other and how children relate to and understand themselves. The chapters in Part II are, as in Part I, filtered through my own position and perspective and echo to some degree my own chronological development and understanding. When I first qualified, and early in my career, I clung tightly to the behaviourist principles of rewards and sanctions and was often so busy simply trying to stay afloat and survive in the classroom, that I was unable to fully understand the complexity of children's behaviour. As I gained more confidence, and some aspects of classroom practice became quicker and easier (planning, marking and so on), I was able to reflect more on how I worked with children and how helpful (or not) the strategies I used were. This coincided with a period of studying for my master's in education which focused on challenging behaviour. The exposure to different views, perspectives and theories gave me pause for thought and allowed me to reflect on my own actions and their impact – specifically on the relationships I was (often not!) developing with the children in my care, particularly those whose behaviours challenged me.

The opportunity to stop and think and the impetus studying provided to read research around behaviours in the classroom changed my entire outlook. The experiences (both in the classroom and in the theory) moved me firmly away from considering my role as a teacher as one of being 'in control' to one of 'being with' and developing positive relationships with children as a key mechanism in supporting behaviour, something that Chapters 4–6 consider.

4
THEORY AND THE CLASSROOM

Chapter 4 examines how beliefs and understandings underpin the way behaviour is managed, whether consciously or not. Galton and MacBeath's (2008) study highlighted tensions between research and classroom practice, suggesting that in relation to managing behaviour, teachers tended to 'play it by ear' and rarely recognised any direct connection between their strategies for managing behaviour and the behaviour of their pupils. Nevertheless, what the underlying causes of behaviour issues are understood to be, the language used to talk about them, the expectations of the school or setting's policy, as well as wider political and educational discourses all shape the actions taken in the classroom to some extent. This happens regardless, as Galton and MacBeath (2008) noted, of whether the impact of these on practice is actively recognised or not. This chapter will consider some of the broad theoretical perspectives on understandings of behaviour and consider how these would influence the way in which behaviour is supported and managed.

This chapter aims to:

- Develop philosophical understandings of the causes of behaviour
- Share examples of how these different philosophical perspectives might guide the actions taken
- Compare and contrast a range of different perspectives
- Consider how dominant behaviourist views have shaped policy and practice

Foundations

This chapter, although moving on from the discussion of behaviour in Part I, does link back to earlier chapters, particularly Chapter 2. It has been argued that:

> There are many ways of conceptualising ... students in the classroom. How children are discussed, perceived and positioned impacts on how teachers position themselves in relation to their pupils and how they respond.
>
> (Roffey, 2010, p. 280)

This view is supported by a number of studies (Postholm, 2013; Wearmouth, Glynn & Berryman, 2005) which link teachers' views of the root causes of behaviour they find challenging, and not only the actions they take but their emotional responses to those behaviours. Despite this, and as noted, some research (Galton & MacBeath, 2008) has suggested teachers do not see the links between their own beliefs and way they manage behaviour, and the way in which students behave. Roffey (2010) highlights that even when the links between practitioner actions and those of the children are seen as linked, teachers are bound by a range of expectations and contexts that limit, or at least direct their actions. This illustrates what Coburn (2005) termed 'bounded autonomy', where she proposed that rather than the high degree of professional autonomy it could be assumed teachers have in the classroom, decision making was limited or 'bounded' by a range of different factors. One example of this might be working within the ethos of the school or setting's behaviour policy. Roffey (2010) also noted the importance of the pervading 'socio-political' environment of the individual school or setting, which may be influenced by issues related to school reputation (and marketisation discussed in Chapter 3) or by concerns over appearing 'soft' (linking with ideas about behaviour and well-being considered in Chapter 1) and how these may limit or 'bound' what is seen as 'good' by the school in relation to supporting behaviour. For example;

> A rule-bound, test-oriented discourse determines that 'good' teachers are constructed as those who keep discipline and get high grades. This may undermine the efforts of those who believe that student well-being is integral to an effective learning environment.
>
> (Roffey, 2010, p. 281)

This was reinforced by Wearmouth, Glynn and Berryman (2005), who noted the 'tensions' resulting from the range of different 'theoretical orientations', beliefs and understandings of what is good practice in supporting and managing behaviour, and how these were at times at odds with the views of others who had different beliefs and 'theoretical orientations'.

The importance of reflecting on how and why we manage or support behaviour in the way we do cannot be overstated. Despite limits which exist on the actions we would like to take, or are able to take, considering what guides our actions is important. O'Brien and Guiney (2005) argued that children whose behaviour challenges are often perceived to exist 'at and on the margins' of schooling and even sometimes of society, and that these children:

> highlight the tensions and dilemmas that exist between systems and force us to look at the goals and values of those systems. In educational settings [they] challenge us to confront the manner in which we balance attitudes, values and beliefs ... they also enable us to reflect upon how we construct meaning.
>
> (p. 143)

This form of introspection is not, unfortunately, something many teachers have the time and space for, yet it is the foundation of work with all children – particularly those whose behaviours challenge. O'Brien and Guiney (2005) further suggest that once consideration of how to meet the needs of children with behavioural difficulties begins, it is often through a focus on their *differences* to other learners, and that these differences are seen as 'more threatening' than their sameness. This suggests that by considering, or describing, children whose behaviours challenge as different to the norm and the rest of the class, they are often actually so, which makes providing support for them even more challenging and more difficult. They conclude that instead, understanding the differences these groups of children have should be seen as part of a solution rather than a problem, and viewing them in this way would enable reflection on the range of 'meanings, understandings, needs, dispositions and goals' that both these children and teachers have. This may provide an opportunity to work with the differences these children exhibit, rather than trying to quash them.

THINKING STOP 1

O'Brien and Guiney (2005) raise some exciting and challenging points in their writing relating to children with behaviours that challenge. When considering 'differences' for these groups of children, they propose that differences are 'constructed within systems' – for example, schools, classrooms, governments – and can be viewed as what they describe as either 'emancipatory' or 'discriminatory'. Reflect on how these different categorisations might affect how schools work with these individuals and groups.

- How might it impact on teachers and peers if schools focused on the 'sameness' of children whose behaviour challenged to others in their class?
- How might the school/setting's behaviour policy reflect the similarities rather than the differences (compared to the norm/class) of these children?
- Do you think children whose behaviour challenges are discriminated against?
- What steps could a classroom teacher/school take to limit or stop any discrimination?

Understanding what we view the causes of behaviour to be, as noted, leads to different ways of acting on, supporting or managing those behaviours. Wearmouth et al. (2005) highlighted how viewing behaviours as caused by the child, the context or the interactions between the two would result in very different interventions to address it. Macleod (2006) used the analogy of 'mad, bad or sad' when considering teachers' understandings of the causes of behaviour issues, touching on the idea of behaviours resulting from some form of problem within the child, or what is also known as a child-deficit model. This understanding of behavioural issues as a child-deficit model has been reinforced and reiterated by a range of policy documents and guidance in England.

Although the child-deficit model is one way of thinking about the root causes of behaviour issues, there are a number of other ways to categorise our explanations of the causes of behaviour that challenges. Wearmouth et al. (2005) proposed cultural, biological and medical, or psychological categories. Gullotta (1996, cited in Cooper & Jacobs, 2011, p. 32) provided four approaches to classifying understandings of behaviour which are helpful when considering the range of different conceptualisations and actions that could be taken. As will be discussed, there is much crossover between these ideas:

Psychological theories encompass a number of different perspectives. This broad category includes a range of understandings, including:

- *Psychodynamic theories*, which consider children's experiences early in their lives and how that might impact on the way they behave now.
- *Behavioural theories*, which look at the influence of reinforcement, both positive and negative, on behaviour.
- *Social psychological theories*, which focus on the influence of others and include considerations of how 'social mechanisms' impact on the way children think and act.

Moving on from psychological understanding are *sociocultural theories*; these consider how the wider context and social environment impact on behaviour and on the child.

- *Structural functionalist theories* examine how social and political influences effect children's understandings of right and wrong.
- *Systems theory* looks at how the child operates in the interactive social systems they are part of (including, for example, families and classrooms) and how the social feedback they receive from these systems shapes them.

Biological theories encompass a range of perspectives including explorations of how genetics and inheritance impact on children and their behaviour. This approach also considers how illness and injury may shape behaviours. These include:

- *Medical models*, in which issues in behaviour are seen as requiring some form of 'treatment', usually by medical professionals (for example, Attention Deficit Hyperactivity Disorder).
- *Biopsychosocial models*, a relatively new perspective that combines biological, psychological and social understandings to provide a holistic perspective on the causes of behavioural issues.

This is a fairly comprehensive overview of a range of standpoints on behaviour. For brevity and simplicity, some of the key theoretical perspectives that are most familiar in schools and are emerging in wider studies and research will be discussed in the next section.

? ACTIVITY STOP 1

Before this chapter moves on to consider these perspectives in detail, and how they might look in the classroom, pause and reflect on what you have read so far:

- Can you link any of the wider theories of behaviour to your own views and beliefs about the causes of children's behaviour?
- If so, what might be the advantages and limitations of these views?
- How might they shape what you do with the children in your care?

Use the diagram (Figure 4.1) to jot down some initial thoughts. You may want to return to it, and continue to annotate it, as your reading through this chapter progresses.

Views on the causes of behaviour:

Advantges of this/these understanding(s):

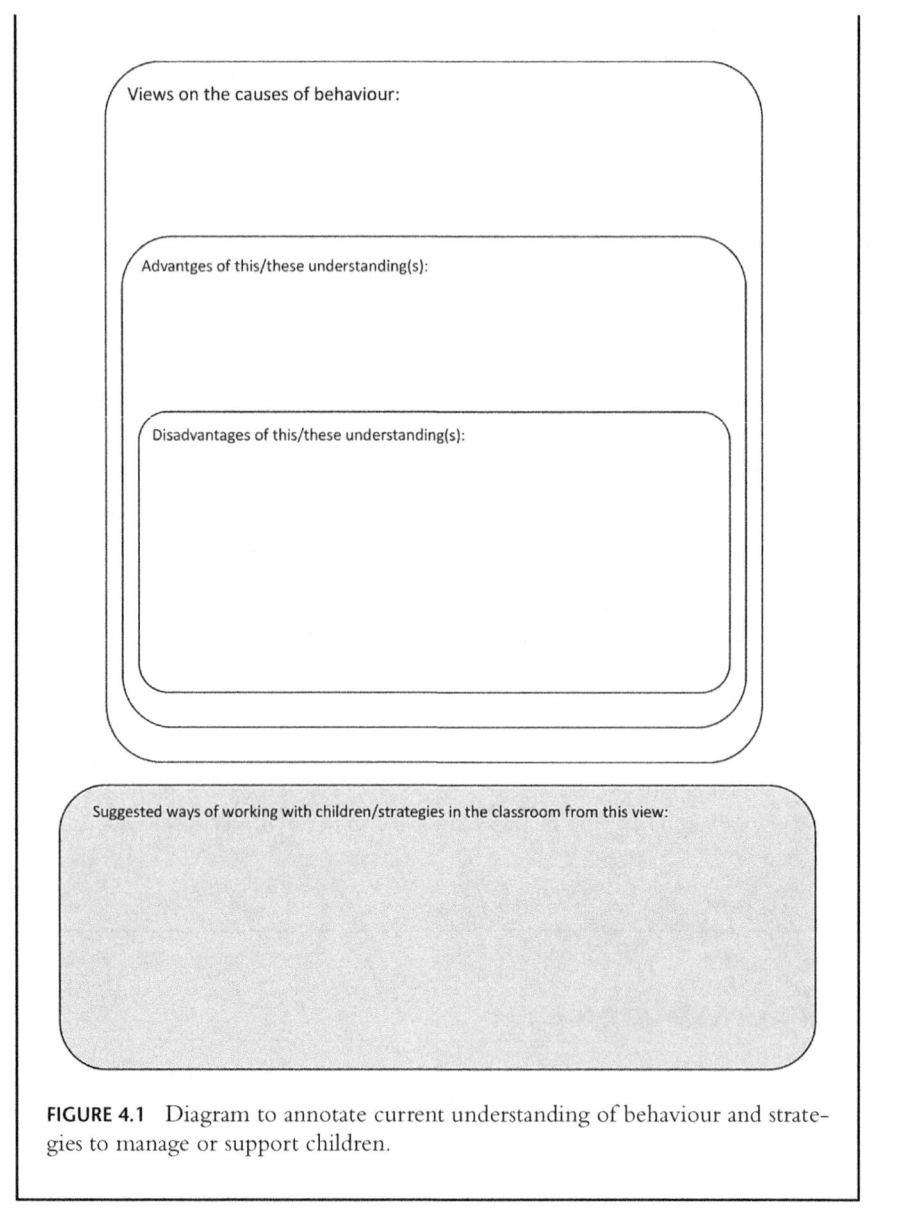

Disadvantages of this/these understanding(s):

Suggested ways of working with children/strategies in the classroom from this view:

FIGURE 4.1 Diagram to annotate current understanding of behaviour and strategies to manage or support children.

Building blocks

The discussions in Part I may have given the impression that these understandings and theoretical positions on viewing behaviour are separate and discrete. In reality, teachers in the classroom work between a range of these understandings at different times and employ strategies (possibly from the same model) in varying ways due to their own views and beliefs on behaviour. The discussion in this section will continue, for simplicity and clarity, under sets of distinct headings. It is important to have in mind as you read through these sections that the different models, understandings and approaches are not always mutually exclusive and that experienced practitioners who understand what is likely to work well for the children in their care can pragmatically blend the strategies they use. Some of the ideas begun here will also be developed in more detail in the following chapters (Chapters 5 and 6 specifically).

Psychological models – behavioural theories

This first model is the one that underpins the most well-known and commonly used approaches in schools – the psychological model, and specifically behavioural theories. From this perspective, the behaviour or issue is within the child – they are child-deficit models – and they focus on external factors to manage behaviour as opposed to internal processes (Cooper & Jacobs, 2011). From this view, there is no specific expectation that relationships with the child are considered as a site of difficulty, or that perhaps the physical classroom environment is contributing to issues in behaviour. Rather, it is seen that there is some issue or problem *within the child* that is causing their behaviour.

One of the most well-known approaches under this umbrella is the behaviourist approach. The behaviourist, or traditional, view of school discipline (Johnson, Whitington & Oswald, 1994), has received both rave reviews and dire criticism over the years. It has been, and remains, the dominant worldwide perspective on behaviour in schools (Cooper & Jacobs, 2011) and its roots can be found in the American psychologist Skinner's (1904–1990) ideas and operant conditioning. Behaviourism is broadly founded on the premise that as a teacher, you have both a right and a responsibility to establish order, and that by definition, the classroom belongs to you as the teacher (Porter, 2000). From this perspective, children operate in a simplified environment of cause and effect (Wearmouth & Connors, 2004), where both positive and negative reinforcements are believed to shape and control behaviour. These negative and positive reinforcements – what is also known as a token economy – commonly take the form of a tangible reward or sanction. This can be seen in the classroom through the use of rewards, such as stickers, golden time or moving up on a chart; as well as sanctions, such as missing break time, moving down on a chart, being sent to another classroom and so on. Other common examples of behaviourist approaches might be 'time out' strategies and a focus on classroom rules. One of the most well-known behaviourist schemes is Canter's (2010) assertive discipline around since the mid-1970s, where it was suggested that the teacher should expect '100% compliance, 100% of the time'. It has been argued that these behaviourist approaches have been adopted in schools without the necessary scrutiny (Payne, 2015). The Education Endowment Foundation (EEF, Rhodes & Long, 2019) also noted that in the UK, there is a lack of research-based evidence on the efficacy of

82 Attitudes, beliefs and perspectives

these approaches, despite the strong and emotive views presented by both sides of the argument.

> Behaviourism poses difficulties, on the one hand, because of its ethical neutrality and, on the other, because it is highly effective. Like any powerful technology it can be used for moral or immoral purposes.
>
> (Cooper & Jacobs, 2011, p. 53)

From the *behaviourist* perspective, Porter (2000, p. 22) suggests that the reasons for behaviours that challenge can include:

- *Self-control* – children may lack the necessary self-government to meet behavioural expectations. This can also be attributed to a lack of respect for the teacher.
- *Lack of teacher confidence* – there is a lack of clarity for children in the sanctions and consequences for any rule infringement.
- *Positive responses* – the behaviour is continuing because it is getting a response (whatever that may be).

Possible strengths in the classroom

The behaviourist model for managing behaviour, as with any other strategy, has a number of advantages and disadvantages. This approach is advocated by the English government through its focus on using rewards and sanctions and encouraging their inclusion in schools' behaviour policies. The appointment of behaviour advisors and 'czars' who support these strategies has also meant the approach is at times unquestioned in its application in English schools. Behaviourism has been suggested to be able to make quick changes (Canter, 2010) and to support schools in developing a consistent approach to managing behaviour, something highlighted as important by a range of research (Rhodes & Long, 2019; Ofsted, 2014; Bennett, 2017; DfE, 2014).

There have also been assertions that behaviourist approaches are easy for staff to learn, as they have straightforward practical guidelines that require limited training and are therefore inexpensive to introduce. The framework of rules, rewards and sanctions has been argued to support staff, as it was seen as 'emotionally safe'; whereas less structured policies, which required teachers to consider their own views and feelings about behaviour, were seen as 'emotionally loaded' (Radford, 2000). Sanctions have also been suggested to provide 'unambiguous cues' that allow children to differentiate clearly between acceptable and unacceptable behaviours (Porter, 2000).

Possible limitations in the classroom

It has been argued that from a behaviourist model, teaching can become reductive and 'unidirectional' – where the teacher teaches, and the pupil learns – usually under tightly controlled parameters (Lewis, 1998). These approaches often take a hard line against any infringement of rules and include zero-tolerance policies at the extreme end of the spectrum despite some research showing they can be both ineffective and counterproductive (see discussions in Chapter 5). It has been suggested that these approaches can do more harm than good by actually increasing incidents of poor behaviour, as well as leading to decreases in academic achievement and positive behaviours (Sugai & Horner, 2008). It has also been argued that behaviourist strategies have been driven by the need for staff to manage relatively large numbers of children, as opposed to being advantageous for children or teachers (Cooper & Jacobs, 2011). The reliance on rewards and sanctions to *manage* behaviours can reduce any behavioural interventions to 'technicist' approaches rather than encouraging a deeper understanding of behaviour, or developing relationships with children (Hanko, 1994, in Wearmouth *et al.*, 2005). The use of rewards (either formal or informal) to reinforce positive behaviours and sanctions to limit unwanted behaviours has also been suggested to oversimplify the complex motivations for behaviour. Although this might be of use when writing behaviour polices, it has been argued that it is naïve to assume managing behaviour can be as simple as 'drawing up such a list (usually depressingly overlong) whereby misdemeanour x irrevocably equals consequence y' (Galvin & Costa, 1995). Indeed, arguments about behaviourist approaches being reductive have been echoed for almost forty years, with Hargreaves (1972, in Wearmouth *et al.*, 2005) warning about the 'damage' that could occur if teachers' interactions with children were framed as only being either approving or disapproving.

Managing behaviour from the behaviourist stance can be impersonal, as it does not take into account the influence of emotions on children's behaviour and does not have any emphasis on responding to an individual's needs. Behaviourist approaches focus on the visible aspects of behaviour and do not engage with its underlying causes. This means that, whilst they may be a quick fix, they do not necessarily produce lasting long-term results or changes to patterns of behaviours. They are also based on an understanding that unacceptable – as opposed to acceptable – behaviour(s) have been learnt, and that these need correcting using rewards and sanctions. At times, the use of sanctions can also outweigh the rewards, for example in 'assertive discipline' (Canter, 2010), one of the most common 'off the shelf' behaviourist schemes, with its focus on sanctions and compliance (Cooper & Jacobs, 2011). There are also wider debates about whether behaviourist schemes overemphasise developing 'behaviour for learning' – through control and managing behaviour – and neglect 'behaviour for life' – encouraging democracy and respect (Maguire, Ball & Braun, 2010).

> Assertive discipline takes no account of the type or reason behind the inappropriate behaviour, or whether learning and simply being 'on-task' constitute the same thing. It does not question whether the ethical development of students is stunted by the emphasis on sheer obedience; it does not question how an obedience model which requires constant supervision, rewards and punishments can serve a larger social purpose.
>
> (Rigoni & Walford, 1998, p. 448)

Radford (2000) had also previously suggested that from behaviourist perspectives, teachers often 'dominated' any discussions or understandings of behaviour and used sanctions more often than rewards, which effectively reduced children's opportunity to develop their own behaviour and relied on teacher control instead. As well as concerns in relation to the overuse of sanctions, there are associated challenges with positive rewards, particularly in the form of praise. It has been suggested that too much praise can lead children to become 'praise-dependent' or 'praise-hungry' and reduce their intrinsic motivation (Wearmouth et al., 2005).

One of the main criticisms of the approach is that the lack of an acknowledgement of the influence of social and emotional factors results in a great degree of teacher power and associated ethical issues (Wright, Weekes & McGlaughlin, 2004). The lack of emotional engagement is also at odds with much research that highlights the importance of relationships with children as effective in managing behaviour (Rhodes & Long, 2019).

? ACTIVITY STOP 2

Vignette: Joanne

Joanne exhibited a range of what seemed unexpected and often violent behaviours in schools (the male teachers stopped wearing ties, and Joanne was expected to remove her shoes in lessons). She was new to the school, and the trail of paperwork which should have accompanied her took significant efforts to track down and receive. Joanne struggled to follow any direct instructions, and her classmates were, on the whole, frightened of her, which led to significant isolation for her. One morning Joanne arrived at school part-way through the first lesson (lateness was an issue the school was working on), only to launch what seemed to be an unprovoked physical attack on the class teacher when he said 'good morning' to her. Although he was unharmed by this, both he and the class were significantly upset by the incident and by witnessing Joanne's subsequent restraint and removal from the classroom.

The discussion on behaviourism has highlighted a range of advantages and disadvantages, for children and more widely with aspects of the ethics of teacher control.

- Using an example from your own experience or the vignette, use the storyboard (Figure 4.2) to help you consider the best possible outcomes from dealing with the issue using behaviourist principles (offering rewards and sanctions), and then the least advantageous outcome on the following storyboard (Figure 4.3).
- How can the advantages of this approach be maximised and the limitations minimised in the classroom?

BEHAVIOURAL INCIDENT MANAGED WITH BEHAVIOURISM BEST OUTCOME			
The incident (what happened)	Outcomes (what happened after the incident)	Impact on the child (short-term and longer-term)	Impact on the teacher (short-term and longer-term)

FIGURE 4.2 Storyboard showing best possible outcome of incident managed with behaviourist strategies.

BEHAVIOURAL INCIDENT MANAGED WITH BEHAVIOURISM WORST OUTCOME			
The incident (what happened)	Outcomes (what happened after the incident)	Impact on the child (short-term and longer-term)	Impact on the teacher (short-term and longer-term)

FIGURE 4.3 Storyboard showing worst possible outcome of incident managed with behaviourist strategies.

Cognitive-behavioural theories

We have considered the dominant behaviourist model; however, there are a number of other models within this paradigm and the cognitive-behavioural model is one that might have some aspects that are common practice in schools too. This view does take account of emotions, although it is still a child-deficit model – the problem behaviour comes from some deficit in the child. Cognitive behaviourism arose in part from a dissatisfaction with pure behaviourism (Cooper & Jacobs, 2011), and unlike the radical behaviourist view, it has some emphasis on feelings and problem solving, and this meta-cognitive awareness can help to develop children's self-management skills. This aspect is very much lacking in the purely behaviourist model, which has no emphasis on self-management of behaviour, only external management by a teacher or other powerful adult. The cognitive-behavioural perspectives begin to move the focus from teacher control to the child's own self-control.

In the classroom, cognitive-behavioural strategies are sometimes seen through self-management logs and challenging and discussing any negative attitudes or behaviours children display. Another aspect of this perspective that has gained traction in schools in recent years is the concept of 'meta-cognitive awareness', which is often associated with learning (Quigley, Stringer & Muijs, 2012). However, it can also be used in relation to behaviour, where it focuses on explicitly teaching children self-management or emotional regulation skills, also known as Social and Emotional (Aspects) of Learning (SE[A]L).

> Social and emotional aspects of learning have a natural focus on the development of a set of personal, self-management skills which are frequently raised as potential issues when individual cases of problem behaviour are identified ... they relate to the development of skills in five principal areas popularised by Goleman (1996) and his work on 'emotional intelligence' and 'emotional literacy'.
>
> (Garner, 2013, p. 3)

These social and emotional skills encompass self-awareness, managing feelings, empathy, motivation and social interactions. They can take the form of whole-class or whole-school programmes, or they can be tailored to suit individuals or groups of children with specific needs (EEF, 2020). A nationwide programme of SEAL was rolled out by the DfE in England in 2005 after it was implemented as part of the National Behaviour and Attendance Pilot in 2003.

From the *cognitive-behavioural* perspective, Porter (2000, p. 68) suggests that the reasons for behaviours that challenge can include:

- *Expectations* – where there is a mismatch between children's understanding of the consequences of certain behaviours.
- *Attributions* – an understanding of what has caused the consequences to occur, but not always correctly attributed to the behaviour displayed.
- *Problem-solving skills* – these may not be suitably developed in children, or they may experience issues in information processing.
- *Emotional state* – this may be linked to their self-esteem(s) and/or stage of development.

Possible strengths in the classroom

A review (Humphrey *et al.*, 2008) of the provision of social and emotional learning found that both staff and pupils noted the small group work had a positive impact on pupils' social and emotional skills, and that this was sustained outside of the small group work environment. These interventions can also lead to an increase in children's motivation to engage with a range of facets of education (Porter, 2000). A key strength of the cognitive-behavioural approach is that, unlike a purely behaviourist standpoint, children can be supported in learning the skills they need in order to behave well, rather than simply correcting any instances of poor behaviour. From a behaviourist perspective, any class rules would be written by the teacher without whole-class participation; unlike in this model, where children would be expected to contribute to setting any rules and consequences, and that these would be based upon their rights and responsibilities, rather than purely on teacher control.

Cognitive-behavioural approaches also prioritise the option for children to make choices about their behaviour and then to subsequently reflect on these and to recognise and manage any strong emotions (Garner, 2013). Research has also noted the impact these programmes can have, not just on children whose behaviours challenge, but on the whole school. This is achieved by promoting better school attendance through a focus on improving motivation and children's enjoyment of school, and through contributing to other aspects of pupil welfare and support (Garner, 2013). The cognitive-behavioural perspective also encompasses theories of motivation as drivers of children's behaviour and an awareness that more than simple external or extrinsic rewards are beneficial. This can mean that unlike behaviourist approaches and token economies, children's intrinsic motivation is often also nurtured.

Possible limitations in the classroom

There are also a number of possible limitations of these approaches in the classroom. Cognitive-behavioural approaches still retain what have been described as 'authoritarian overtones' (Porter, 2000) which can be seen by some children as confrontational. A review of SEAL interventions found that the success of the programmes was influenced by a range of factors, including the skills and experience of the facilitator and the availability of an appropriate physical space to conduct the sessions (Humphrey *et al.*, 2008). This means that unlike behaviourist strategies, which require little specific training, some form of INSET or time to become familiar and skilled with the materials used with cognitive-behavioural approaches is needed for teachers and other staff. Other issues highlighted which limit the efficacy of these approaches (Humphrey *et al.*, 2012) included a lack of time and space for SEAL interventions, something which could be argued is even more challenging now for schools.

The importance of a positive rapport between the teacher or member of staff providing the activities and the children involved has been noted. This may be problematic if the interventions are, for example, run by TAs in withdrawal groups, as they may not have an established relationship with the children. The importance of 'follow-up' in lessons after sessions was also noted as important; again, time constraints and staffing issues may make this challenging in some schools and settings. This was also noted by Garner (2013), who highlighted the importance of senior leaders' understanding the core underlying philosophy of SEAL and that any form of 'bolt-on' approaches are largely ineffective, reiterating the importance of these approaches being embedded in the school's ethos.

Cognitive-behavioural approaches also depend on children being motivated to engage with self-management strategies and to have the verbal abilities to express – at least to some extent – their thoughts and feelings. Nevertheless, at their core, cognitive-behavioural strategies and interventions are still closely linked to behaviourism and behavioural methods, with a clear model of consequences, sanctions and rewards and where the ethical position of the teacher or professional deploying these is paramount.

ACTIVITY STOP 3

The discussion on cognitive-behavioural approaches has highlighted a range of advantages and disadvantages for staff and children.

- Using the same example as from the previous 'activity stop' (either the vignette or your own), use the storyboard (Figure 4.4) to help you consider how the same incident might have played out differently with this approach.
- How can the advantages of this approach be maximised and the limitations minimised in the classroom?

BEHAVIOURAL INCIDENT MANAGED WITH COGNITIVE-BEHAVIOURAL APPROACHES			
The incident (what happened)	Outcomes (what happened after the incident)	Impact on the child (short-term and longer-term)	Impact on the teacher (short-term and longer-term)

FIGURE 4.4 Storyboard to consider the outcomes of a cognitive-behavioural intervention on a behaviour incident.

Sociocultural models

Sociocultural models, or sociological perspectives more broadly, differ from the behaviourist standpoint we have just discussed in that they not only consider addressing behaviour but look deeper to understand what might be causing the external manifestations of behaviours that can be seen in the classroom (or the lack of behaviours in the case of those children who internalise rather than externalise). Unlike psychological understandings, sociological perspectives are not child-deficit models; rather, they consider the causes of behaviour as existing within the systems the child engages with – relationships, family, peers and so on. From these perspectives, behaviour is:

> the product of an individual's way of thinking, or it may be the product of the interactions an individual has with other people, or (and most importantly) it may reside entirely in the minds and actions of people other than 'the symptomatic individual'
>
> (Cooper & Jacobs, 2011, p. 54)

The approaches that nest within this range of philosophies are usually pro-active and preventative, as opposed to psychological approaches which, in the main, tend to be reactive and tariff or token based. There are a range of approaches within this sociological umbrella, but for the sake of brevity and simplicity, two of those that might be seen in the classroom will be discussed – humanism and systems theory. Humanism broadly considers whether problems in behaviour are the cause of unmet needs in the child, while from a systems theory view (sometimes known as ecosystemic), behaviour issues arise from problems in the child's environment – including their relationships with peers and teachers.

In sociological models, the teacher does not try to enforce control, but rather works with and alongside the child. Whereas behaviourism can see quick changes in behaviour but long-term issues with intrinsic motivations to behave in sanctioned ways, sociological models try to support the child in making long-term changes to their behaviour. These models flip behaviourism's focus on aspects including order, compliance and obedience on their head, and instead try to support children in developing autonomous ethics, emotional regulation, cooperation and integrity. It can be seen, just by looking at the key words used to sum up these approaches, how they lie at very different ends of a continuum to behaviourist approaches. As a result, they need very different whole-school approaches to managing behaviour and suggest a range of different underlying practices.

Humanistic approaches

This broad category of approaches rose in prevalence in the 1970s and 1980s in schools in part as a reaction against labelling and 'treating' children whose behaviours challenged. Humanism moves away from teacher-centred to child-centred engagements, from control to self-discipline, and has a focus on educating the whole person (Sharp, 2012). This perspective makes clear links between the emotional and cognitive aspects of learning, acknowledging the importance of thinking and feeling – linking closely with Maslow's hierarchy of needs (Maslow, 1943), which was itself informed by indigenous American (Blackfoot Nation) beliefs. From this perspective, children are viewed as having rights just like adults, and that without the need for punishment or reward, they will be motivated, make constructive choices, and be trustworthy (Porter, 2000). Goodman's (2006) view that children make mistakes 'because they are young not bad', and that any interventions should 'offer support and guidance', mirrors the humanistic philosophy.

> At the heart of a humanistic approach is the principle that all human beings deserve respect because they are human beings, and a carefully developed theory that states the solution to many social and psychological ills resides in the rigorous application of this principle. This agrees with contemporary perspectives on human rights, in particular the rights of the child, and accounts for the popularity of this approach.
>
> (Cooper & Jacobs, 2011, p. 54)

It has been argued more recently that the 'clinical and child-centred' understandings of behaviour still seen in much government policy in England have continued to effectively deflect attention away from developing schools to be 'more humane, more inclusive places' (Armstrong, 2014; Maguire *et al.*, 2010; Thomas & Loxley, 2001) – something humanism focuses on. Humanistic approaches are guided by Rogers's (1980, in Cooper & Jacobs, 2011) key principles of honesty, empathy and unconditional positive regard and one of the most recognisable facets in the classroom are 'circle time' activities.

A key driver from a humanistic perspective is the development of children's self-esteem or range of multiple 'esteems', as O'Brien and Guiney (2004) have argued. According to research (Miller & Moran, 2005, cited in Glazzard, 2016), much practice in primary schools has aims to encourage positive self-esteem among pupils. Yet, other studies have noted that even where teachers know their classes very well, they still struggle to identify individual children who are specifically in need of interventions to develop self-esteem (Miller & Parker, 2005 cited in Glazzard, 2016). This reinforces the need for whole-class circle time activities as opposed to individual interventions.

As noted, many of these approaches, although discussed separately here, are combined in practice despite their at-times contesting philosophical standpoints. Humanistic approaches, for example, are often combined with psychological approaches in nurture group provision and settings.

From a *humanistic* perspective, Porter (2000, p. 114) suggests that the reasons for behaviours that challenge can include:

- *Secondary problems* – these can be 'symptoms' of the problem, as opposed to the problem or issue itself. For example, not wanting to complete work might be a secondary problem where the primary problem is that the work is too difficult.
- *Exploration* – in line with physical exploration, children also explore different behaviours often without the understanding that these might do harm to others.
- *Being emotionally overwhelmed* – this can often stem from being unable to successfully regulate their emotions and feelings.
- *Socially influenced behaviour* – either using the wrong behaviour at the wrong time, or by copying other children whose behaviour is inappropriate in that context.
- *Unmet needs* – this can occur when children have experiences they are unable to cope with and/or are beyond their understanding and may include a range of adverse childhood experiences (ACEs).

Possible strengths in the classroom

The humanistic approach has been suggested to be implementable in a range of settings including mainstream classrooms. Humanistic approaches are also relatively easy to learn and are more immediate in their effects than other 'therapeutic' approaches. Warm and positive relationships are necessary in these approaches, and much research (see Chapter 1) makes links between positive relationships between teachers and children and increased well-being, academic engagement and lower incidences of referral for mental health conditions.

The approaches used in the classroom from this standpoint are preventative and focus on developing children's own sense of responsibility, moving towards democratic processes in the classroom. In this sense, children are being supported in developing skills for their whole lives. Humanism advocates a 'consultative' approach to supporting children with behaviour, where teachers do not direct or advise children but instead act as a 'sounding board' to help them reflect on and develop their behaviour and reactions. In these models the underlying causes of behaviour, rather than the surface manifestations, are addressed. Kohn (1996) believed that one of the problems with managing behaviour from, for example, the behaviourist perspective was that it limited the opportunities for children to become 'morally sophisticated, think for themselves and care about others'. This can seem far removed from many behavioural interventions and from the 'traditional' views of school discipline. However, it addresses Payne's (2015) concerns about the mismatch between the ways in which behaviour and learning are currently supported. This form of humanistic approach also aligns much more closely with current learning strategies (for example, mantle of the expert, child-led learning) and reflects the way in which most early years' and foundation stage learning is successfully delivered. This may address for some children (and teachers) the incongruity between approaches to learning and approaches to behaviour.

Possible limitations in the classroom

Approaches under the humanistic umbrella can be diverse and do not easily form a coherent model (Wearmouth *et al.*, 2005), and this means that they can be difficult to pin down. In addition, there are few immediate or prescribed interventions to follow, as these approaches cannot be reduced to 'off the peg' tips and tricks, but rather are established and cemented over much longer periods. As such, children may initially test the teacher's integrity, so it is important that staff are wholly committed to these philosophical standpoints, or they risk being seen by children as inauthentic and dishonest.

The primary curriculum has been noted by many to be overly packed, and that has led some schools to focus on more narrowly academic curricula to meet external pressures (testing, league tables and so on). This means that finding time for pastoral activities and wider social learning interventions is challenging at best if it is not a whole-school priority. Humanistic approaches overall have also been criticised for their usually protracted nature (solution-focused approaches being the exception to this rule – see Chapter 6), although specific interventions such as Circle Time can result in quicker changes to behaviour.

Humanistic approaches also rely on a genuine and sustained positive relationship with the adult involved, and it has been suggested that much skill is needed to facilitate Circle Time programmes (Wearmouth et al., 2005). This can be problematic, as noted, if these approaches are led by an adult who is external to the school or class. It is also difficult to mandate on a whole-school level for the necessary warm relationships between staff and pupil(s), or to write this into a consistently applied behaviour policy. Instead, these types of relationships are naturally individualistic to some level and can be difficult to draw up into a step-by-step policy; as such, they would require regular and possibly extensive training.

> ### ❓ ACTIVITY STOP 3
>
> The discussion on humanist approaches has highlighted a range of advantages and disadvantages.
>
> - Applying the same example as from the previous 'activity stop' (the vignette or your own), use the storyboard (Figure 4.5) to help you consider how the same incident might have played out differently with this approach.
> - How can the advantages of this approach be maximised and the limitations minimised in the classroom?
>
> | BEHAVIOURAL INCIDENT MANAGED WITH HUMANISTIC APPROACHES | | | |
> |---|---|---|---|
> | | | | |
> | The incident (what happened) | Outcomes (what happened after the incident) | Impact on the child (short-term and longer-term) | Impact on the teacher (short-term and longer-term) |
>
> **FIGURE 4.5** Storyboard to consider the management of a behaviour incident from a humanist perspective.

Systemic approaches

Systemic approaches offer a significant challenge to the black-and-white, stimulus and response models of behaviourist thinking and move away from simple cause and effect thinking to offer what has been described as a 'serious challenge' to some of the government's recommendations (Cooper & Upton, 1991). Within systems theories, or what Cooper and Upton (1991) amongst others also term 'ecosystemic' practices, there is a focus not so much on the individual, but on the dysfunctions of the school and/or the general environment. Unlike some of the psychological (and medical) approaches, labelling is avoided from these sociological perspectives, and they move thinking from a process of attributing blame to one of finding solutions. Sociological approaches shift the perspective away from viewing the world as being made up of parts and instead see children as being part of a larger whole or 'system'. These systemic approaches specifically provide:

> [a] synthesis of other approaches ... the interventions that flow from this approach often combine features of behaviourism, humanism and, most commonly, cognitive behaviourism. Their distinctive feature is the target for the application of the intervention.
>
> (Cooper & Jacobs, 2011, p. 55)

These can include specific Circle Time activities and interventions, or a range of other therapeutic approaches.

Systemic approaches assume an empowering focus, where teachers support children to solve problems themselves and respect their inherent ability to do so – clearly linking closely to humanist perspectives. Rather than a focus on changing a child's behaviour as with behaviourism, there is an understanding that change cannot be imposed or forced upon children, and the teacher's role is to respond in new ways to behaviours that challenge and help children to break the cycle they are in (Porter, 2000). The focus is on the problem within the child's interactions in their system – for example, between them and their peers, friends, teachers, parents, siblings and so on – and that these behaviours might serve the needs of the system of interactions in some way, but may be detrimental to the child. 'Re-framing' or changing the viewpoint or emotional feelings around the behaviour is a typical form of intervention (Cooper & Upton 1991). Cooper and Jacobs (2011, p. 52) note that reframing can often take the form of:

> constructing a version of the supposed problem which shifts the focus from the individual ... to people and circumstances outside of the individual and the related patterns of interpersonal and social interaction. The proclaimed value of a systemic approach is that it encourages lateral thinking and innovative action in situations which seem deadlocked.

It is understood that changing any part of the system will have knock-on – hopefully positive – repercussions in the rest of the systems. This means that anyone who is not actively working towards finding a solution to the problem(s) is actually part of the problem. Unlike with some other theoretical positions, there is no possibility of neutrality in these approaches (Wearmouth *et al.*, 2005).

From *systemic* perspectives, Porter (2000, p. 163) suggests that the reasons for behaviours that challenge can include:

- *Applying the wrong solution* – it can follow from teachers attempting the 'if you don't succeed at first ...' pattern of action.
- *Behaviour safeguards relationships* – the behaviours children are exhibiting are 'working' in some way. This differs from behaviourist views that the behaviours receive attention by considering how these behaviours might serve some purpose and/or stabilise some relationships.
- *Internal problems* – these may take the form of some type of special educational need or disability, medical or psychological diagnosis.

Possible strengths in the classroom

These models focus on facilitating solutions and respect for individuals, and as such, this gives teachers a broad scope of possible methods for supporting children. As has been suggested, systemic interventions can also be used to circumnavigate any deadlocks in behaviour, as from this perspective there are a multitude of possible ways to support the child and engage with them and with others. This can also be supportive for the teacher involved, as they are working as part of a wider system to support the child; and rather than the fear of 'losing control', those working with the child can investigate other strategies to support them. Multi-agency working, due to the systemic underpinnings of these strategies, is advocated so that the teacher is part of a team working with the child as opposed to assuming sole responsibility for the success – or otherwise – of the interventions and supports utilised.

Unlike behaviourist and cognitive-behavioural strategies, there is no focus on teacher power, and as a result, many of the ethical issues levelled at these approaches are not relevant when working from a systems perspective. Unlike these models, the solutions for the behaviours that challenge are sought and teachers persevere until these solutions are effective, and so systemic approaches can offer the possibility of long-term, child-motivated changes in behaviours.

Possible limitations in the classroom

Due to their broad focus, this umbrella of approaches has received criticism for being complex, with individual interventions at times being difficult for individual teachers to design and carry out. It can also be seen as 'insincere' if staff are not wholly committed to the ethos behind the interventions they use. Like humanist approaches, they can also require time to introduce and embed, and as a result, they do not always see quick changes in children's behaviours.

? ACTIVITY STOP 5

The discussion on systems theory approaches has highlighted a range of advantages and disadvantages for staff and children.

- Applying the same example as from the previous 'activity stop' (the vignette or your own), use the storyboard (Figure 4.6) to help you consider how the same incident might have played out differently with a systems theory approach.
- How can the advantages of this approach be maximised and the limitations minimised in the classroom?

BEHAVIOURAL INCIDENT MANAGED WITH SYSTEMS THEORY APPROACHES			
The incident (what happened)	Outcomes (what happened after the incident)	Impact on the child (short-term and longer-term)	Impact on the teacher (short-term and longer-term)

FIGURE 4.6 A behaviour incident supported using systemic approaches.

Medical and biopsychosocial models

Understanding behaviour from a medical perspective is also a child-deficit model, where the 'problem' causing the behaviour is within the child and can be addressed, at least in part, by medical interventions; for example, attention deficit hyperactivity disorder (ADHD). The medical model was at one time used to justify removal from mainstream schools (Wearmouth, 2004). Children whose behaviours challenge, from this perspective, are understood as requiring some form of 'treatment' and are seen from the viewpoint of existing only within the child and not within the context(s) they are in (Wearmouth *et al.*, 2005). From a medical perspective, the solutions to children's behavioural issues lie with other professionals; for example, doctors, psychiatrists and so on, which means that teachers can be left relatively powerless to act to support children (Didaskalou & Millward 2004). There can also be something of an ideological clash between medical and education professionals, which can make it hard to develop relationships based on agreed and reciprocal understandings of terms and working practices.

It has been argued that by only looking at medical explanations for behaviour, support mechanisms at home and school are ignored. Ethical issues abound with prescribing medications for some conditions which deviate from the normal expectations of behaviour (Wearmouth *et al.*, 2005), and this has been described as a 'failure-driven' model. Cooper and Shea (1999, cited in Cooper & Jacobs, 2011, p. 28) highlight:

> It is also important to stress that while medication may be of value to the student taking it, it is never an adequate substitute for effective teaching and appropriate school organisation, behaviour management and other features of the educational context to maximise a student's social, emotional and academic engagement.

The purely medical model offers little in the way of practical application for teachers working with children in the classroom whose behaviours challenge. This approach has largely given way to the more recent perspective of the biopsychosocial model which considers how biological, psychological and social factors interact and influence behaviour (Visser, 2017), and forms a bridge between the three different perspectives. The term was coined by the neurologist and psychiatrist, Grinker in the 1950s, being first applied to medicine before eventually making its way into the field of education (Reisinger, 2014). It has been noted that it is much more closely aligned with systemic theories than other understanding of behaviour, as it considers behaviour in a range of different 'systems' – biological and psychological and social – and how these interact (Cooper & Jacobs, 2011). As such, the biopsychosocial model offers a different perspective on complex behaviours by enabling an understanding from multiple sources, as well as considering how these different facets engage with each other.

Cooper (2005) argues, fairly incontrovertibly, that 'the more we understand about a child's difficulties, the better placed we are to provide effective support'. The biopsychosocial model enables us to consider the causes of behaviour from a range of perspectives and therefore develop a better understanding of the possible causes of behaviours that challenge. Because this model considers a range of different reasons for behaviours that challenge, it has a broad spectrum of possible interventions and supports for children, drawn from different theoretical positions. Cooper and Jacobs (2011) suggest that interventions from a biopsychosocial perceptive might include using some form of behaviourist training, including the use of rewards and sanctions and/or cognitive-behavioural strategies such as anger management training and/or various sociological therapeutic interventions, such as counselling. In line with this perspective are trauma-informed approaches which are becoming increasingly prevalent in the UK.

> The vigour behind the movement stems from the growing awareness of the prevalence of exposure to trauma among youth and an increased understanding of the corrosive impacts resulting from the biological, psychological, and social adaptations to chronic exposure to trauma.
>
> (Overstreet & Chafouleas, 2016, p. 1)

Trauma-informed practice considers how children's experiences have impacted on them and how to support them in making the social, emotional, neurobiological, psychological or behavioural adaptations that may be needed. Like many facets of sociological models more broadly, trauma-informed schooling focuses on the importance of warm and positive relationships with children and like systemic practices, shifting the focus from asking what is 'wrong' with the child to asking what is 'wrong' with the situations the child has been in. Trauma-informed approaches can encompass a range of wholistic interventions that are 'less emotionally harmful than restrictive interventions' (Holmes, 2020), such as zero-tolerance policies and automatic hierarchies of sanctions. Instead, trauma-informed approaches include a focus on ensuring interactions and relationships with all adults in the school are safe and consistent, that the whole school is culturally responsive and mindful of the range of cultures and cultural norms within its pupils (and staff) and that targeted strength-based interventions are offered through peer and individual pathways (Cavanaugh, 2016). (This will be discussed further in Chapter 6.)

In the biopsychosocial model a range of factors can fall under the *biological* aspect and are also sometimes referred to as 'developmental disorders'. However, there is also an understanding that the biological elements of any behaviours are affected by the wider environment the child is in. These can include early childhood experiences that affect the child's neurology, including diet and nutrition, how they were parented and the peer influences they were exposed to, as well as the extent to which they were positively stimulated and interacted with through the early stages of their development. Within this is also the acknowledgement that any form of neglect, abuse or range of adverse childhood experiences (ACEs) can negatively affect children's social and cognitive functioning. It also considers the impact of neurological 'plasticity' – the ability of the brain to change and develop new neural pathways or to essentially rewire itself depending on the environment it is in and the experiences it receives (Cooper & Jacobs, 2011). Rather than being stuck in the time-old nature-vs-nurture debate on the causes of behaviours that challenge, the biopsychosocial model is capable of considering the impact of nature – biological factors – and nurture – social and psychological factors – together.

Under the psychological and sociological aspects of the model, a range of different approaches can be applied. These can range from behaviour plans to therapeutic interventions, and anything in between. What makes this approach different from the perspectives we have discussed earlier is the idea that the strategies used are synthesised together, and that there is a clear view on how the biological, social and psychological factors interlink and overlap. The approaches (plural is key here) used from the biopsychosocial perspective consider the impact of all three factors on the child's behaviour, rather than viewing them in isolation. Cooper and Jacobs (2011) suggest that this consideration of a range of factors *together* makes the biopsychosocial approach 'truly holistic' and helps to understand the 'complexities', both of a range of challenging behaviours and of the associated interventions.

From the *biopsychosocial* perspective, the reasons for behaviours that challenge can include any from the previous models. However, unlike some of the previous perspectives, this understanding enables a more complex view of how these causes may interact with each other.

Possible strengths of these approaches in the classroom

Because this model considers a very broad range of causes of behaviours that challenge, it enables a broad spectrum of interventions and approaches. Therefore, for teachers there is a lot of scope to try different strategies rather than be bound by a strict set of interventions or approaches; for example, using only rewards and sanctions. As this understanding is predicated on a number of systems working together, it is inherently multimodal and, as a result, encourages multidisciplinary support and intervention, which can take the pressure off individual class teachers and allow them to feel more supported by working as part of a team.

Possible limitations of these approaches in the classroom

Some of the advantages of this perspective may also be limitations. The myriad of approaches that can be utilised means staff need knowledge of, and training in a number of different approaches to work with children whose behaviours challenge and to understand how to skilfully combine different theoretical potions so they complement, rather than contradict each other.

> ## ❓ ACTIVITY STOP 6
>
> The discussion on biopsychosocial approaches has highlighted a range of advantages and disadvantages for staff and children.
>
> - Applying the same example as from the previous 'Activity Stops' (the vignette or your own), use the storyboard (Figure 4.7) to help you consider how the same incident might have played out differently with this approach?
> - How can the advantages of this approach be maximised and the limitations minimised in the classroom?
>
> | BEHAVIOURAL INCIDENT MANAGED WITH BIOPSYCHOSOCIAL APPROACHES ||||
> |---|---|---|---|
> | | | | |
> | The incident (what happened) | Outcomes (what happened after the incident) | Impact on the child (short-term and longer-term) | Impact on the teacher (short-term and longer-term) |
>
> **FIGURE 4.7** Storyboard to consider supporting a behavioural incident with biopsychosocial approaches.

Theory and the classroom **99**

The following chapters (Chapters 5 and 6) in this section will consider some specific approaches and practical strategies that fall under the umbrella of sociological and biopsychosocial approaches.

Review

This chapter has covered a lot of information! There has been a discussion on how what we understand, and what we believe about the causes of behaviour, can either consciously or subconsciously drive our actions in relation to it. There then followed a consideration of some of the major philosophical and theoretical understandings of the causes of behaviours that challenge, and how these influence our work with the children in our care. The possible strengths and limitations for the classroom use of each model has also been evaluated. The table (Figure 4.8) summarises some of the key terms associated with the approaches and standpoints discussed.

It can be seen that within the different theoretical understandings of behaviours are different rationales for teacher power. Although very simplified and artificially separated – as discussed, many of us will move between different models at different times and for different children – the diagram (Figure 4.9) shows how teacher power changes with different models and how an emphasis on teacher control influences the role of the children or child.

Paradigm	Key terms					
Behaviourism	Authoritarian		Teacher control	Easy to learn	Quick changes to behaviours	Relies on extrinsic motivation
Cognitive-behavioural	Authoritative	Child-deficit	Teacher control and self-management	Relatively easy to learn	Some quick changes to behaviours	Uses extrinsic motivation but can improve children's intrinsic motivation
Humanist	Democratic	Systems-deficit	Growing child autonomy, teacher supports	Requires positive teacher/child relationships	Can be a prolonged process	Uses child's own intrinsic motivations
Systems theory	Facilitator					
Medical	Implementor	Child-deficit	Other professionals in control	Beyond scope of teacher	Can be very quick but not sustained	Relies on extrinsic/medical intervention
Biopsychosocial	A combination of the above					

FIGURE 4.8 Key terms for each approach discussed in this chapter.

100 Attitudes, beliefs and perspectives

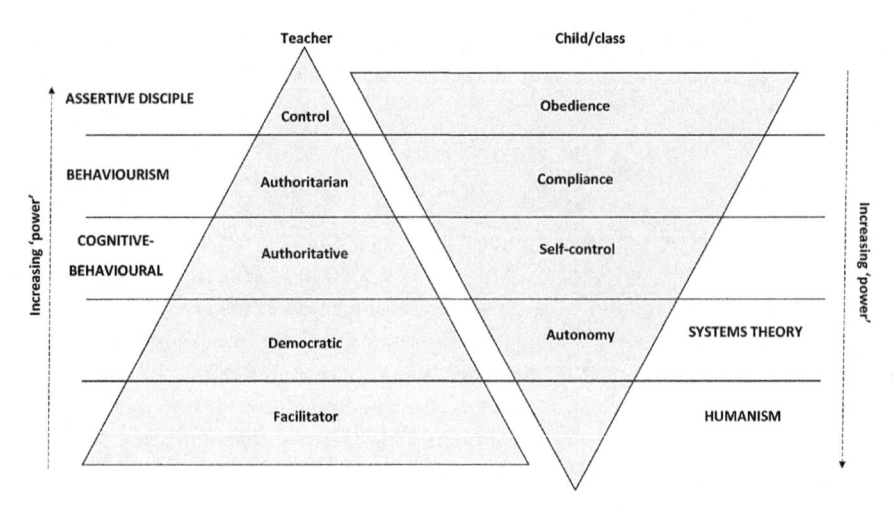

FIGURE 4.9 Power in the different theoretical understandings of behaviour.

THINKING STOP 2

Regardless of the philosophical and/or theoretical position we take as Cooper and Jacobs (2011, p. 55) highlighted, there are key questions that should be asked and answered in relation to any position adopted and actions taken. These include:

- What interests are being considered and served by selecting a particular intervention or approach?
- What interests are being considered and served by identifying the intended outcome from this intervention?
- Who is the greatest beneficiary of this intervention?

This was also noted by Kohn (1996) who argued we should always ask, 'Cui bono' – who benefits?

- Think about the way in which behaviour is managed in your school or setting.
- Can you reflect on these questions in relation to policy and your own practice?

Whole-school actions might include some or all of the following:

- Consider the training needs of staff. Could training be developed or bought in to share the philosophical and theoretical underpinnings of the approaches used in the school? This would help to support all staff in developing a clear and/or deeper understanding of approaches to ensure they are not relying on strategies without any underpinning.
- Ensure that the philosophical standpoint of the school or setting, or its ethos, is clearly embodied in the way behaviour is managed, and that this 'golden thread' or joined-up thinking is evident in the strategies used to manage behaviour.
- Encourage all staff to read widely about current issues in education – particularly behaviour; maybe even start a reading club!

Individual teacher actions might include some or all of the following:

- Take the time to consider your own philosophical position on behaviour and how that consciously and subconsciously guides the actions you take with the children in your care.
- Your own beliefs and views will affect the way in which you manage behaviour.
- Ensure the strategies you use to manage behaviour are in line with your school or setting's ethos and the behaviour policy.
- Continue to read widely – and critically – about supporting children's behaviour.

Possible mental health and well-being implications:

- Relationships between pupils and teachers, and between pupils and peers, have been repeatedly highlighted as protective factors for children's mental health. Different philosophical positions advocate different forms of relationships. If pure behaviourism is used to manage behaviour, this may need support with a range of opportunities for PHSCE or SEAL activities to provide time for relationships to develop.
- A sense of 'belonging' to a school community and not being 'labelled' was key for those with behaviours that challenge, and specifically those children at risk of exclusion (either fixed-term or permanent) (Graham *et al.*, 2019). Some philosophical positions enable greater agency for pupils and ownership over setting behavioural expectations in the classroom. These may be advantageous in developing this sense of community for pupils, where teachers are working *with* them, rather than doing things *to* them. Some positions also move away from labelling and pathologizing children's behaviours. Graham *et al.* (2019) found that children at risk of exclusion found these approaches particularly positive.

Practitioner-related take-away:

- Personal beliefs and attitudes related to children's behaviour will impact on the actions taken in the classroom – consciously or not – often more than any published guidance.

Practitioner reading:

Wearmouth, J., Glynn, T., and Berryman, M. (2005). *Perspectives on Student Behaviour in Schools: Exploring Theory and Developing Practice.* Abingdon: Routledge.

References

Armstrong, D. (2014). Educator perceptions of children who present with social, emotional and behavioural difficulties: A literature review with implications for recent educational policy in England and internationally. *International Journal of Inclusive Education,* **18**(7), pp. 731–745.

Bennett, T. (2017). *Creating a Culture: How School Leaders Can Optimise Behaviour.* London: DfE.

Canter, L. (2010). *Assertive Discipline* (4th ed.). Bloomington: Solution Tree Press.

Cavanaugh, B. (2016). Trauma-informed classrooms and schools. *Beyond Behavior,* **25**(2), pp. 41–46.

Coburn, C. (2005). The role of nonsystem actors in the relationship between policy and practice: The case of reading instruction in California. *Educational Evaluation and Policy Analysis,* **27**(1), pp. 23–52.

Cooper, P. (2005). Biology and behaviour: The educational relevance of a biopsychosocial perspective. In Clough, P., Garner, P., Pardeck, J., and Yuen, F. (Eds.), *Handbook of Emotional and Behavioural Diffiuclties* (pp. 105–122). London: SAGE Publications.

Cooper, P., and Upton, G. (1991). Controlling the urge to control: An ecosystemic approach to problem behaviour in schools. *Support for Learning,* **6**(1), pp. 22–26.

Cooper, P., and Jacobs, B. (2011). *Evidence of Best Practice Models and Outcomes in the Education of Children with Emotional Disturbance/Behavioural Difficulties: An International Review.* Co. Meath: University of Leicester and NCSE.

Department for Education. (2014). *Behaviour and Discipline in Schools.* London: DfE.

Didaskalou, E., and Millward, A. (2004). Breaking the policy log jam: comparative perspectives on policy formulation and development for pupils with emotional and behavioural difficulties. In Wearmouth Glynn, J., Richmond, T. and Berryman, M. (Eds.), *Inclusion and Behaviour Management in Schools: Issues and Challenges* (pp. 52–67). London: David Fulton Publishers.

Education Endowment Foundation. (2020). *Social and Emotional Learning: Social and Emotional Learning Teaching and Learning Toolkit.* London: EEF.

Galton, M., and MacBeath, J. (2008). *Teachers Under Pressure.* London: SAGE Publications Ltd.

Galvin, P., and Costa, P. (1995). Building better behaved schools: Effective support at the whole school level. In Gray, P., Miller, A., and Noakes, J. (Eds.), *Challenging Behaviour In Schools* (pp. 145–163). London: Routledge.

Garner, P. (2013). *Social and Emotional Aspects of Learning.* Northampton: University of Northampton.

Glazzard, J. (2016). The value of circle time as an intervention strategy. *Journal of Educational and Developmental Psychology,* **6**(2), pp. 207–215.

Goodman, J. (2006). School discipline in moral disarray. *Journal of Moral Education*, **35**(2), pp. 213–230.

Graham, B., White, C., and Potter, S. (2019). *School Exclusion: A Literature Review on the Continued Disproportionate Exclusion of Certain Children*. London: DfE.

Holmes, J. (2020). *Trauma-Informed Approach in Schools Helps Staff and Benefits Students, New Report Says*. News from BACP. https://www.bacp.co.uk/news/news-from-bacp/2020/9-january-trauma-informed-approach-in-schools-helps-staff-and-benefits-students-new-report-says/

Humphrey, N., Kalambouka, A., Bolton, J., Lendrum, A., Wigelsworth, M., Lennie, C., and Farrell, P. (2008). *Primary Social and Emotional Aspects of Learning (SEAL) Evaluation of Small Group Work*. Manchester: University of Manchester School of Education.

Johnson, B., Whitington, V., and Oswald, M. (1994). Teachers' views on school discipline: A theoretical framework. *Cambridge Journal of Education*, **24**(2), pp. 261–276.

Kohn, A. (1996). *Beyond Discipline: From Compliance to Community*. Alexandria: Association for Supervision & Curriculum Development.

Lewis, J. (1998). Embracing the holistic/constructivist paradigm and sidestepping the postmodern challenge. In Clark, C., Dysin, A., and Millward, A. (Eds.), *Theorising Special Education* (pp. 90–106). London: Routledge.

Macleod, G. (2006). Bad, mad or sad: Constructions of young people in trouble and implications for interventions. *Emotional and Behavioural Difficulties*, **11**(3), pp. 155–167.

Maguire, M., Ball, S., and Braun, A. (2010). Behaviour, classroom management and student 'control': Enacting policy in the English secondary school. *International Studies in Sociology of Education*, **20**(2), pp. 153–170.

Maslow, A. (1943). A theory of human motivation. *Psychological Review*, **50**(4), pp. 370–396.

O'Brien, T., and Guiney, D. (2004). Self-esteems and emotional differentiation. In Wearmouth, J., Richmond, R., Gkynn, T., and Berryman, M. (Eds.), *Understanding Pupil Behaviour in Schools: A Diversity of Approaches*. London: David Fulton Publishers.

O'Brien, T., and Guiney, D. (2005). The problem is not the problem: Hard cases in modernist systems. In Clough, P., Garner, P., Pardeck, J., and Yuen, F. (Eds.), *Hanbook of Emotional and Behavioural Diffiuclties* (pp. 141–154). London: SAGE Publications Ltd.

Ofsted. (2014). *Below the Radar: Low-Level Disruption in the Country's Classrooms*. London: Ofsted.

Overstreet, S., and Chafouleas, S. (2016). Trauma-informed schools: Introduction to the special issue. *School Mental Health*, **8**, pp. 1–6.

Payne, R. (2015). Using rewards and sanctions in the classroom: Pupils' perceptions of their own responses to current behaviour management strategies. *Educational Review*, **67**(4), pp. 483–504.

Porter, L. (2000). *Behaviour in Schools: Theory and Practice for Teachers*. Buckingham: Open University Press.

Postholm, M. (2013). Classroom management: What does research tell us? *European Educational Research Journal*, **12**(3), pp. 389–402.

Quigley A., Stringer, E., and Muijs, D. (2012). *Guidance Report: Metacognition and Self-Regulated Learning*. London: EEF.

Radford, J. (2000). Values into practice: Developing whole school behaviour policies. *Support for Learning*, **15**(2), pp. 86–89.

Reisinger, L. (2014). Using a bio-psycho-social approach for students with severe challenging behaviours. *LEARNing Landscapes*, **7**, pp. 259–270.

Rhodes, I., and Long, M. (2019). *Guidance Report: Improving Behaviour in Schools*. London: EEF.

Rigoni, D., and Walford, G. (1998). Questioning the quick fix: Assertive discipline and the 1991 education white paper. *Journal of Education Policy*, **13**(3), pp. 443–452.

Roffey, S. (2010). Classroom support for including students with challenging behaviour. In Rose, R. (Ed.), *Confronting Obstacles to Inclusion: International Responses to Developing Inclusive Education* (pp. 279–292). London: Routledge.

Sharp, A. (2012). Humanistic approaches to learning. In Steel, N. (Ed.), *Encyclopedia of the Sciences of Learning* (1469–1471).Boston: Springer US.

Sugai, G., and Horner, R. (2008). What we know and need to know about preventing problem behavior in schools. *Exceptionality*, **16**(2), pp. 67–77.

Thomas, G., and Loxley, A. (2001). *Deconstructing Special Education and Constructing Inclusion*. Buckingham: Open University Press.

Visser, J. (2017). Classroom behaviour: Finding what works for you. In Colley, D., and Cooper, P. (Eds.), *Attachment and Emotional Development in the Classroom: Theory and Practice* (pp. 279–290). London: Jessica Kingsley Publishers.

Wearmouth, J. (2004). Introduction: Issues in inclusion and the management of student behaviour in schools. In Wearmouth, J., Glynn, T. Richmond, R. and Berryman, M. (Eds.), *Inclusion and Behaviour Management In Schools: Issues and Challenges* (pp. 1–14). London: David Fulton Publishers.

Wearmouth, J. and Connors, B. (2004). Understanding student behaviour in schools. In Wearmouth, J., Richmond, R., Glynn, T. and Berryman, M. (Eds.), *Understanding Pupil Behaviour in Schools: A Diversity of Approaches* (pp. 1–15). London: David Fulton Publishers.

Wearmouth, J., Glynn, T., and Berryman, M. (2005). *Perspectives on Student Behaviour in Schools*. London: Routledge.

Wright, C., Weekes, D. and McGlaughlin, A. (2004). Teachers and pupils – relationships of power and resistance. In Wearmouth, J., Richmond, R., Glynn, T. and Berryman, M. (Eds.), *Understanding Pupil Behaviour In Schools: A Diversity Of Approaches* (pp. 67–88). London: David Fulton Publishers.

5
RESTORATIVE PRACTICE
Reconciliation and restitution

This chapter builds on the preceding and largely theoretical chapter by considering the practical application in the classroom of some of these approaches. It moves the focus from a theoretical and rather abstract discussion to sharing how using restorative practices might support and develop aspects of your classroom practice and how they differ from the 'traditional' behaviourist strategies of rewards and sanctions.

This chapter aims to:

- Share what restorative practices are and how they have been developed
- Consider how they can be used to support children whose behaviour challenges
- Evaluate the possible strengths and limitations of this approach
- Contrast restorative practices with behaviourist rewards and sanctions-based strategies
- Discuss what impact these approaches might have on mental health and well-being

Foundations

Research (Cooper & Jacobs, 2011) has suggested that behavioural and cognitive-behavioural interventions are the most common strategies used with children whose behaviours challenge. However, as Chapter 4 discussed, a raft of other evidence-based approaches have been shown to be highly effective that can mitigate some of the limitations and ethical issues associated with the behaviourist and some of the cognitive-behavioural strategies.

DOI: 10.4324/9781003035527-9

106 Attitudes, beliefs and perspectives

> **? ACTIVITY STOP 1**
>
> Before this chapter begins in earnest, jot down some notes (they may be brief or copious!) in the diagram (Figure 5.1), reflecting on:
>
> - What you already know about restorative practices.
> - Which beliefs they may align most closely with.
> - What you would like to find out about restorative practice.
>
> [Diagram with three boxes labelled: "What I know:", "What I want to know", "Where they fit:"]
>
> **FIGURE 5.1** Record of ideas about restorative practices.

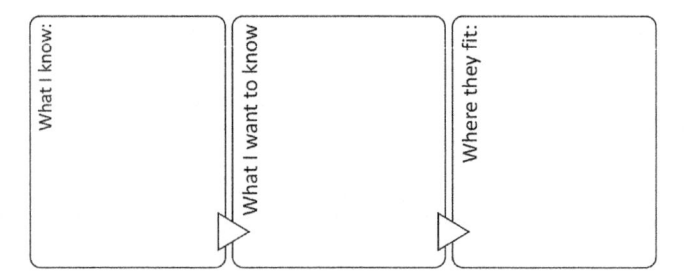

Restorative practices nest largely within the humanistic person-centred perspectives (McCluskey *et al.*, 2008a) of the sociological approaches but have also been suggested to link to biopsychosocial interventions (Cooper & Jacobs, 2011). They have developed from restorative justice models and are part of a family of approaches used in a range of settings in the UK; for example, by the police force, in youth justice, probation services and social work as well as in schools. These approaches are also used in a range of contexts in North America, Europe, Australia and New Zealand (Wearmouth, Glynn & Berryman, 2005). In education, restorative practices are, and can be, used in specialist SEMH schools and alterative provision as well as mainstream primary and secondary schools. At their heart, they are focused on making the distinction between 'managing behaviour' and 'managing relationships' (Hansberry, 2016). One of the clearest descriptions of restorative practices comes from the work of McCluskey (2016), where she outlines the key aims and intentions of a restorative approach which:

> emphasises the human wish to feel safe, to belong, to be respected and to understand and have positive relationships with others. It recognises the fundamental importance in schools of both effective support and clear control and boundaries. Restorative Practices comprise key principles and values,

skills and strategies on a continuum ranging from whole school approaches to those used in more challenging situations or with individual students in difficulty.

(p. 19)

It has been suggested that, unlike behaviourist approaches which reduce behaviour to a rather simplistic cause-and-effect model without considering wider influences, restorative practices recognise the complexity of education and offer a model which takes into account the wider demands on schools (McCluskey et al., 2008b). This wider and more holistic understanding of behaviour and its enmeshed nature with other issues has been argued to account for the increasing interest in this way of working in schools. It has been suggested that unlike purely behaviourist approaches, restorative ways of working with children support a range of well-being and mental health issues, with headteachers aware of:

> the complex pressures on children and young people: the numbers of young carers, of looked after children, of children coping with a range of family and personal difficulties, of increasing concern about wellbeing and mental health among the young; and expectations about body image, self-presentation and success.
>
> (McCluskey et al., 2008a, p. 406)

Restorative practices are not in any way 'new' and have their roots in mediation and ages-old community-based approaches such as the *hui whakatika* in Maori culture and in a range of ingenious practices in Australia and North America. The focus on community values provides a clear and structured alternative to sanctions and punishment, moving away from:

> the primacy of assigning blame and punishment to finding a mutually agreeable way forward by negotiation. The prime focus is on 'putting things right' between all those involved or affected by wrong-doing.
>
> (Wearmouth et al., 2005, p. 182)

Braithwaite (1997, cited in Wearmouth et al., 2005) argued that the community-based aspect of restorative practices is a key strength as well as a significant difference compared to other ways of supporting children. He highlights that this practice moves away from considering children and young people in isolation and as isolated, and instead considers them in the context of the wider community (for example, peers, class, school, neighbourhood) of people who know and care about them. He asserts that this community aspect can offer care and support for children who may not have a family or close relationship that are able to provide this. From this perspective there is an element of both 'nurturing learning', 'unconditional' support and 'social responsibility' involved, as well as possible wider positive repercussions for the (school) community. Many of these factors are replicated in Visser's (2007) concept of the eternal verities (Chapter 8) and address some of the wider concerns about the behaviour for life versus behaviour for learning debate touched on in the previous chapter. In line with this, it has been highlighted that restorative practices must not be viewed or used as a 'bag of tricks' but rather firmly rooted in a pedagogical and philosophical understanding (Hansberry, 2016).

> ### THINKING STOP 1
>
> We have considered Armstrong's (2014) view that schools are often not 'humane' places in relation to behaviour management. The list of terms pertaining to restorative practices discussed earlier in the chapter would seem to address some of these concerns about being 'humane'. They have included: community, context, nurturing, support and responsibility.
>
> - What do you think stops some schools or settings from enacting these values?
> - How many of them are limited by school-based factors?
> - For those that are limited by factors outside of schools, what might these factors be?
> - Are there any that embody your current practice or those of your school?
> - How do you manage that?

One of the key strengths – and for some, a key challenge – of working restoratively is that it moves away from punitive and punishment-based approaches. It is acknowledged that in many countries, 'the will to punish is deeply embedded' (Parson, 2005, cited in Macleod, 2006) and that moving away from this can be very difficult for some children and staff. However, restorative practices eschew the false dichotomy between punishment and permissiveness and instead focus on offering a balance of support and accountability through a 'forward looking and hopeful approach' (McCluskey et al., 2008a). As we discussed in Chapter 4, many of the theoretical perspectives on behaviour consider the role of power – either the power of the teacher or how empowered children are. If you return to the diagram (Figure 4.8) in Chapter 4, restorative practices are situated within the bottom halves of each triangle where there is a focus on self-control, autonomy and democracy for children. Indeed, power and how it impacts on the way we work with children and their relationships with each other is specifically considered in restorative practices:

> Restorative practices admit the centrality of power relations and the complexity of social structures, offering the opportunity for all those involved to

explore more deeply the relationship between the internal and external tensions of schools and to focus on how and where possible solutions might lie.

(McCluskey *et al.*, 2008a, p. 213)

An interesting way to visualise this is by using the social control window (Figure 5.2). This shows the impact of control and support and how the outcomes of each can be different. For example, the figure suggests that low support and low control combine to form a 'neglectful' position for – in this case – the teacher or school. Here, teachers may be described as 'uninvolved, passive or resigned' (Hansberry, 2016). Few, if any, would suggest that this combination could lead to positive outcomes for any, pupils or staff. Moving across to the next box along the bottom of the figure is a permissive way of working, where staff can be seen as acting in ways which are 'rescuing/protecting, excusing, over-reasoning' (Hansberry, 2016). High support and low control are proposed to create a permissive culture – a criticism that some have levelled at restorative practices, and that will be discussed in this chapter. Looking across the top boxes of the diagram, high control and low support can create an 'authoritarian, stigmatising' (Hansberry, 2016) environment in the classroom and has echoes of some assertive discipline and zero-tolerance approaches. The final box highlights what good restorative practices should offer: a balance between high control and high support, where teachers work in a 'authoritative, reintegrative, collaborative and responsibility-taking' way (Hansberry, 2016). The key words in each section of the window are also exemplars of the teacher's role in behaviour from each of these approaches; for example, interventions or, more traditionally, 'discipline' *cannot* be done at all, or be done *to, for* or *with* children. It is the core belief of restorative practices that they are done with children and not imposed on them or done for them.

THINKING STOP 2

Take a moment to reflect on the social control window (Figure 5.2).

- Where would you position 'good' practice with children whose behaviours challenge?
- Why?
- Where would you position less effective practice with children whose behaviours challenge?
- Why?
- Where would you place your practice now? Does it match with where you would want it to be?
- If not, what do you need to develop your practice?

FIGURE 5.2 Social control window.

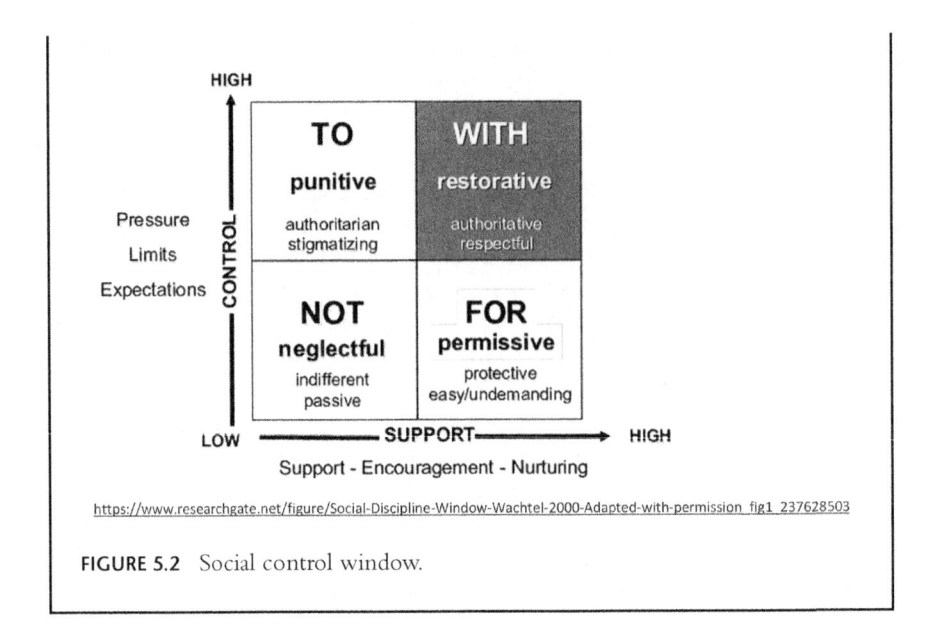

Axes: Pressure / Limits / Expectations (CONTROL, LOW to HIGH vertical); Support - Encouragement - Nurturing (SUPPORT, LOW to HIGH horizontal).

- **TO** — punitive (high control, low support): authoritarian, stigmatizing
- **WITH** — restorative (high control, high support): authoritative, respectful
- **NOT** — neglectful (low control, low support): indifferent, passive
- **FOR** — permissive (low control, high support): protective, easy/undemanding

https://www.researchgate.net/figure/Social-Discipline-Window-Wachtel-2000-Adapted-with-permission_fig1_237628503

Hansberry (2016) noted that being seen to be 'doing something' immediately to deal with behaviour – for example, by using rewards, sanctions or zero-tolerance policies (top left box of the window, Figure 5.2) – is able to address some of the pressures over a school's accountability. This fast action can also be 'powerfully reassuring for staff, students and the community', and yet, there is no evidence that these approaches are actually more effective or result in increased safety – particularly in relation to zero-tolerance approaches (Hansberry, 2016). Figure 5.3 shows how restorative practices compare with traditional authoritarian ways of working.

One of the issues with behaviourist approaches (as discussed in Chapter 4) was that they were often separated from expectations related to children's learning, and Payne (2015) suggested that approaches to learning and behaviour in schools often conflicted. Poikela (2010, in Gellin, 2018) argues that due to the reflective nature of managing behaviour in restorative practices, strategies for learning and behaviour are much more closely aligned. This, he suggested, happens in two ways: by using concrete experiences as a basis for reflection, and by being supported and scaffolded by staff and peers to make sense of these new learning opportunities.

In Finland, a mediation and a restorative focus in schools has been practiced since 2001, and this dovetails with the Finnish curriculum's view (2014, in Gellin, 2018, p. 253) that schools are a site of both academic and social development, where children are expected to 'learn cooperation, have opportunities to practice skills for negotiation, mediation and conflict management as well as critical thinking'. The implications and outcomes of this will be explored in more detail in Chapter 9. In the UK, Scotland has done much work on using restorative practices in both their primary and secondary schools, and many authorities in England have also

Authoritarian approach	Restorative approach
The focus is on:	**The focus is on:**
• Rule-breaking	• Harm done to individuals
• Blame or guilt	• Responsibility and problem-solving
• Adversarial processes	• Dialogue and negotiation
• Punishment to deter	• Repair, apology and reparation
• Impersonal processes	• Interpersonal processes
and, as a result:	**and, as a result:**
• Needs of those affected often ignored	• The needs of those affected are addressed
• The unmet needs behind the behaviour are ignored	• The unmet needs behind the behaviour are addressed
Accountability = being punished	**Accountability = putting things right**

FIGURE 5.3 Comparing and contrasting restorative and authoritarian approaches.
Source: Howard (2009).

developed their use of restorative practice, including schools in Surrey, Hackney, Dudley, Leeds, Tower Hamlets and Stockport, among others. Research (McCluskey et al., 2008b) into the impact of these approaches has provided some very positive findings. A study of a pilot in 10 secondary schools, 7 primary schools and a special school in Scotland highlighted the 'cultural change' that had been evidenced in those schools – which mirrors the embedded nature of restorative practises rather than their bolt-on nature. Findings from McCluskey (2016) highlighted the profound impact this way of working had on staff when supporting children whose behaviour was very challenging, with teachers noting how 'their experiences of working restoratively in these situations was profoundly moving' (McCluskey, 2016, p. 19). The research suggested that the schools were demonstrably calmer, and the pupils' responses about schooling were overall more positive, with them describing teachers as 'fair and listening to "both sides of the story"' (McCluskey et al., 2008b). The implementation in the special school (although this was only one) was stated to have had a significant impact, whilst the success in implementation in the secondary schools had been 'patchy' and had resulted in a more 'diverse' range of restorative practices. The report drew out some key factors that affected the impact of restorative ways of working, and these included both an enthusiasm for change and a balance of clarity and flexibility about the aims of the approaches. Here, staff agency was key – where schools believed that they had the capability and capacity to improve situations. Additionally, and perhaps most importantly, the influence of high-quality training and leadership were also identified (McCluskey et al., 2008b). This final point is often at the root of some of the well-publicised criticism of restorative approaches in the media and by some high-profile educationalists. In a report on secondary schools in Scotland, teachers suggested that working restoratively added to their workload and that they lacked the time and, crucially, the training to implement it (Seith, 2019). However, a study using randomised control trails in America (Augustine *et al.*, 2019) found that across 54 schools, teachers suggested there was an improvement in the 'school climate' and a reduction in the number of exclusion – both fixed term and temporary – but that academic standards did not improve, and some children's attainment even went backwards. Aspects of this research were also supported by the Scottish study's findings, that the greatest positive change was seen in primary rather than secondary schools.

One of the issues that can face restorative ways of working is their reduction to one or two aspects, rather than being viewed as an embedded practice. One of the most recognisable features of restorative practices is the restorative conference where individuals meet with a facilitator – usually a teacher – and progress through a scripted list of questions. While this is a central tenet of restorative practice, alone it is not enough to make the systemic and cultural changes needed, and it may address some of the previous criticisms of the approach in relation to time and workload. Wachtel (2003) asserted that this was just one aspect in a suite of strategies and restorative interventions, which can usually be grouped under two main headings: *restorative conferences*, which repair relationships after an incident; and wider *restorative approaches*, which develop the skills to build and maintain relationships. Wachtel (2003) also discussed the importance of understanding this complete range of restorative practices and, despite being a self-confessed 'conferencing advocate', asserted that it would be naive to assume that any single intervention could lead to a significant change. He highlighted the importance of a whole-school ethos and environment that is 'characterized by the everyday use of a wide range of informal and formal restorative practices' (p. 84). Figure 5.4 shows some of the range of approaches used in restorative practices.

The importance of this breadth of restorative interventions has also been noted by others. In their American study, Augustine *et al.* (2019) reported a range of restorative interventions and strategies which provide a comprehensive list that helps to develop a fuller understanding of the variety of strategies, and away from a focus on only one aspect of working restoratively. The table (Figure 5.5) shows the scope restorative practices have, and how they can be used individually, as a whole class and a whole school.

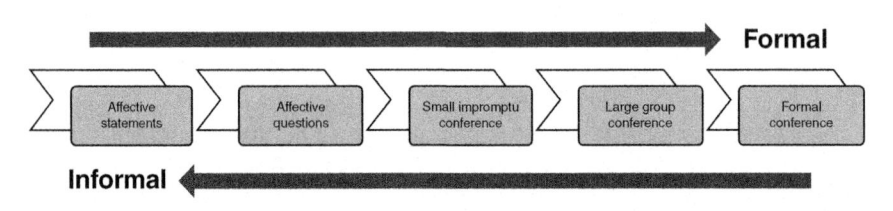

FIGURE 5.4 A range of formal and informal restorative practices.

Restorative practice **113**

Element	Definition
Affective statements	Personal expressions of feeling in response to specific positive or negative behaviors of others
Restorative questions	Questions selected or adapted from two sets of standards questions designed to challenge the negative behavior of the wrongdoer and to engage those who were harmed
Small impromptu conferences	Questioning exercises that quickly resolve lower-level incidents involving two or more people
Proactive circles	Meetings with participants seated in a circle, with no physical barriers, that provide oppertunities for students to share feelings, ideas, and experiences in order to build trust, mutual understanding, shared values, and shared behaviors
Responsive circles	Meetings with participants seated in a circle, with no physical barriers, that engage students in the management of conflict and tension by repairing harm and restoring relationships in response to a moderately serious incident or pattern of behavior affecting a group of students or an entire class
Restorative conferences	Meetings in response to serious incidents or a cumulative pattern of less serious incidents where all of those involved in an incident (oftern including friends and family of all parties) come together with a trained facilitator who was not involved in the incident and who uses a structured protocol

FIGURE 5.5 A range of restorative practices in school.
Source: IIRP (2011, cited in Augustine *et al.*, 2019, p. xi).

Building blocks

As discussed, the key factor that marks restorative practices as different from behaviourist rewards and sanctions-based approaches is the way in which the behaviours are perceived. Rather than a focus on breaking rules – although this is included – there is an emphasis on how the behaviour or incident has impacted on the people and relationships in the school, and possibly the wider community too (Roffey, 2010). Hansberry (2016) suggested that in restorative practices, there is a focus on changing the way individuals see and feel about each other, which in turn changes people's behaviours, and that better relationships create better behaviours – for staff and pupils. McCluskey *et al.* (2008b) found that this could be a transformative process for teachers as well as children, noting that the staff involved in some of the schools piloting restorative practices in Scotland 'asked new questions of themselves as professionals'. Through the process of reflecting on some of the key principles of restorative practices, and recognising that 'the person is not the problem, the problem is the problem', some schools in the study were able to fundamentally reassess their teaching of, and relationships with, students (McCluskey *et al.*, 2008b). Hendry (2009, cited in Hansberry, 2016) also highlighted not only the different way of *working* with children in restorative practices, but also the different way of *thinking* about them, due to their key tenets of: genuineness, valuing people, empathy, responsibility and accountability and optimism. Following this, restorative practices are underpinned by an understanding that children and young people are able to take responsibility for their own behaviours, that people can change and that individual's rights should be respected.

Restorative practices have been described as 'active, problem-solving and balanced' (Wearmouth *et al.*, 2005), and as discussed, a key aspect of restorative approaches is the importance placed on maintaining, repairing and building relationships. This has resonance with discussions in Chapters 1 and 4 about the important role positive relationships play, not only in supporting children's behaviour but also in maintaining mental health and well-being. The range of restorative practises additionally support children (and staff) in developing a range of key life skills, including active listening, emotional literacy, patience, objectivity, anger management and dealing with difficult situations. In practice, these skills are nurtured and accountability is provided through a range of formal or informal restorative conversations or restorative meetings, as opposed to rewards and sanctions. In his own practice and experience, Wachtel (2003, p. 84) highlighted a number of criteria to improve the efficacy of restorative practices, including:

- *Fostering awareness* – this could be either very informal or formal, and it includes asking those involved in an incident how they think their behaviours might have affected others. This can also include the teacher expressing their own feelings to those involved.
- *Avoiding lecturing* – this focuses on the importance of encouraging empathy and an understanding of how children's behaviours affect others. It is suggested that when sanctioned, punished or 'lectured', children (and adults) can become defensive and feel victimised, which prevents them from noticing and considering how their actions have impacted on others.
- *Involve all actively* – punitive interventions are suggested to make children passive because we are doing things to them rather than with them. But from a restorative approach, all involved are encouraged to speak up and take part in some way. Participation might be through listening to others, deciding how to repair any harm done or keeping their commitments to repair damaged relationships and so on.
- *Accept ambiguity* – this relates to accepting that sometimes it is difficult to get to the root of the problem and that, for example, in a fight between two people, the person at fault can often be unclear. When this is the case, working restoratively encourages all individuals to take as much responsibility as possible for the situation, and that any intervention belongs to the participants.
- *Separate the deed from the doer* – this reminds us to try to maintain a neutral and objective position. The aim in restorative practices is to reinforce children's worth and may include disapproval of their actions, but not of them.
- *See every instance of wrongdoing and conflict as an opportunity for learning* – this returns to the idea that 'the problem is the problem' rather than focusing on the child as a 'problem'. By changing the focus of thinking, negative incidents can be transformed into constructive ones by building empathy and developing a sense of community, both of which reduce the recurrence of negative incidents in the future.

❓ ACTIVITY STOP 2

Look at the factors Wachtel (2003) described as key a restorative 'mindset'. Using the diagram (Figure 5.6) can you compare these to your current school or setting's behaviour policy and consider:

- Is there scope for any of these practices?
- If so, which ones?
- Would you want them all to be facilitated by the behaviour policy?
- For the facets that are not yet possible, what changes would need to be made to the policy?

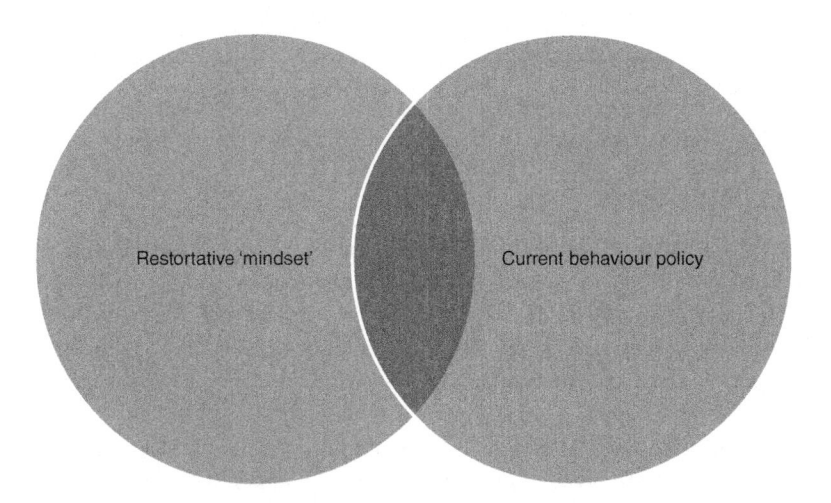

FIGURE 5.6 Diagram to consider any overlaps between a current school/setting's behaviour policy and a restorative mindset.

In practice (as shown in Figure 5.4), there are a range of opportunities and different ways to engage with children restoratively. The least formal and most everyday of these is by using affective statements and questions. Hansberry (2016) defined these as being used when 'respectfully confronting a student' – for example, for an incident of low-level disruption – but highlights that children can, and should, also be supported in developing this way of communicating with their peers. Affective questions and statements are suggested to encourage fair and respectful dialogue and encourage children to take responsibility for their own actions. They are easy to use and to teach as they follow a pattern. Usually these begin with some sort of *affirmation* of the child's worth, followed by identification of the problematic *behaviour*, then an *affect* or feeling description and an additional *affirmation* to end. In practice this might sound something like:

> Evelyn, I can see you are really enthusiastic (*affirmation*), but when you shout out I find it hard to listen to everyone else (*behaviour*). It makes me disappointed (*affect*) but I know you are kind and will let everyone else join in (*affirmation*).

This should be followed by an opportunity for the child to reply. One of the additional advantages of these conversations is that once the habit has been established, the only preparation needed is to ensure you are calm and collected before talking to the child.

? ACTIVITY STOP 3

Vignette: Shaun

Shaun has a history of being disengaged with schooling, attendance issues and problems making friends. He is quick to perceive any input from an adult as a confrontation and often reacts aggressively. Shaun was removed from a lesson after responding sarcastically to a request from his class teacher to hand out some exercise books. Both the teacher and Shaun later separately agreed they had overreacted.

Thinking about this restorative recipe for conversations, reflect on a time where an interaction with a pupil did not go as planned. (I can think of lots!) You could also use the example conversation in the preceding vignette too. Use Hansberry's (2016) steps – affirm the pupil, challenge the behaviour, use an affect (feeling) word, reaffirm the pupil, give a right of reply – to replay the conversation.

- How might it have been different if you had used Hansberry's structure? If using the vignette, you might like to rewrite it following the outline Hansberry suggested.
- How might the pupil have felt using this structure?
- How might it have made you feel?
- What might be the short- and longer-term implications for you and the pupil – specifically around restoring, repairing and developing relationships?

Moving on from these quick and easy affective questions and conversations, the next level of intervention can be small and impromptu conferences; these could be either for individual children or for small groups. They can range from informal to increasingly formal and can also be termed a 'restorative chat'. These follow a script and, when used regularly, support children in developing their own thinking about incidents around these questions, which may mean that these conferences become quicker as they become more embedded in the school routine. The questions that form the basis of these are the same as those (possibly more familiar) in the formal conferences, and Hansberry (2016, p. 133) suggests asking:

- What happened?
- What were you thinking at the time?
- What do you think now?
- Who has been/could be affected by this and how?
- What needs to happen to fix this?

Any restorative conference, whether big or small, formal or informal, needs to be followed up to ensure those agreeing to actions have fulfilled them. This follow-up may also need to take the form of some sort of record-keeping which will allow staff to check that incidents are not always happening on the same day, place or time, or with the same children. If incidents have a regular geography or context, then this may signal a wider issue that needs to be addressed. For example, if there are common behavioural issues when children are exiting or entering the buildings for breaks, or at lunchtimes, then there may need to be a wider discussion about how to address these. If the same children's names are recurring in informal (or formal) conferences, then some level of additional follow-up would be needed, and this might include the following additional questions (Hansberry, 2016):

- What might be a fair way to deal with this if it happens again? Or,
- What should happen if we see, hear, etc. you do this again?

The responses here might then include some form of sanction.

If the incident is more serious, or has involved more children, then the process might need to be escalated to a larger and more formal small group conference. Like the individual conferences, these too can be impromptu or scheduled and require no specific preparation from the teacher or those involved. The same questions can be used as noted in the individual conference, but with a group conference, additional follow-up may be needed. Hansberry (2016) suggests checking with those involved whether the agreed methods to repair the hurt done need to be formally recorded or can remain as a verbal agreement between the group. This same process is also utilised for large, formal conferencing; however, these require preparation and greater follow-up due to either the number of children involved and/or the severity of the incident. At its simplest level, preparation might include ensuring the room is set out appropriately – for example, there are enough chairs for everyone – or it might involve discussing the incident with staff that were present, and so on. Hansberry (2016) highlights that when working with children who have experienced trauma, ACE or attachment issues, it is much more effective to delay any restorative work until around an hour after the incident to ensure they are able to neuro-regulate effectively and engage in the process. Restorative Justice 4 Schools (http://www.restorativejustice4schools.co.uk) suggests conferences are guided by the following questions, although there is flexibility to amend them based on the age and understanding of those involved, as well as any specific contextual issues:

- Can you tell us about what happened and how you became involved?
- (If necessary) What happened next and/or what else (ask this until their story unfolds)?
- What were you thinking at the time this happened?
- What have your thoughts been since?
- Who has been affected/upset by this and in what way?
- What has been the hardest thing for you?

These questions are asked of all involved, and when the questions have been asked and answered, a conference agreement is drawn up which is formally recorded. This is a record of the initial problem or incident, what has been agreed between the children at the conference, as well as a possible section detailing what will happen if the agreement is broken, or the incident happens again. An important next step is to set a time to review the agreement to make sure that it is suitable and working. This key step helps to develop and maintain what Hansberry (2016) terms 'the 3 E's' of 'engagement, explanation and expectation'. These ensure children are actively involved in the process and understand what they need to do, as well as being clear on any new expectations for their behaviour.

> It is essential that these conferences – at any level – are embedded within a wider structure of restorative practices and not seen as a stand-alone element or an off-the-peg trick. When seen as a holistic ethos, research suggests that working restoratively can support children broadly by:Building relationships, learning empathy, reinforcing academic content and practicing problem solving in a structured and predicable manner
>
> (Evanovich, Martinez, Kern & Haynes, 2020, p. 34)

It would be true to say that working restoratively is very different from a behaviourist rewards and sanctions-based approach. The teacher's and children's roles in behaviour are perceived differently. For some teachers and children, this can be an exciting and collaborative way to support each other; for others, there is a great challenge in this very different way of relating to children. Restorative ways of working and engaging with children are significantly emotional practices and that this can be seen as both an advantage and a disadvantage.

? ACTIVITY STOP 3

Using the storyboard (Figure 5.7), think of an incident of poor behaviour that you have experienced or been involved in. You might like to use the previous vignette (or one from the other chapters) to help too.

- Can you draw how the episode might have played out differently and what the short and longer-term implications might have been for those involved if restorative practices, perhaps conferencing in particular, had been used?

BEHAVIOURAL INCIDENT MANAGED USING RESTORATIVE PRACTICES			
The incident (what happened)	Outcomes (what happened after the incident)	Impact on the child (short and longer-term)	Impact on the teacher (short and longer-term)

FIGURE 5.7 Storyboard to consider how restorative practices might impact on the children and teacher.

Possible advantages of this approach in the classroom

Research (Kokotsaki, 2013, cited in Hansberry, 2016) has identified a range of advantages to working restoratively, which include: pupils feel their teachers are fair, and that they show care and respect; pupils feel safer and more comfortable at school; attendance improves; there is a reduction in low-level disruption which is associated with higher levels of participation and engagement in lessons and as a result, improved attainment. Restorative practices have also been suggested to have particular benefits for vulnerable children and those with SEMH needs, as it develops emotional intelligence and can empower change and growth for children, as it enhances their own individual levels of responsibility (Hansberry, 2016). Staff have also found that these interventions had helped to prevent low-level incidents from escalating to the stage where fixed period exclusions were necessary (Graham, White & Potter, 2019).

DfE guidance makes clear links between their anti-bullying documentation and the possibility of utilising restorative practices, noting that schools which excelled at tackling bullying were those where pupils had a 'clear understanding of how [their] actions affect others' (DfE, 2017). The Restorative Justice Council (restorativejustice.org.uk) also highlighted a 2001 DfE publication which noted their research found 'two-thirds of schools use restorative approaches in response to bullying and 97% of teachers rated restorative approaches as effective'.

A key advantage for teachers and children is the structured approach restorative practices – and the conferences in particular – have. There is a sense of security and familiarity for all of those working in this way that they know what will happen and the expectations of those involved. Many restorative practices require no preparation or resources (such as conversations and individual conferences) and are quick and easy to do.

When embedded as part of the school's ethos and practices, the community-based focus in restorative approaches can support not only individual children, but whole classes and key stages too. From a broader perspective, these benefits can also extend to the wider community and even the local area, as the skills children learn through restorative practices can be used both in and outside the school-environment.

Possible disadvantages of this approach in the classroom

However, like all approaches, Howard (2009) suggests that there are also some disadvantages under certain contexts to working restoratively. As noted, restorative practices are fundamentally emotional, and remaining neutral in their work with children can be problematic for some teachers. Issues in restorative practices are specifically highlighted if there is not support from the Senior Leadership Team for staff, or if they are not embedded in the school's ethos and values. As part of a commitment to working restoratively, staff need to be provided with ongoing training to support them in their work. One of the key complaints from staff using restorative practices in Scottish schools was a lack of training (Seith, 2019).

Although restorative practices reconsider the power dynamic that might be familiar to many in traditional and authoritative ways of working, there can also still be issues of power and teacher control in this model. There are still questions of power and control that need to be considered when staff are running conferences, and power-sharing between staff and pupils can be difficult for some schools. Because restorative approaches are a community-based approach, it is also very important to consider how those whose culture is not the same, as either the school or the dominant group's, are supported (Wearmouth *et al.*, 2005).

Restorative practices definitely are not a 'quick fix', McCluskey *et al.* (2008b) suggested that between three and five years are needed for sustained change, while other findings proposed it was more like 5–10 years (Augustine *et al.*, 2019). This shows that schools expecting swift changes are often disappointed and that many years of work are needed for restorative practices to become fully embedded in the way a school works.

The central challenge of working restoratively in schools has been argued to be the implicit and often taken-for-granted systems of discipline and control. In some schools the deeply entrenched nature of a will to punish takes much work – from all involved, children, staff and parents – to overcome and adjust to. As a result, there needs to be a genuine commitment on the part of all of those involved to work this way with children – restorative interventions are necessarily voluntary for all those involved. This can be both and advantage and a disadvantage depending on the school or setting's climate.

Review

This chapter has discussed some of the key aspects of restorative practices, and how they differ from a behaviourist focus on rewards and sanctions. Restorative approaches are a whole-school intervention based on respect, responsibility, repair and reintegration. They change the traditional dynamic of the teacher being 'in control' and look at creating a culture of democracy, autonomy and self-direction. Restorative practices must be embedded across the whole school to be effective and need to focus on developing and maintaining relationships through explicitly teaching and modelling skills and engaging with children in restorative conversations. Restorative conferencing should be used to repair relationships and reintegrate children, and they are significantly less effective if they are used only as a stand-alone intervention.

Whole-school actions might include some or all of the following:

- Support from the SLT is crucial to make this whole-school approach work for children *and* teachers. As a result, this needs to be a decision taken by a critical mass of staff, rather than imposed from above by school leaders.
- Training is also very important, and staff need access to regular and ongoing training to support them and their developing practice. This is also essential to maintain motivation, as embedding practice and change is not a quick process.
- A clear understanding of restorative practices is needed to ensure that it is the foundation of all interventions and everyday interactions, as opposed to moving visible aspects (such as conferencing) and adding them on to pre-existing or even opposing practices and policies as a bolt-on.
- Restorative practices take time and work, and it is key that this message is shared and that staff do not feel under pressure to 'turn behaviour around' quickly.

Individual teacher actions might include some or all of the following:

- Take all opportunities to engage with training and sharing of good practice as your skills in using restorative practices develop.
- Ensure that the philosophy underpinning restorative practices become embedded in all of your interactions with children, not just those related to behaviour.
- Be consistent and clear in your application of restorative practices, and do not be disheartened if change is not immediate.
- Follow-up on all restorative conferencing – big or small – to ensure actions are followed through.

Possible mental health and well-being implications:

- Restorative practices are fundamentally community-based approaches. These strengthen the positive relationships between all involved, staff, children and their peers. Much research highlights the importance of strong, positive relationships for promoting well-being and good mental health.
- Restorative practices focus on repairing the relationships that inevitably get bumped and bruised as part of school life and reintegrating children, skilling then with valuable techniques for later life and for use outside school in a range of situations.
- Research (Marshall, Shaw & Freeman, 2002) highlights the ability of restorative practices to provide children with the vocabulary to describe their feelings; this in itself is empowering. If children are to be able to talk about their own well-being and mental health and ask for help when they need it, being able to talk about their feelings and emotions is essential.

Practitioner-related take-away:

- Restorative approaches develop children's autonomy and skills for life rather than focusing on compliance.

Practitioner reading:

- http://www.restorativejustice4schools.co.uk
- https://restorativejustice.org.uk

References

Augustine, C., Engberg, J., Grimm, G., Lee, E., Wang, E., Christianson, K., and Joseph, A. (2019). *Can Restorative Practices Improve School Climate and Curb Suspensions? An Evaluation of the Impact of Restorative Practices in a Mid-Sized Urban School District*. California: RAND Corporation.

Cooper, P., and Jacobs, B. (2011). *Evidence of Best Practice Models and Outcomes in the Education of Children with Emotional Disturbance/Behavioural Difficulties an International Review*. Co. Meath: University of Leicester and NCSE.

Department for Education. (2017). *Preventing and Tackling Bullying: Advice for Headteachers, Staff and Governing Bodies*. London: DfE.

Evanovich, L., Martinez, S., Kern, L., and Haynes, R. (2020). Proactive circles: A practical guide to the implementation of a restorative practice. *Preventing School Failure*, **64**(1), pp. 28–36.

Gellin, M. (2018). Mediation in Finnish schools: From conflicts to restoration. In Nylund, A., Ervasti, K., and Adrian, L. (Eds.), *Nordic Mediation Research* (pp. 247–266). New York: Springer International Publishing.

Graham, B., White, C., and Potter, S. (2019). *School Exclusion: A Literature Review on the Continued Disproportionate Exclusion of Certain Children*. London: DfE.

Hansberry, B. (2016). *A Practical Introduction to Restorative Practice in Schools*. London: Jessica Kingsley Publishers.

Howard, P. (2009). *Restorative Practice in Schools*. Reading: CfBT Education Trust.

Macleod, G. (2006). Bad, mad or sad: Constructions of young people in trouble and implications for interventions. *Emotional and Behavioural Difficulties*, **11**(3), pp. 155–167.

Marshall, P. Shaw, G., and Freeman, E. (2002). *Restorative practices: Implications for educational institutions*. Third International Conference on Conferencing, Circles and Other Restorative Practices, Minneapolis, MN. https://pdfs.semanticscholar.org/39cd/3856f624a81f501e6afdaf95116cfcee9b3d.pdf

McCluskey, G. (2016). Restoring the possibility of change? A restorative approach with troubled and troublesome young people. *International Journal on School Disaffection*, **7**(1), pp. 19–25.

McCluskey, G., Lloyd, G., Stead, J., Kane, J., Riddell, S., and Weedon, E. (2008a). 'I was dead restorative today': From restorative justice to restorative approaches in school. *Cambridge Journal of Education*, **38**(2), pp. 199–216.

McCluskey, Gillean, Lloyd, G., Kane, J., Riddell, S., Stead, J., and Weedon, E. (2008b). Can restorative practices in schools make a difference? *Educational Review*, **60**(4), pp. 405–417.

Payne, R. (2015). Using rewards and sanctions in the classroom: Pupils' perceptions of their own responses to current behaviour management strategies. *Educational Review*, **67**(4), pp. 483–504.

Roffey, S. (2010). Classroom support for including students with challenging behaviour. In Rose, R. (Ed.), *Confronting Obstacles to Inclusion: International Responses to Developing Inclusive Education* (pp. 279–292). London: Routledge.

Seith, E. (2019, May). Restorative-practice approach to behaviour 'ineffective'. *Times Educational Supplement*. https://www.tes.com/news/ubiquitous-non-punitive-approach-behaviour-often-ineffective

Visser, J. (2007). Key factors that enable the successful management of difficult behaviour in schools and classrooms. *Education 3–13*, **33**(1), pp. 26–31.

Wachtel, T. (2003). Restorative justice in everyday life: Beyond the formal ritual. *Reclaiming Children and Youth: Summer 2003*, **12**(2), pp. 83–87.

Wearmouth, J., Glynn, T., and Berryman, M. (2005). Addressing behaviour at school-wide level. In Wearmouth, J., Glynn, T., and Berryman, M (Eds.), *Perspectives on Student Behaviour in Schools* (pp. 180–217). London: Routledge.

6
SOLUTION FOCUSED WORKING
Celebrating success

This chapter will discuss the possibilities solution focused approaches have to support children and their behaviour. As in the previous chapter, although there are strategies associated with this way of working, it is an ethos and holistic approach as opposed to a 'bag of tricks'. Solution focused approaches move even further along the continuum in the opposite direction to behaviourist strategies and do not use sanctions or rewards in any way. Instead, it is a strengths-based approach (in contrast with the child-deficit understandings examined in Chapter 4) and, like restorative practices, it is focused on working *with* the child rather than doing things *to* them. This way of working rests firmly within the sociological views of understanding behaviour and uses systemic theories to work therapeutically with children, groups, classes or even whole schools.

This chapter aims to:

- Share what solution focused approaches are and how they have been developed
- Consider how they can be used to support children whose behaviour challenges
- Evaluate the possible strengths and limitations of these approaches
- Contrast with behaviourist rewards and sanctions-based strategies
- Discuss what impact these approaches might have on children's mental health and well-being

Foundations

Solution focused approaches are already used in a range of schools and settings, both by teachers and a number of other professionals, including educational psychologists. Solution focused ways of working have their roots in the work of Steve de Shazer and his team of family therapists in America in the 1980s (Simmonds, 2019). De Shazer and his wife Insoo Kim Berg worked with a team of therapists and researchers to trial different approaches which ultimately led to the establishment of Solution Focused Brief Therapy (SFBT) (Ratner & Yusuf, 2015), which is used by a wide range of professionals with children, adults, individuals and groups. It was the focus within this model on what was already working and concentrating on people's strengths rather than their issues, that De Shazer and his team found has the most impact on the people they were working with.

As noted at the start of this chapter, solution focused approaches move away from the child-deficit, problem-based and psychological understandings of behaviour where children (rather than sometimes their behaviours) can become labelled and 'pathologised', and where any problems lay firmly with the child as an individual. Theses labels or categories can then define what intervention is most suitable, often without consulting the child or considering their own strengths. From a solution focused approach any labelling is avoided, and instead of prescribing an intervention, the aim is to utilise the innate problem-solving skills and resourcefulness children (and all individuals) have. Milner and Bateman (2011) warned that if we are sure what the problem is, we often stop listening to what children are actually saying. Instead, they argue that, from a solution focused perspective, we should see the children in our care as 'experts in their own lives' – this is quite a shift from 'traditional' ways of understanding and working with children.

? ACTIVITY STOP 1

Considering children as experts is not often a common way of viewing them in schools. Usually, the teacher is the 'expert' and the child the 'novice'. Using the diagram (Figure 6.1), think about some of the attributes often associated with the word 'novice' and with the word 'expert'. How does the language associated with each term affect how we relate to them?

- How might much classroom practice change if children were viewed as 'experts' in some areas?
- How might our role and practice as teachers change?
- What might be some of the advantages of this?
- What might be some of the limitations of this?

126 Attitudes, beliefs and perspectives

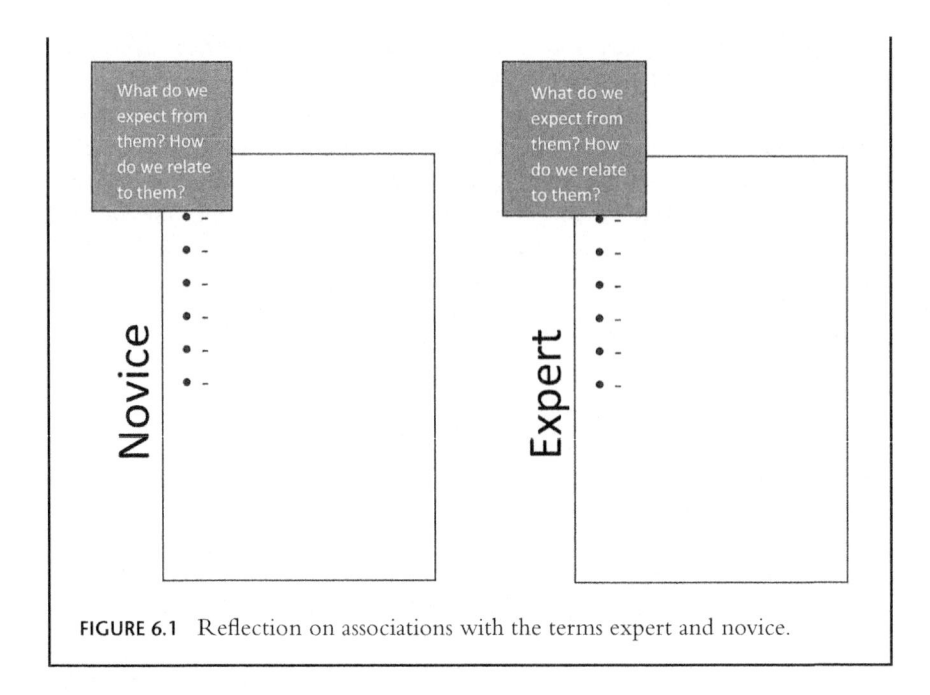

FIGURE 6.1 Reflection on associations with the terms expert and novice.

Solution focused approaches gained prominence in schools well over 10 years ago when the Primary National Strategy – Behaviour and Attendance (DfES, 2004) publication encouraged the provision of solution focused training for schools by educational psychologists (Simm & Ingram, 2008). Following on from this, the government (DfES, 2005, p. 5) published training guidance for schools on solution focused working, in which they suggested that it:

> encourages teachers, and others involved in developing effective approaches to behaviour issues, to adopt a positive stance in which energy is directed towards finding satisfactory ways forward rather than focusing on what is going wrong in a situation.

Lam and Yuen (2008) found from their research in primary schools that many teachers felt counselling-based approaches would support the children in their care and be effective at managing behaviour problems but were concerned about adding to their workload. They found solution focused approaches met this need, as they are intended to be brief and easily manageable ways of working:

> in my opinion [it is] ideally suited to school-type work, since it does not presume any psychological training, doesn't delve dangerously into children's psyche and is pragmatic in its intentions. It is easy to tailor it to suit your personal style without compromising its essential worth and efficacy.
> (Colley 1999, p. 1, cited in Lam & Yuen, 2008, p. 104)

Like restorative practices, solution focused approaches offer new ways of relating to and working with pupils, as well as structured step-by-step strategies to support children (to support themselves!). There is an understanding in this way of working that behaviours repeat because solutions have not yet been found and so new strategies and approaches need to be sought, while more of the same needs to be avoided (Porter, 2000). Ratner and Yusuf (2015) argue that this form of working with children is particularly useful due to the way children perceive time. They suggest that their concerns are often more immediate (yesterday and tomorrow) rather than wanting to engage in discussions about a historic or ongoing issue that has not happened that day. Focusing on the 'problem' was also highlighted as being a particularly uncomfortable and restrictive way of working with children, whereas solution focused conversations avoid negative labelling and 'remind the child there is much more to them then their problem or worry' (Ratner & Yusuf, 2015). This is key when children are still developing their own self-concept and sense of identity. Solution focused ways of working are future-oriented and focus not on the child or individual's problem, but rather on working towards their best hopes for the future.

> Essentially, the focus is on successes, solutions, strengths and positives. Solution focused approaches centre on the premise that change is possible by utilising the skills and resources which already exist.
>
> (Fernie & Cubeddu, 2016, p. 199)

Simmonds (2019) argued that solution focused approaches are defined by a 'specific way of thinking and speaking' which is based on a set of principles. These include: treating people as experts in their own lives; assuming that people have the capacity and resources to resolve their own difficulties; working with the person and not the problem; exploring the person's best hopes for the future and exploring what is already working for them. Ratner and Yusuf (2015) also highlight that the underlying assumptions made about children are very different from a solution focused perspective than any other, suggesting that rather than the more traditional view of teachers 'leading a child to water', teachers here position themselves in a way that is 'following the child to their own oasis'.

THINKING STOP 1

Ratner and Yusuf's (2015) suggestion is a radical departure from the traditional authoritarian position of the teacher. Take a moment to consider this:

- What might be the limitations of this teacher–pupil position?
- What might be the advantages of this teacher–pupil position?
- What skills would children need (to be taught) to make the most of this way of working?
- What changes would teachers need to make to the ways in which they worked with and related to children to make this happen?

128 Attitudes, beliefs and perspectives

As you read through the rest of this chapter, refer back to these initial ideas and see if you can add to your first thoughts here.

In common with restorative practices, solution focused approaches are fundamentally relationship-based. Rather than having a focus on managing behaviour, solution focused approaches are concerned with developing children's own problem-solving skills and resourcefulness so they are able to begin to positively and autonomously regulate their emotions and behaviour rather than focusing on the teacher to do this for them. Looking at the social control window from the previous chapter (Figure 5.2), solution focused approaches are firmly embedded in the top right-hand corner of the diagram. They encourage even greater autonomy from children than restorative approaches, with teacher power reduced so they act as a facilitator working alongside children to support and develop their autonomy. Solution focused approaches are suggested to be empowering for children, in part due to this change in the traditional teacher–pupil power dynamic, but also because they support pupils in making changes for themselves. Ratner and Yusuf (2015) note that inevitably, much of a child's environment and the experiences they have are controlled by others; for example, teachers, parents or carers and so on. However, a solution focused way of working supports children in seeing change as a process that not only happens to others and by others, but one that they can be responsible for in their own contexts.

Research by Fernie and Cubeddu (2016), using a solution focused intervention (WOWW – Working on What Works) in Scottish primary schools, showed that after as few as six sessions, the teacher reported a significant increase in children's relationships with each other, acceptance and tolerance of each other, respect and collaboration, as well as (possibly associated) an increase in teacher confidence. In the same study, the children also significantly increased their own ratings for how well they worked with, and listened to, each other. As solution focused approaches are an embedded and ethos-driven way of working with children, they can also be combined with other specific interventions. For example, a research project showed that girls working on a reading intervention scored more highly and felt more confident when it was combined with a solution focused approach than those who just completed the intervention (Bond, Woods, Humphrey, Symes & Green, 2013). Research (Bond *et al.*, 2013) has suggested that solution focused approaches may be particularly useful for children who internalise rather than externalise their problems. It has been suggested that internalised behaviour can be seen as most concerning for teachers and difficult to support children with.

Building blocks

Simm and Ingram's (2008) research showed that in schools, solution focused approaches were used in a range of ways that included:

- Introducing change
- Working with individual children and parents

- Working with groups and classes
- Meetings
- Target setting
- Writing individual education plans
- Teaching pupils how to use solution focused approaches

This fairly comprehensive list shows that these approaches can be tailored to fit many needs and are flexible. This makes them well suited to the ever-changing classroom environment.

A key difference between solution focused approaches and other classroom practices, which may sound surprising, is that the problem is not important. From this perspective, teachers are 'too busy helping children find solutions to difficulties' to be investigating the problem itself (Milner & Bateman, 2011). That is quite a switch in thinking for many. Milner and Bateman (2011) found that children 'may not wish to, or feel unable to explore the reasons why they are struggling'. They suggest that 'digging into the problem' even when our intentions are to help can be 'disrespectful and possibly painful' for the child. The idea of not forcing the child to discuss the 'problem' also links to the bigger view in solution focused approaches that teachers are neither the expert in, nor responsible for, finding a solution to children's problem(s). Again, both of these are radical shifts in most teacher's practice, particularly the traditional methods of managing behaviour where teachers often tell children what their 'problem' is – i.e. 'you can't sit still', 'you can't concentrate', 'you can't stop talking' – and then make themselves the holder of the solution – 'you need to move seats', 'stand up', 'stay in at playtime' and so on. With solution focused approaches, the solutions to the 'problem' and the best way forward are all the responsibility of the child, and the teacher's role is to support children in finding a solution. Here the child (rather than teacher, educational psychologist, doctor, etc.) is the 'expert' in their own lives and possesses all the skills and knowledge they need to arrive at the solution – something which is achieved through developing supportive conversations that allow children to use their own knowledge, strengths, skills and abilities to work towards a range of solutions to difficulties.

Solution focused approaches are, as noted previously, quick and easy to use and require little training. They can be used in a range of situations and comprise a set of assumptions that provide the foundation to all of our engagements with children. However, there are key strategies associated with solution focused ways of working that fit when working with individuals, groups or whole classes. Like restorative practices, solution focused approaches are a very structured way of working, which provide teachers with a 'security blanket' when using strategies that are new. Although, as discussed in the previous section, all work from this approach is underpinned by a philosophical understanding of children and a way of working with and talking to them, there are a number of sequential and structured steps that accompany this work.

The miracle question

The first step is considering the child, group or classes' long-term goals by asking a structured question, sometimes referred to as the 'miracle question'. James's (2016) version of this is simply, 'Suppose things are going to get better; what would you notice that's different?' The more comprehensive 'miracle question' is:

> Suppose that while you are sleeping tonight, a miracle happened. The miracle is that the problem you have is solved. However, because you are sleeping, you don't know the miracle has happened. So, when you wake up tomorrow morning what will be different that will tell you that the miracle has happened and the problem is solved?'
>
> (Milner & Bateman, 2011, p. 51)

Both of these questions focus on possible solutions rather than any specific problem or problems. Simply asking a child or a group to envisage a time when things are better immediately has a positive effect. It might then be necessary to narrow down their answer a little, possibly by asking questions that focus on what they will be doing. For example, if after giving the child or children time to think and absorb the question they reply, 'I'll be happy', you might need to make it more specific by asking them, as Milner and Bateman (2011) suggest, 'What are you going to be doing when you're happy?' 'How will other people know when you're happy?' A focus on what the child will 'see' and 'do' helps make their goal more concrete and less abstract. One of the aims of this question is to help the individual(s) set goals, so the more detailed and specific their answers are, the easier that will be. This initial part of the process needs time invested in it, as being able to have a clear 'picture' in their heads of a time when things are 'better' or going as well as they possibly can is important for children before moving on. Ensuring the focus is on what the child or children *will* be doing, rather than what they *won't* be doing, or what anyone else may or may nor do, is also important. This might be, for example, 'I will smile at my teacher', rather than 'I won't shout at her'. If the child's answers include something generic, trying to bring the focus back to them is key; for example, if they reply that they 'will not mess around', they need to be able to suggest what they would do instead. If children's replies focus on the actions of others again, they might need supporting in considering what *they* would do. This might be by asking them what they would be doing differently, particularly if their reply to the miracle question is beyond their control, such as 'I will play for Manchester City football team' or 'X teacher will leave'. In practice, the conversation might look like this example (with just one child rather than a group for brevity):

TEACHER: Suppose things are going to get better, what would you notice that's different?
CHILD: I don't know …
T: Suppose that you did know, what would you notice that was different?
C: That Nancy would be nice to me and the class wouldn't pick on me.
T: What would you be doing differently then?

C: Maybe I would be nice to them.
T: What would that look like?
C: I could ask them to play my game.
T: What else?
C: I might try to smile at them sometimes.
T: What else?
C: I would be happy.
T: What would you be doing if you were happy?
C: I wouldn't get so cross and upset.
T: I see, what would you be doing instead of being cross and upset?

There are a range of suggested prompts to encourage children to focus on their own actions. These can include some of those mentioned in the example conversation, but also;

- What will other (possibly named, i.e. family, friends, teacher) people notice about you?
- Who might be the first person to notice these changes?
- How will you know they are pleased?
- What effect would that have on you?
- What effect would that have on them?
- How will things be different at home, in the playground, in the classroom, before school, after school, etc.?
- What might you say to yourself at the end of the day?

Ajmal and Ratner (2020, p. 6) suggested five key aspects any solution focused conversation should focus on, and the 'miracle question' conversation should also include these:

> '*The great instead*'. This is intended to keep the focus on what the child(ren) will be doing instead as opposed to what won't be happening or what they won't be doing, e.g. 'So, what will you be doing *instead* of being cross?'
>
> '*Difference questions*'. This considers the impact the behaviours children suggest in response to the previous question will make and to whom, e.g. 'What *difference* will your best friend notice?'.
>
> '*Other person perspectives*'. These, as suggested, focus on how the changes will be noticed and felt by others, what difference it would make not only to the child but the people they interact with, e.g. 'What would be the first change your *best friend* would notice?'
>
> '*Keep it small*'. This might include asking children to think about the first sign of change or what the smallest sign might be that things are changing for the better. This keeps the discussion manageable and concrete. Making very small changes always feels more manageable than one huge change.

For example, *smiling at a teacher at the start of the day* feels more achievable than *always being happy to be at school*, e.g. 'What might be *the first tiny sign* I notice that you are …?'

'*What else?*' This should be the most frequently asked question in any solution focused conversation. Asking this question means the child needs to give more details, and the more details they can suggest for the ways in which any changes could happen, the more options that are available to them and the more hopeful it is that a change could occur. As part of this process children can also be asked an 'exception' question. For example, if the child suggests when things are going well, they won't be 'shouting out', ask them if they can think of a time they were about to or could have shouted out but didn't. Children often find this tricky, so they can be supported by reinforcing that it is a really difficult question, and that 'I don't know' is an acceptable first answer. Like the 'what else' question, the aim is to keep encouraging the child to think of one occasion where they didn't shout out, etc. This 'exception' then shows children that they are actually already making progress towards their goal.

Although solution focused work can be brief, in reality the first 'miracle question' conversation needs time and space and is not something that can be rushed. Once children (and staff) become more familiar with this way or working and the questions they will be asked the conversations are quicker, but should never be rushed. The next step, however, is quicker, and whilst the 'miracle question' may not be used regularly, scaling is a quick and easy activity that can be used as often as desired.

Scaling

While the aim of the 'miracle question' is to think about what things might be like when they are at their best – or what is also known as a 'preferred future' – scaling shows children how much progress they are making towards the goal(s)

? ACTIVITY STOP 2

Using the image from the NSPCC's (2015) solution focused toolkit (Figure 6.2), ask yourself the questions in relation to your practice in supporting and managing behaviour, then consider:

- How might you (or would you) use this with children?
- How would you want to adapt it?

FIGURE 6.2 Solution focused starter taken from NSPCC (2015) (https://learning.nspcc.org.uk/research-resources/2015/solution-focused-practice-toolkit).

they described in their answer to the miracle question. Scaling is simply where the child, group or class rate themselves on a scale, which might be between 1 and 10, using traffic lights, ladders or anything that allows some form of quantification. This is very helpful as it provides a visual signal to children about how much progress they are making, and it can be done as often as necessary (at the end of every lesson, morning, day, week or whatever is required). Figure 6.3 shows images taken from the NSPCC solution focused toolkit to help children scale their progress.

Once explained, scaling only takes moments to do, so it is easy to fit into a busy school day. On the scale (for example, a 1–10 scale), 1 represents no achievement towards their goal and 10 represents meeting their goal. Ajmal and Ratner (2020) note that when scaling, 10 should be the 'presence of something not the absence of the problem'. This strategy is for the child – the teacher cannot impose their views, as it is the child's perception of their progress and current position, rather than an objective assessment. For example, if the child feels they are a '5' on the scale, the

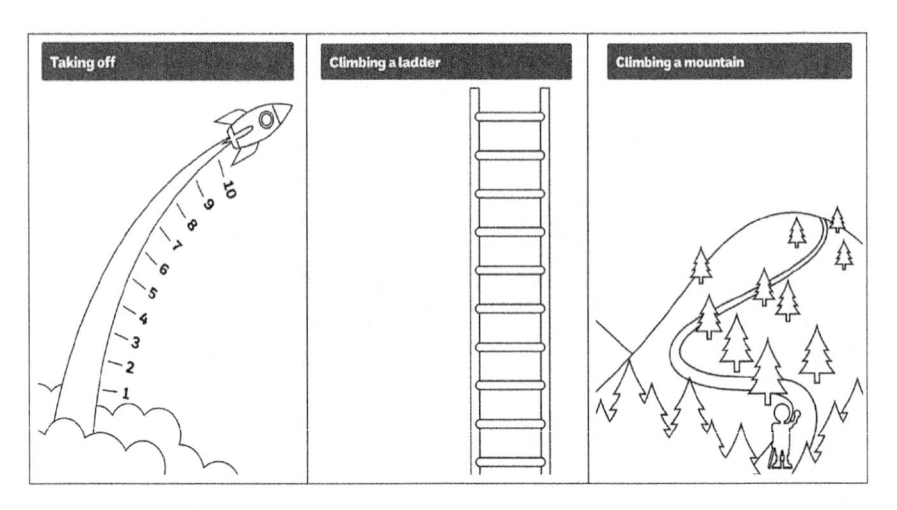

FIGURE 6.3 NSPCC (2015) resources to support scaling.

teacher cannot step in and say, 'But you're shouting out, you're only a 2!' The key to making this process meaningful is the solution focused conversation held about where the child has scaled themselves. Here, the position on the scale is not overly important, it focuses more on the opportunity to highlight to the child all of the positive things that have happened so far and to encourage them to identify the skills and traits they have that have helped them to reach this point. The conversation that follows could use some of these prompts (Milner & Bateman, 2011, p. 116) to deepen the child's thinking and reflection:

- How did you get to this point?
- What does number x represent?
- Where would you like to be on the scale?
- Where would be good enough?
- What do you need to do to get there?
- What help might you need?

As well as a discussion about where the child is and how they could move up their scale, it is also important to highlight all of the work they have done to get to, or remain where they are. Questions to get children to reflect on their progress might include variations of these;

- How did you get to this score?
- How else?
- How else? – as many as possible
- What skills, qualities and abilities did you need to get that far?

(Milner & Bateman, 2011, p. 134)

? ACTIVITY STOP 3

Following on from the previous activity, try to scale yourself in relation to your best hopes for managing behaviour using Figure 6.4? You might also want to use the follow-up questions that have just been discussed on yourself! If you have trialled the questions:

- Were they easy to answer?
- Which one(s) was/were the trickiest?
- Would you want to adapt the questions to use in the classroom?
- Which ones?
- Why?

FIGURE 6.4 Scaling example from NSPCC (2015) (https://learning.nspcc.org.uk/research-resources/2015/solution-focused-practice-toolkit).

If a child places themselves at the bottom of their scale, or even below, there are still opportunists to help them reflect on the things that they are doing well. Simply acknowledging that things must be very hard, and then asking them what skills and qualities they have that help them cope with things being as bad as they are, could be a useful place to start. Conversely, if the child scores themselves a 10, it might provide an opportunity to ask them what they might like themselves, or others, to keep noticing about them that shows they are a 10 (Ajmal & Ratner, 2020). Scales are often used to show a child or group's progress towards a goal or preferred future. Ajmal and Ratner (2020) suggest a broader range of applications which could include a scale of confidence, commitment, coping or effort. A great way to end a solution focused conversation is with a compliment; this might be related to some changes in the child's behaviour, about progress they have made, or the way they are engaging with the process. As the child develops it might even be that they can give themselves a compliment. It can be seen, just through this brief overview, that these conversations focus on what is working; strengths and the successes that already exist are positive and uplifting for all involved. This way of working is in many respects the 'light at the end of the tunnel' for a lot of children and teachers, where conversations with the child are positive and enjoyable rather than focusing on what is not working. The repercussions for maintaining and deepening positive and supportive relationships for children when they regularly have these conversations with teachers and adults is significant.

Because solution focused approaches are fundamentally conversational, they can be used in a range of contexts. For example, whole classes could scale their confidence in writing a report, adding fractions, working as a team and so on – the possibilities are endless. If the focus is on 'what will I (the teacher) notice when we as a class are working at a x', then it makes it easy for the teacher to spot these positive behaviours and acknowledge them. Children could also be encouraged to spot these positive behaviours in each other. For some children, being 'noticed' and praised by a peer can be even more meaningful than being praised by a teacher. This type of activity can also encourage children (as well as some staff) to move from 'telling tales' and noticing others' behaviour when they are not meeting expectations, to beginning to notice all of the positive behaviours, effort, confidence and so on. This may in turn become more formalised; for example, something Ajmal and Ratner (2020) refer to as 'sparkling moments' or the 'compliment game'. When writing about this, they included a quote from a year 6 girl who said that after this game became routine, she looked forward to the teacher calling her name as she knew that they were always going to say something nice about her.

THINKING STOP 2

What an amazing impact this way of working had on that year 6 pupil. Although this is just one comment from one child, take a minute to reflect on it.

- What impact would it make if just one child in your class felt this way?
- What impact would it make if 5 did, or 10?
- How would it affect them?
- How would it affect you?

The 'compliment game' is simple, quick, incredibly effective, can be done at any time and in any lesson. The teacher models initially – often the children will automatically contribute without being encouraged to do so – by stopping the class and telling them 'I am thinking of someone who is…'. This might be a child that is 'trying really hard', 'always helpful' 'persevering', 'friendly' and so on; the 'compliments' can be tailored for any age, subject or context. The teacher than asks the class who they think it might be. As the children volunteer suggestions, the teacher replies along the lines of 'Oh, I wasn't thinking of them today. What have you noticed them do that showed perseverance/effort/friendship, etc.?' The child identified and their volunteer can then be congratulated, and the suggestions can continue until the child the teacher was thinking of has been identified. This can last for 1, 5 or 10 minutes, or for however long you think it is needed. As with all solution focused work, this can help to initiate a virtuous cycle, where children begin to recognise and value their own strengths as well as those of their peers.

Possible advantages of this approach in the classroom

Research (Simmonds, 2019) has suggested that solution focused approaches are a cost-effective, time-sensitive, simple and practical method of supporting a range of children. It is also a flexible and pragmatic approach, so the same strategies can be used with individuals, groups and classes. They can also be used where there is behaviour which is very challenging as well as to maintain existing positive behaviours.

Solution focused approaches are not done to, or imposed on children. Rather, they centre on a collaborative partnership between children and teachers and as such, they have the ability to develop self-efficacy (Ratner & Yusuf, 2015). This emphasis on the pupil's ownership over the approach and of the actions taken has been found to motivate children to perform better (Brown, Powell & Clark, 2012). Additionally, the targets and goals that children set for themselves were found to be consistent with the criteria set for good goals by Berg and Shilts (2005) – concrete, measurable, simple, realistic, achievable, participative, collaborative and social (Brown et al., 2012). Solution focused ways of working are also intrinsically positive. When reporting on the implementation of a solution focused project, Brown and her collegaues (2012) found that 84% of pupils indicated they had enjoyed the project all of the time, with only 16% indicating they enjoyed it some of the time. These findings suggest that solution focused approaches are enjoyed by children, and that as a result they are likely to willingly engage with them.

Unlike authoritarian strategies where there can be ethical concerns over teacher power, solution focused approaches empower children, and the teacher acts as a facilitator and supporter, as opposed to controlling the behaviours in the classroom. As a result, concerns about teacher power and control are not an issue in solution focused approaches.

Possible disadvantages of this approach in the classroom

Conversations are key to solution focused approaches, and there are children for whom this might not be suited in its original form. The approach may need adapting to support children who have English as an additional language, who have specific speech and language difficulties or have learning difficulties (Simmonds, 2019). Lam and Yuen (2008, p.104) also found from their research that for the approach to be of most use, children needed to have:

> Sufficient autonomy to be able to plan and regulate their own actions, recognise their own strengths and weaknesses, and take some responsibility for self-management. In addition, they must have adequate metacognition to monitor their own thinking.

A consistent theme, of both solution focused approaches and restorative practice is the reconceptualisation of the teacher's role in managing behaviour and the different assumptions needed about children for these approaches to work. If the staff using this approach are not committed to its aims and values, they risk being seen by children as inauthentic, which damages rather than strengthens relationships and undermines the approach. For some teachers, the lack of rewards and sanctions can be challenging, and staff may need much support initially when transitioning to this way of working with children. Also, unlike when using traditional behaviourist approaches, quick changes in children's behaviours are not always possible.

❓ ACTIVITY STOP 4

Vignette: Hannah

Hannah appeared isolated and withdrawn in class. She had spent the previous academic year, and sometime (less consistently) before that as an elective mute. She appeared to have little interest in making friends and was often alone. There were no behavioural issues – she had never been sanctioned, or rewarded, using the formal school systems – but staff were increasingly concerned about Hannah's internalised behaviours and lack of friends. Hannah was largely unwilling to engage in 'chit-chat' with staff, and her class teacher was unsure how to begin addressing the issues.

Using the storyboard (Figure 6.5), think of an incident of poor behaviour that you have experienced or been involved in. Draw how the episode might have played out differently and what the short and longer-term implications might have been for those involved if solution focused approaches had been used.

Solution focused working **139**

BEHAVIOURAL INCIDENT MANAGED USING SOLUTION FOCUSED APPROACHES			
The incident (what happened)	Outcomes (what happened after the incident)	Impact on the child (short and longer-term)	Impact on the teacher (short and longer-term)

FIGURE 6.5 Storyboard of possible outcomes of a behavioural incident supported with solution focused approaches.

Review

This chapter has shared some of the key strategies for working with children using a solution focused approach. It has considered the main premises of this philosophical way of supporting children and outlined how it differs from other approaches. It has provided practical strategies to use to support children in identifying their own and others' strengths. Some of the main advantages and issues identified by research on solution focused approaches have been discussed and the strengths and limitations of this way of working with individuals, groups and classes has been explored.

Whole school actions might include some or all of the following:

- For solution focused approaches to be embedded, school-wide practice is needed, and for this support from the senior leadership team (SLT) and opportunities for staff (and children) to feedback are essential.
- Although solution focused approaches do not need resources, access to ongoing training for all staff is necessary to develop and refine practices and ensure that this way of working is not seen only as an 'intervention'.
- Solution focused approaches should not only be used in work with children but need to permeate exchanges with all staff and children. This needs to be modelled and supported by the SLT.
- The whole-school behaviour policy is likely to need to be rewritten in line with solution focused practices. Consideration might need to be given to additional short-term interventions for children who require more support.
- Solution focused approaches, although quick once staff and children are familiar with them may need additional time to be explained and taught (for example, the use of the miracle question). Consideration will need to be given to where this additional time is found and whether this could go hand-in-hand with (additional) time for subjects such as PHSCE.
- Parents/carers would benefit form an opportunity (perhaps an open evening/ drop in sessions) to understand how and why solution focused approaches

work and what this might look like in the classroom for their children. There may also be the possibility of directing parents/carers to outside training or resources on solution focused approaches if they wish to use them with their children at home.

Individual teacher actions might include some or all of the following:

- Berg and Shilts (2005) highlighted that for both teacher and student to succeed, they must cooperate with each other, and one cannot succeed without the help of the other. For some teachers, this may mean a significant shift in their classroom dynamics which may require time and support.
- This approach is new to many and additional time/staff meetings/INSET to read around the approach or attend training would be particularly useful.
- Timetables and routines may need to be adapted initially to provide time for more detailed solution focused conversations/miracle questions/scaling until this becomes a routine part of classroom practice.
- Support staff deployment may need to be considered to enable either the teacher or TA(s) to support solution focused work with individuals or groups during sessions.

Possible mental health and well-being implications:

- Solution focused approaches nurture and develop a focus on children's (and staff's) strengths. This in turn can help them to 'realise that they can manage their problems and learn how to cope with future ones' (Simmonds, 2019, p2).
- Working in this way with children (and adults) is fundamentally positive and forward looking, as it focuses on the positives already in people's lives and their own expertise.
- Much research highlights the contribution positive relationships have on mental health and well-being, and solution focused approaches actively develop and deepen relationships between staff and children.
- Solution focused approaches are structured to empower children and support them in recognising the strengths they already have.

Practice-related take-away:

- A structured focus on children's strengths, the progress they are making and their own autonomy changes the traditional role of the teacher.

Practitioner reading:

Ajmal and Ratner (2020). *Solution Focused Practice in Schools: 80 Ideas and Strategies*. London: Routledge.

References

Ajmal, Y., and Ratner, H. (2020). *Solution Focused Practice in Schools: 80 Ideas and Strategies*. London: Routledge.

Berg, I., and Shilts, L. (2005). *Classroom Solutions: WOWW Coaching*. London: BFTC.

Bond, C., Woods, K., Humphrey, N., Symes, W., and Green, L. (2013). Practitioner review: The effectiveness of solution focused brief therapy with children and families: A systematic and critical evaluation of the literature from 1990-2010. *Journal of Child Psychology and Psychiatry and Allied Disciplines*, **54**(7), pp. 707–723.

Brown, E., Powell, E., and Clark, A. (2012). Working on what works: Working with teachers to improve classroom behaviour and relationships. *Educational Psychology in Practice*, **28**(1), pp. 19–30.

Department for Education and Skills. (2004). *Primary National Strategy: Behaviour and Attendance*. London: DfES.

Dperatment for Education and Skills. (2005). *National Strategy Focusing on Solutions: A Positive Approach to Improving Behaviour*. London: DfES.

Fernie, L., and Cubeddu, D. (2016). Theory, research and practice in educational psychology WOWW: A solution orientated approach to enhance classroom relationships and behaviour within a primary three class. *Educational Psychology in Practice*, **32**(2), pp. 197–208.

James, G. (2016). *Transforming Behaviour in the Classroom: A Solution-Focused Guide for New Teachers*. London: SAGE Publications.

Lam, C., and Yuen, M. (2008). Applying solution-focused questions with primary school pupils: A Hong Kong teacher's reflections. *Pastoral Care in Education*, **26**(2), pp. 103–110.

Milner, J., and Bateman, J. (2011). *Working with Children and Teenagers Using Solution Focused Approaches*. London: Jessica Kingsley Publishers.

NSPCC. (2015). *Solution-Focused Practice Toolkit*. London: NSPCC. https://learning.nspcc.org.uk/research-resources/2015/solution-focused-practice-toolkit

Porter, L. (2000). *Behaviour in Schools: Theory and Practice for Teachers*. Buckingham: Open University Press.

Ratner, H., and Yusuf, D. (2015). *Brief Coaching with Children and Young People: A Solution Focused Approach*. London: Routledge.

Simm, J., and Ingram, R. (2008). Collaborative action research to develop the use of solution-focused approaches. *Educational Psychology in Practice*, **24**(1), pp. 43–53.

Simmonds, S. (2019). A critical review of teachers using solution-focused approaches supported by educational psychologists. *Educational Psychology Research and Practice*, **5**(1), pp. 1–8.

ATTITUDES, BELIEFS AND PERSPECTIVES

Conclusion

The chapters in Part II have built on those in Part I and have introduced a range of theoretical views and beliefs around behaviour and the causes of behaviours. The first chapter considered a range of viewpoints for understanding the causes of behaviours that challenge and how these shape and affect the actions taken with children in the classroom. A number of psychological and sociological understandings were reviewed as well as the medical and overarching biopsychosocial model. How teacher power and control were enacted from these different conceptualisations was discussed, as well as how this alters the responsibilities of children. The chapters then moved on from the abstract to the concrete, to discuss two different approaches under the sociological and biopsychosocial perspectives.

Restorative practices were introduced and the history and range of settings and situations they are used in was shared. The differences in restorative practices and more traditional authoritarian and psychological approaches were evaluated and practical strategies to develop restorative practices with individuals, groups and whole schools were considered. The strengths and limitations that restorative practices might have in the classrooms and the ways in which working restoratively can support mental health and well-being concluded the chapter.

The final chapter in Part II considered solution focused approaches. Like restorative practices, this relational way of working with children assumes a different perspective on children and their skills than psychological understandings and strategies do. The chapter looked at a range of ways solution focused approaches could be embedded in our work with all children, groups and classes and how they reconceptualise traditional teacher–pupil relationships. The advantages and disadvantages of solution focused working with children were evaluated and a number of strengths for supporting well-being and mental health were shared.

These chapters all feed into the 'new perspectives' focus of the book, not necessarily by being 'new', but by making explicit links to how the actions taken in the classroom to support/manage/sanction/control, etc., behaviour are largely driven by the fundamental beliefs and attitudes of those in power – the adults. These adults may include the politicians and advisors who write policy, the SLT who filters this down through whole-school expectations, the multi-agency workers providing collaborative support, authors and those on social media platforms and others. These views are all filtered in some way by the teacher or practitioner who works day in and day out with the child or children whose behaviour(s) challenge, but what often mediates actions are the beliefs, views and attitudes of the teacher.

This contribution of Part II, then, in relation to 'new perspectives' is not necessarily the content of the chapters, though for some this may be new, but rather an opportunity to consider what your core beliefs are, how they align with overarching theory and as a result how these guide your actions. It may also be that by reading and reflecting on the content of these chapters and the associated reading suggested by them, your beliefs have changed or shifted in some way, or you have been able to consider the ways in which your beliefs are similar to and different from those who make policy and set behavioural expectations in schools.

💭 THINKING STOP 1

- Have you read anything that has surprised you?
- Have you learnt anything new?
- Have you read anything that has made you reflect on the way in which you work with children in the classroom?
- Will anything change for you as a result of reading these chapters?

Returning to the idea of a 'behaviour suitcase' (Sproson, 2004), is there anything you have read in Part II that you can add to your 'suitcase' of ideas to support children and their behaviour? If so, make a note of it in Figure C2.1. Review your previous 'suitcase':

- Is there a theme to the skills or ideas you are adding?
- What actions do you need to take to develop these further?

FIGURE C2.1 Sproson's (2004) 'behaviour suitcase'.

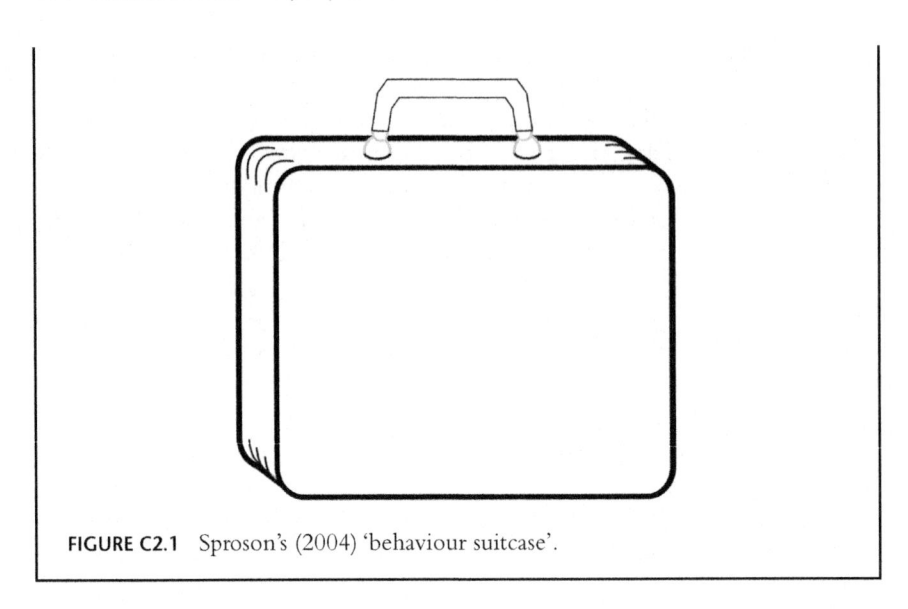

References

Sproson, B. (2004). Some do and don't: Teacher effectiveness in managing behaviour. In Wearmouth, J., Glynn, T., Richmond, R., and Berryman, M. (Eds.), *Inclusion and Behaviour Management in Schools: Issues and Challenges* (pp. 311–321). London: David Fulton Publishers.

PART III
Beyond strategies to embedded ethos

Part III of the book shares wider classroom practice as well as international comparisons to consider other ways to support behaviour. Rather than discussing specific ways of working with children, the chapters outline a range of opportunities to understand practice better (by developing an understanding of children and supporting them as individuals in Chapter 7, by reflecting on the key attributes of successful teachers in Chapter 8, and comparing English and Finnish approaches in Chapter 9).

As I hope the previous parts and chapters in this book have made clear, managing behaviour and supporting well-being and mental health are not a series of discrete and specific approaches or strategies, but rather are embedded in all of the engagements with children, in the views and beliefs held and in the language used to talk about children. For me – as all of these previous chapters have detailed – behaviour is supported, managed and nurtured through the relationships we form. Parts I and II have reflected the skills and knowledge I gained from relationships with the children in my classes and the dedicated and highly skilled teachers I taught alongside, as well as from my years of study and research.

The chapters in this section have come about as a result of the relationships and connections I have formed with other academics, both within and beyond my own context. Chapter 7 has been contributed by a long-time friend and mentor who through formal, but mostly incidental, conversations (often in pubs) has continued to develop my understanding of working with children in a range of situations and also the value of using philosophy in the classroom. Chapter 8 was written by my academic hero, who I was privileged enough to have as a supervisor for my PhD (along with the wonderful Philip Garner!). John's writing and research was highly influential for me when I was studying for my master's, and the guidance and support John (and Philip) provided during my doctorate developed my own professional learning significantly.

DOI: 10.4324/9781003035527-12

Chapter 9 was contributed by international colleagues who I met during a research trip to Finland. My ongoing relationship with my Finnish colleagues has enabled me to visit schools, talk to teacher trainees and significantly expand my understanding of supporting behaviour by considering it from an entirely different cultural (and snowier) perspective.

Working with a range of colleagues has enabled me to draw on relationships with experts in the fields, making use of their significant skills to develop, deepen and support my own learning. Drawing on my own professional leaning community for support and expertise mirrors good practice in school where, when children's behaviours present a challenge (something every teacher who has ever taught has experienced) and our own repertoire of skills is not as extensive as those of others, we collaborate!

7
PHILOSOPHICAL INQUIRY AS A TOOL FOR WELL-BEING

Aimee Quickfall

This chapter examines using philosophy in schools with children. Philosophy, at its simplest, is engaged with actively thinking and reflecting about a range of topics and ideas. As we have seen in the chapters throughout this book, many approaches to supporting children, specifically those that step away from behaviourism, have a reflective and 'thinking' element. This was seen in the preceding chapters on restorative practices and solution focused approaches, but is a recurrent thread in sociological and systems theory approaches to behaviour. Aimee's chapter will consider in depth how philosophy can support children's well-being and impact on their behaviour.

This chapter aims to:

- Explore the research literature on philosophical inquiry with children
- Describe one of many ways in which philosophical inquiry can be used with children
- Consider three case studies of children in communities of inquiry

This is the first chapter from a contributing author. Aimee was asked to write this chapter as using philosophy with children is an area of expertise for her, both practically and in related research in this area. My knowledge of using philosophical inquiry to support children's well-being and behaviour arose through informal conversations with Aimee, and my own understanding and interest in the area is largely a result of listening to Aimee and watching her in action, talking to other colleagues engaged in research, teachers and teacher-trainees as well as children. Aimee's post-doctoral research is also focused on using philosophical inquiry, and it was an area she was passionate about using in the classroom when she was a teacher and senior leader in schools. Philosophical inquiry was not something I used in the classroom with my children when I was a teacher, but I am convinced – retrospectively – that

DOI: 10.4324/9781003035527-13

it would have been incredibly beneficial, not just for children whose behaviours challenged me, but for all of the children in my classes.

Philosophical inquiry is not in and of itself a tool, strategy or intervention to manage behaviour. However, it does facilitate the opportunity for children to speak and be heard, and as a result, to develop their confidence voicing views and opinions (that might be different from others) and provide a structured way to do this. As Aimee will suggest, this develops confidence and independence in children as well as supporting them in understanding each other and working together.

> *Happiness can be found, even in the darkest of times, if one only remembers to turn on the light.*
>
> —— *J.K. Rowling*

Foundations

What is philosophy with children?

Philosophy with children, when it is embedded in classroom practice, is about children being empowered to turn on the light (as J.K. Rowling describes it); to open up different points of view, build communities and foster respect for other thinkers in the community. In this chapter, I argue that going through the process of establishing a community of philosophical inquiry with a group of children can also turn on the light for adults, encouraging us to review our role in the community and how classroom management strategies can close down independent and group thinking if used in clumsy ways.

The study of philosophy and philosophical inquiry (what philosophy with children is generally based on) are two very different ideas. Philosophical inquiry is about your own thinking, your own ideas and the thoughts and ideas of your community of inquiry, rather than starting with the thoughts of famous philosophers and weaving arguments between them. In greater depth, philosophical inquiry is about approaching an idea in a certain way, which can be easily learnt, constructing an argument and testing it in different scenarios from your experience or fantasy.

? ACTIVITY STOP 1

An example of a philosophical inquiry: The community consider a stimulus, in this case, a photograph of a beached whale. After pursuing their individual thoughts, then talking with a partner, they construct a question and begin a discussion: 'Is it ever right for humans to interfere with nature?' Children then put forward views based on their understanding of the world. They give examples from their own experience, such as Dad swerving to avoid running over a hedgehog, or taking an injured gull to a local wildlife rescue centre. Using Figure 7.1, consider the following:

- What skills would children need to be able to engage in an activity like this?
- What skills would the teacher/adult need to lead a session like this?
- How many of these skills are linked to managing or supporting behaviour?

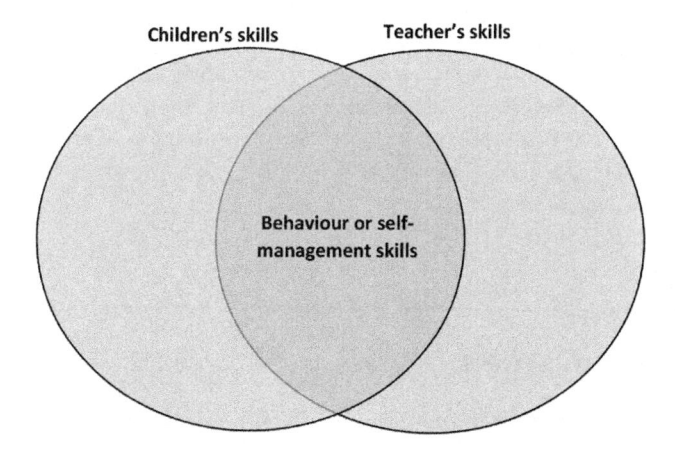

FIGURE 7.1 Philosophical inquiry skills and self/behaviour management skills.

Philosophical inquiry is more than a curriculum subject. In the community of inquiry, 'children are acknowledged as independent thinkers, capable of seeing clearly and contributing in valuable ways to our understanding of our shared world' (Cassidy & Mohr-Lone, 2020, p. 16). Children are natural philosophers in many respects (Quickfall, 2019), but strategies within a community can refine the inquiry process and also broaden the reservoir of ideas and experiences that the inquiry draws upon. For individual children, philosophical inquiry has a positive impact on socio-emotional development, confidence and engagement in learning, as well as maths, reading and writing progress (Gorard, Siddiqui & See, 2017; Tolmie et al., 2010; Topping & Trickey, 2007). Research also suggests that involvement in weekly philosophical inquiry sessions has a lasting effect, with children exhibiting positive effects of inquiry two years later in secondary education, even though the philosophical inquiry sessions had not continued (Topping & Trickey, 2007).

In terms of community and relationships, philosophy with children can have many benefits (Hedayati & Ghaedi, 2009). It makes the community work within a more defined arrangement in terms of communal practices and agreed standards, and it teaches children how to respectfully disagree, make connections, identify weaknesses in evidence and think about their thinking (Murris, 2000). In a community of children, philosophical inquiry helps them to see each other in different ways (Murris, 2000), and research suggests that children engaging in regular inquiry sessions display increases in social and communication skills, teamwork, resilience and empathy (Siddiqui, Gorard and See, 2019). Dialogic advantages of inquiry sessions have been demonstrated, for example in a study by Cassidy and Christie (2013) where children were involved in a one-hour-per-week session which provided 'a context for genuine collaborative engagement in learning where the actual process of learning itself is a shared one' (Cassidy & Christie, 2013, p. 1081, see also Barrow, 2010). The study took place in six primary schools in Scotland, with a range of socio-economic and rural/urban contexts. The researchers used a story as a stimulus for the sessions, and children quickly became adept at using and explaining metaphor and examples from their own experience, and they also learnt to define the terms they were using to ensure the community had a shared understanding of points being made.

> ### THINKING STOP 1
>
> The discussion here has considered the research on the positive impact of philosophy with children. Given this, why do you think it is not widespread practice?
>
> - What might prevent schools form using this approach with children?
> - Can you think of any additional advantages for the children in your care?
> - How do you think these types of activities, and this form of thinking and discussion could impact on behaviour in the short term?
> - And in the long term?

In terms of positive impacts on classroom behaviour management and well-being, the research in this area is scarce; possibly because setting up a community of inquiry leads many practitioners to question their beliefs about managing behaviour and what education is all about, together with the adult/child relationship (Durlak,

Weissberg, Dymnicki, Taylor & Schellinger, 2011). Cassidy and Mohr-Lone (2020) collected responses from children in their inquiry sessions that ably describe other ways of looking at the teacher and pupil distinction:

> Madison: When you think about it, childhood and adulthood are just ideas people thought of and then they put boundaries around these names to create something that isn't actually real. There really is no such thing as "being a child" or "being an adult." They're just labels. We're all people.
> (Cassidy & Mohr-Lone, 2020, p. 20)

This links with the ideas discussed in chapters in Part II of this book, which emphasise that how we view children impacts on how we manage or support their behaviour. For example, the teacher's understanding and view of children is very different when we compare behaviourist and solution focused interventions, or psychological and humanist perspectives. As Cassidy and Mohr-Lone point out, 'in order to facilitate this transformation, the view of children as irrational, uncritical, under-socialised, and lacking in competence needs to be addressed' (p. 18). Whilst practitioners very rarely hold these views of the children they teach, the main critiques of using philosophical inquiry with children are based on children's inability to grapple with complex concepts, a lack of knowledge and experience and stage models of child development which restrict conceptions of what is possible at specific chronological ages. As practitioners, our training and the traditions of our profession have been shaped by these models and are worth re-examining and reflecting upon as part of the process of setting up a community of inquiry.

Cassidy, Marwick, Deeney and McLean (2018) found that the structure of inquiry sessions (see the next section, 'Building blocks') supported 'children's engaged participation and self-regulation' (p. 81) in a study focused on children with emotional and behavioural challenges, and a similar intervention with children living in secure accommodation (Heron & Cassidy, 2018). As Heron and Cassidy note:

> enhancing self-regulation using argumentation and dialogue might help to promote more adaptive behaviours, including better reasoning and judgement, which can give highly vulnerable children greater control over their own lives.
> (p. 255)

I would argue that the same applies to other children in less rigid settings, in that learning to disagree with respect and to take on board other points of view is beneficial to anyone, and that practising these skills as a community is a worthwhile aim of education.

> ## 🗨 THINKING STOP 2
>
> ### Vignette: Josh, who learnt to talk it through
>
> Josh was in my community of inquiry for two years, as part of an after-school club in a school with high percentages of children with behavioural issues and special educational needs. Josh was nominated to come to the club by his class teacher, who explained that he hoped it might help Josh with his behaviour towards peers, as he could be very aggressive when upset, and the hope was that inquiry sessions may encourage Josh to listen to other points of view. Josh had been diagnosed with ADHD and ASD, and funding had been awarded for him to have a one-to-one assistant during lessons. However, Josh's behaviour at breaks and in less structured activities in the classroom was disruptive, and other children had reported feeling frightened of his outbursts, which often stemmed from a difference of opinion.
>
> Josh found the inquiry sessions very difficult to start with, and I found myself, several times, talking him into coming back into the building after he had decided to walk home on his own. Over time, he began sharing his ideas more readily, perhaps after recognising that the community valued his contributions. He would still find disputes and challenges very difficult, and I would never claim that the inquiry sessions had solved his issues with aggression towards other children, but what Josh did find was a place to talk through his thoughts. Over time it became easier for him to talk about his feelings, even if this was just with members of the community of inquiry. Children from the community had different perceptions of Josh.
>
> Josh's behaviour changed over this period – and perceptions of Josh's behaviour from his peers also changed.
>
> - What impacts do you think these changes may have had on the well-being of Josh?
> - His peers?
> - His teacher?

Building blocks

In this section, I will explain how to set up a community of inquiry with a class, and a model for running a basic session. From a teacher's perspective, the role in the classroom is different during philosophy with children inquiry sessions. Once the community is established, the teacher becomes a facilitator, or may step out of the discussion altogether. In terms of behaviour management, classroom management more broadly, and even professional identity, this can be a culture shock. The process of setting up the conditions for philosophical inquiry involves everyone in the room having equal rights to express their opinions and ideas – including the adults. However, as recent research has shown;

> Pro-social behaviour is only encouraged when children see it in adults, and learn to trust adults in schools on the basis of their fair treatment and just values.
>
> (Siddiqui, Gorard and See, 2019, p. 148)

Taking on this approach, even for an hour a week, will potentially change the way you see your role in the classroom, and may change the way children perceive their place in the community, too.

THINKING STOP 3

Vignette: Jack, the boy who no one noticed

I had noticed Jack at the beginning of Year 5, mostly because he wasn't often noticeable. He got on with his work, he was quiet and, I think it is fair to say, he would be considered 'average' in many respects. He was on track academically but didn't excel. He seemed to like having a kick-about at playtime, but he wasn't interested in joining the football team. Jack could slip through the day at school without attracting much attention from his peers or adults. When we started using philosophy with children, as you might expect, Jack continued to 'fly under the radar'. For the first few sessions, he didn't volunteer any thoughts but would nod in agreement and contribute to votes (see the inquiry process). Then, something remarkable happened. In the fourth session, we talked about a book in which the beloved pet of the protagonist dies and the children were interested in whether the character would get another dog, knowing the pain that another loss would cause to him. The community voted for a discussion question: If you know something is going to be really painful, is it ever right to continue with it? Towards the end of the discussion, the children seemed to agree that if possible, you should try to avoid pain. Jack signalled that he wanted to speak, and told us about his grandma, who was dying in hospital. He explained that no matter how painful it was to lose her, his memories of her were worth hundreds of times more than dodging the pain, and that having known her had made him a stronger person. The rest of the class were stunned – they saw Jack in a different way after that session. I am not going to claim that he became captain of the football team, but their perceptions of him as someone with real insights to offer had shifted.

> Reflecting on the vignette about Jack;
>
> - Do you have a 'Jack' in your class?
> - When does your Jack get a chance to share their strengths, feelings and thoughts with the community?
> - What difference might it make if your jack got a planned and regular opportunity to do this?
> - Who might see and feel that difference the most?

I have been using philosophical inquiry in my classrooms for 15 years, and the model I use has been adapted over time – yours will, too, if you decide to commit to using inquiry in your teaching. Many other models can be found described online or in the literature, but most tend to follow a basic sequence of steps (Haynes, 2002).

Starting up

- Agree how your community will operate – what is important to you? This can be written as rules, an agreement, or discussed at the beginning of each session. It is vital that children understand that disagreements are a strength of the community and should be welcomed, if handled respectfully by all (Cassidy & Christie, 2013).
- Discuss what philosophical inquiry is and who can be a philosopher. We are all philosophers, and with a community of inquiry, we can learn to be better philosophers.
- Consider your place in the community. As the teacher in the room, you will have a key role in setting up the community, but once established, the children should lead the sessions and listen to each other, rather than wait for the adult to give the 'correct answer'. Considering your place in the community at regular points will help.

Preparing for a session

- Choose a stimulus for the inquiry – this could be a photo, story, dilemma, something that has really happened in school –music and smells can also work with an established community.
- Think about roles for the children. In the story of Sophie that follows, I considered giving Sophie a role such as inquiry scribe, so that she could record the discussion rather than dominating it. You may have children who would benefit from being a timekeeper, fairness overseer, scribe or facilitator at different times.

Process for a session (approximately an hour)

1. Play a game with a community objective; for example, a game that builds listening skills, turn taking and noticing.
2. Share the stimulus and give children time to think.
3. Thinking individually – ask children to generate a word that sums up the stimulus for them.
4. Thinking with a friend – share your word with a partner and generate a question from your ideas. Write down the question, or appoint a scribe to record them.
5. Share all the questions with the whole community.
6. Make connections between the questions– give children opportunities to spot links between the questions, with no correct answers! Agree on sets of questions that go together if you can.
7. Read a representative question for each set and do a 'secret vote' to choose one for the discussion.
8. Begin the discussion – the original authors should be invited to explain how they came up with the question and define any terms.
9. Don't be afraid of silences! If the discussion needs re-invigorating, you (or the facilitator!) can re-read the question.
10. Try to conclude the session with a summary of the discussion. If you have had a scribe, go through the notes/pictures and ask children to pick out the key points.

? ACTIVITY STOP 2

Try this warm-up game: Everyone stands in a circle, in silence. The aim is to get everyone sitting down. The rules are that each person who sits down must say the next number, e.g. the first person sits down and says '1'. If two people speak at once, everyone stands up and starts again. You must not say a number after a person standing next to you has said one. This takes ages the first time and gets faster and faster as the group learn to read the signs that someone wants to speak next – a vital skill for debate.

> ### 💭 THINKING STOP 4
>
> **Vignette: Sophie, who found her favourite game**
>
> Sophie was a really 'bright spark' in my Year 6 class. She often dominated discussions and team work, known as someone who was bright and knowledgeable. My worry was that on introducing philosophical inquiry sessions, Sophie would either dominate, or the rest of the children would just agree with her after listening to her insights into the topic. I didn't need to worry. After the first session, Sophie stayed behind (a common feature of these sessions – children often don't want them to end) and asked me what we could do to get other children to participate in the discussions. She had noted that with so much time given over to the discussion of the community question, it would be much more fun and productive if others were confident to disagree, explain their ideas and contribute to examples. Sophie had been used to giving short, verifiable answers to closed questions, or to giving concise summaries of her ideas to open questioning. She had not experienced a proper debate, with its twists and turns, evolution, dead-ends and disagreements at school before. Over the next two sessions, Sophie worked on encouraging others to make their points, taking on the role of facilitator and looking out for children who wanted to speak, reminding the community of the question and giving balance when a point was missed.
>
>> Philosophical inquiry sessions are based on ideas of fair contributions and respect for others, and a reduction of the disparity in power between adults and children. Are there other times in school when fair treatment is more clearly defined or felt?
>
> Using the vignette to reflect on Sophie (the one described, or a 'Sophie' of you own):
>
> - How could Sophie's new skills be utilised in other sessions?
> - How can this be balanced with her right to express her own ideas?

Experiences of behaviour and strengthening well-being

In the case studies included in this section, I have briefly summarised the experience of working with three very different children in communities of inquiry; Josh, in an after-school club focused on improving behaviour; Jack, as part of his class but very much on the periphery at the beginning of the community; and Sophie, a confident child who could easily dominate class discussions in other sessions. In this section, I am going to talk about those three examples of children, but they represent many individuals who I have worked with over the years, and undoubtedly share much with children in your class and school.

In terms of their well-being, I saw improvements for all three of these children in different ways. Josh, like the children in Heron and Cassidy's work (2018), learnt other ways to express himself that gave him options for handling disagreements and situations that he found tense. Over time, this changed the perception of Josh's behaviour amongst his peers, and it gave Josh choices. He didn't always choose to use the skills of philosophical inquiry, but at least he had some alternative ways of behaving, and I feel this did improve his well-being and his relationships with other children. His behaviour was modified in many subsequent situations, but I think it is fair to say that his well-being was also positively impacted.

Jack's behaviour changed in a subtle way, following the inquiry sessions. He grew in confidence and again, the perception of Jack by his peers changed, too. In some respects, some observers may consider Jack's behaviour to have been modified negatively; with some newfound confidence, he was more likely to shout out in class (although not often!) However, his well-being was surely positively impacted. Jack's contributions, whilst not as frequent as others, were insightful, other children looked at him in a different way, and each session reinforced the idea within the community that Jack was someone worth listening to. As a teacher, watching a child grow in confidence over a year is a privilege; one that can be brought about by many different topics, subjects, competitions and interactions – philosophical inquiry provided this opportunity for Jack.

Sophie's behaviour certainly wouldn't have been pointed out as problematic, or in need of modification. However, in a short time, she realised that her impact on the community was considerable and needed to be carefully reflected upon. Sophie identified where she could benefit the community in more than one way; her contributions were always well thought out and interesting, but she also had the trust of the community and the skills to help others share their ideas. Sophie could easily have been pushed out of discussions, so her well-being had to be carefully considered, too – but this was greatly cushioned because she had the freedom to reflect and make decisions about her role in the community.

Review

Whilst there are theoretical critiques of using philosophical inquiry with children, there are many examples from research where there have been benefits to children. Whilst I have personally found philosophical inquiry beneficial for my class and my pedagogy, you may not hold with the underpinning ideas, particularly around the management of behaviour during an inquiry session and the shifting identity of the teacher as part of this process. I would never suggest taking on something like philosophical inquiry if, as a professional, someone decides it is not compatible with their views. However, I would advocate that if you do not use philosophical inquiry, there are other opportunities in your class for community building, voicing opinions and sharing different and sometimes conflicting points of view.

? ACTIVITY STOP 3

This chapter has considered a focus that has not been touched upon in previous chapters. However, there are lots of cross-overs and common themes. Use the diagram (Figure 7.2) to see if there are any links for you between this chapter and some of the ideas or theories introduced in the previous chapters.

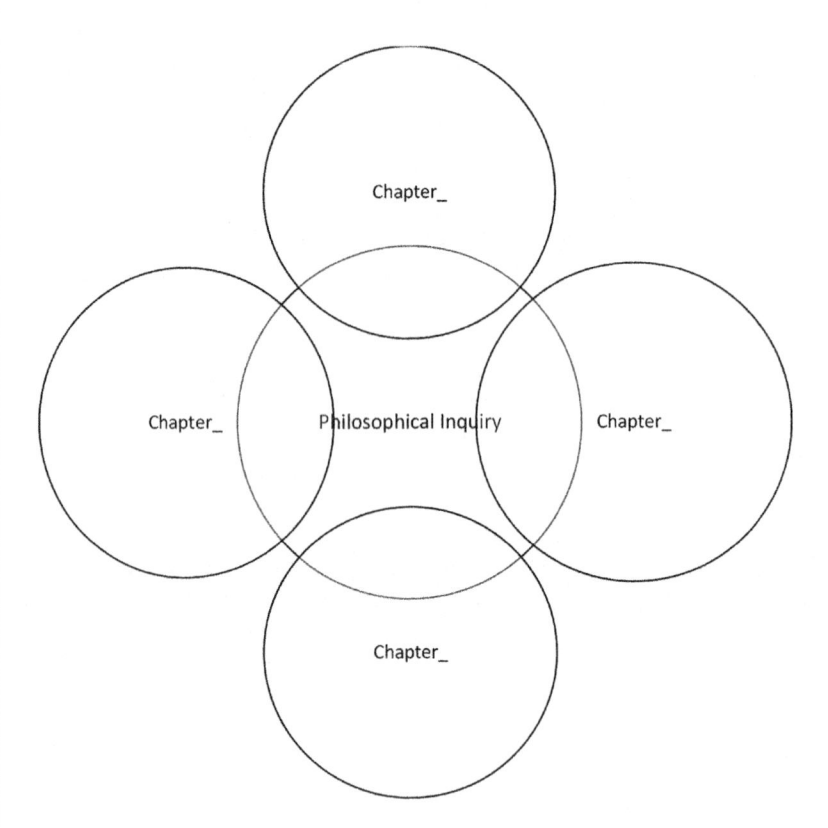

FIGURE 7.2 Identifies cross-overs between philosophical inquiry and other chapters.

This chapter has:

- Explored the research literature on philosophical inquiry with children.
- Described one of many ways in which philosophical inquiry can be used with children.
- Considered three case studies of children in communities of inquiry.

In doing so, you have been prompted to consider the role of the adult in the classroom during philosophical inquiry sessions, and how these (possibly) different roles for you and the children may have positive impacts on well-being, social interactions and peer relationships.

Whole-school actions might include the following:

- Investigating philosophical inquiry as a whole-school project, making time and space for a one-hour session per week in each class.
- Considering how philosophical inquiry can be introduced to other sessions, as a discussion activity with a shared understanding of the value of different opinions.
- Support staff continued professional development in facilitating and introducing philosophical inquiry.

Individual teacher actions might include some or all of the following:

- Research resources and approaches to philosophical inquiry with children, which are freely available online.
- Have a go at using philosophical inquiry with your class – bearing in mind that a community of inquiry takes time to establish!
- Use further reading to enhance your understanding of philosophical approaches in the classroom.

Possible mental health and well-being implications:

- There is a clear link between children's well-being and fair treatment at school (Pretsch *et al.*, 2016). Whilst research in this area is scarce, anecdotally, the fair treatment and respect that is fostered in a community of inquiry has a positive impact on well-being and a sense of belonging.

If you decide to set up a community of inquiry with your class, I would love to hear about it:

Aimee.quickfall@bishopg.ac.uk.

Practitioner-related take-away:

- Communities of philosophical inquiry give structure and support children in voicing their views or opinions. This same structure and confidence in being heard can support them in managing their own and others' emotions and behaviours.

Practitioner Reading:

Quickfall, A. (2019). Philosophy and learning to think. In, Ogier, S. (Ed.) *A Broad and Balanced Curriculum in Primary Schools: Educating the Whole Child*. London: Learning Matters.

References

Barrow, W. (2010). Dialogic, participation and the potential for philosophy for children. *Thinking Skills and Creativity*, **5**(2), pp. 61–69.

Cassidy, C., and Christie, D. (2013) Philosophy with children: Talking, thinking and learning together. *Early Child Development and Care*, **183**(8), pp. 1072–1083.

Cassidy, C., and Mohr-Lone, J. (2020). Thinking about childhood: Being and becoming in the world. *Analytic Teaching and Philosophical Praxis*, **40**(1) pp. 16–26.

Cassidy, C., Marwick, H., Deeney, L., and McLean, G. (2018). Philosophy with children, self-regulation and engaged participation for children with emotional behavioural and social communication needs. *Emotional and Behavioural Difficulties*, **23**(1), pp. 81–96.

Durlak, J., Weissberg, R. P., Dymnicki, A. B., Taylor, R. D., and Schellinger, K. B. (2011). The impact of enhancing students' social and emotional learning: A meta-analysis of school-based universal interventions. *Child Development*, **82**(1), pp. 405–432.

Gorard, S., Siddiqui, N., and See, B. (2017). Can 'Philosophy for Children' improve primary school attainment? *Journal of Philosophy of Education*, **51**(1), pp. 5–22.

Hedayati, M., and Ghaedi, Y. (2009). Effects of the philosophy for children program through the community of inquiry method on the improvement of interpersonal relationship skills in primary school students. *Childhood & Philosophy*, **5**(9), pp. 199–217.

Heron, G., and Cassidy, C. (2018). Using practical philosophy to enhance the self-regulation of children in secure accommodation. *Emotional and Behavioural Difficulties*, **23**(3), pp. 254–269.

Murris, K. (2000). Can children do philosophy? *Journal of Philosophy of Education*, **34**(2), 261–279.

Pretsch, J., Ehrhardt, N., Engl, L., Risch, B., Roth, J., Schumacher, S., and Schmitt, M. (2016). Injustice in school and students' emotions, well-being, and behavior: A longitudinal study. *Social Justice Research*, **29**(1), pp. 119–138.

Quickfall, A. (2019). Philosophy and learning to think. In Ogier, S. (Ed.), *A Broad and Balanced Curriculum in Primary Schools: Educating the Whole Child*. London: Learning Matters.

Siddiqui, N., Gorard, S., and See, B. H. (2019). Can programmes like Philosophy for Children help schools to look beyond academic attainment? *Educational Review*, **71**(2), pp. 146–165.

Topping, K., and Trickey, S. (2007). Impact of philosophical enquiry on school students' interactive behaviour. *Thinking Skills and Creativity*, **2**(2), pp. 73–84.

8
VERITIES REVISITED
Keeping behaviour in perspective

John Visser

The second chapter in Part III is also written by an invited author. John's original writing on his concept of 'eternal verities' is a seminal piece. It is based on his extensive long-standing work with children in a range of contexts and brings together both research findings and practice. As with the preceding chapter, there is nothing in this chapter that will explicitly set out strategies to manage behaviour and, again, the focus on more on the holistic practice of the teacher and their personal qualities, embedded in everyday exchanges that are suggested to make the biggest difference to managing behaviour. In his chapter, John discusses a range of themes that have recurred throughout the book so far. He uses his wealth of practical and research experience to provide an overview of approaches to behaviour, labels and language as well as policy expectations. He revisits his eternal verities or truths that should shape our work with children whose behaviour challenges. This chapter's (and author's) contribution to the 'new perspectives' in the book is that it is the first review of the 'eternal verities' and is therefore new in itself, but also the all-inclusive consideration of the skills teachers bring to supporting behaviour through their own personalities and beliefs. This focus on teacher attributes and values is one which is rarely explicitly discussed but mirrors and develops the themes of values, attitudes and beliefs in Part II.

This chapter aims to:

- Consider some of the common myths and misconceptions around behaviour and how it has changed (or not)
- Revisit the use of labels, particularly that of 'challenging behaviour'
- Our iterative approach to behaviour and interventions to manage and support it
- A discussion of the need for consistency in whole-school behaviour polices

DOI: 10.4324/9781003035527-14

There are no specific thinking or activity stops in this chapter, however, as it draws together many of the themes that chapters in this book have covered so far. It may be a good time to pause and review the activities and reflections up to this point and see how your thinking has changed or developed.

Classrooms and behaviour

Some 50 years ago I walked into my first primary classroom as the adult in charge of the learning of 35 children who today would be referred to as year 4. The school had a very mixed catchment of deprivation and prosperous housing. Newly qualified, I had successfully completed four 'teaching practices' but this would be the first time I was on my own and responsible for the outcomes and impact my teaching would have on the lives of the children in my class. My training had adequately given the basics of learning theory, child development and some of the rudiments of keeping control. The operative word here is rudiments. I had then, and have still today, a nervousness and anxiety as I go before an audience who are there to listen to me. Will I be able to 'control' the situation so that my message gets across and my audience learns? Will they do as I ask? What if they go berserk and out of control? Sharing those concerns with other teachers and learning from experience gave me some of the 'secrets' of classroom management that have helped to control those fears!

My point in the opening paragraph is to show the universality of the concern about the behaviour of children and young people. In an age of constant and instant social messaging, the media and political pundits are quick to focus upon behavioural issues. In education, as in other spheres of life, bad news makes news. There is within the cultural memory a view that there once was a golden age of education. Was there ever a time when children all sat quietly and did exactly as they were told all the time? If such a time ever existed, it isn't recorded in any of the literature about schools and schooling I have come across. Managing behaviour cannot be achieved by following a particular prescriptive scheme. My experience as a teacher in a very wide range of schools is that the pursuit of a one-size-fits-all approach is futile (Royer, 2001). Learning takes place in our classes which have a mixture of schools, curriculums, teachers, children, families and carers, all different and in very different atmospheres, ethos and ambiences. Buckley and Maxwell (2007) in discussing the problematic nature of behaviour which was described as violent in schools, quote the Commissioner for Children in New Zealand as saying:

> we simply do not know if there is more violence within schools, more violence within our communities and families or if we are tolerating less violence than before and responding differently to this violence.
>
> (p. 2)

Given the wide range of factors which affect behaviour in our classrooms, it is first of all necessary to realise that very few behaviours are universally disapproved of and lead to physical harm. The behaviours of which teachers describe as the 'irritant' ones are those that often arise in the course of teaching and interrupt the flow of the lesson. They are of the order of 'calling out', 'non-compliance', failing to engage with tasks, absence of the right equipment for particular lessons, talking 'out of turn', swearing and verbal abuse. Whilst these types of behaviours can be challenging, they can also be viewed as part of most young people's behaviours at some time. A reading of national reports on behaviour in schools over the past 70-plus years exemplifies this (Underwood, 1955; Elton, 1989; Daniels, Visser, Cole & de Reybekill, 1998; Visser, 2003; Ofsted, 2005; Steer, 2009).

Writing about behaviour in schools is seldom simple and doesn't lend itself to being captured by a sound bite or simplistic phrase. A Google search for classroom management of behaviour quickly finds a vast range of material that offers schemes/ strategies/procedures and structures for classroom management. This plethora of material can be confusing and conflicting. How do you decide what is best and worth an investment of your time to follow and master? What criteria should you use to choose a particular 'package'?

I came to this question after working through and experiencing many different 'packages' in my work with children who, when I started teaching, were called the maladjusted, and then became those with social and emotional behavioural difficulties, and now have a wide range of descriptions. I came across a wide range of methodologies for working with these children and found nearly all of them worked. What I slowly realised was that the key to their working was the person(ality) carrying out the method or technique being espoused. One key starting point was their differentiation between the behaviours and their philosophical understanding of human behaviour.

'Good behaviour' and 'misbehaviour'

When is a behaviour seen as inappropriate or of such a nature that interferes with what you as a teacher deem to be good behaviour? When talking about behaviour, what is the terminology that goes alongside it? What labels do you use or have you come across which describe children and young peoples' behaviours? The range of behaviours which children and young people display which are disruptive and at times challenging is large, and your perception of those behaviours will be coloured by many different factors. What for one teacher is a low-level irritant may well be for another a source of anxiety and concern. That is not to say that either perception is 'right', but rather to understand that our perception is part of the judgement of a child's behaviour.

Though not on a continuum between the rare and the frequent, 'low level' behaviours lie another range of which have a qualitatively different 'feel' to them. They often are intense, unpredictable, constant and difficult to ignore, while still other behaviours which are equally intense and constant are overlooked because the behaviour doesn't impact on that teacher's perception of control of the classroom. Educationalists over time have used a variety of terms to label these behaviours and more latterly have increased the range, incorporating some of the more controversial ones in their repertoire, such as attention deficit hyperactivity disorder (ADHD) (Visser & Zenib, 2009). Educationalists do not have one term they use consistently to describe the behaviours or the children whose behaviour they deem to be inappropriate (Visser, 2003).

How any given child becomes labelled depends on so many different variables in the process as to believe that there is a serendipity about which label is ascribed when. The ascription of labels by teachers and other professional groups in education is determined by prevailing fashions and 'routes' to intervention. Many writers have also discussed the problematic nature of moving from the 'label' to defining the behaviours appropriate to that label (see for example Cooper, 1996, 2001; Cooper, Jacobs & Martin, 2009; Cole, Visser & Upton, 1998; Thomas & Glenny, 2000). Many of the terms used by educationalists to describe behaviours within schools are idiosyncratic to education. Terms such as ADHD, autism and others which derive from a medical perspective of behaviour can be equally idiosyncratic in their ascription to any individual child or young person. While educationalists may use terms such as 'antisocial' and 'criminal' behaviour, it is as well to remember that these will largely be ascribed to behaviours occurring *outside* of the school day.

The ascription of a label like 'challenging' or 'ADHD' can be useful; however, it can also lead us to assume the 'problem' is entirely within the child, and thus there is little or nothing that we can do as teachers. Take as an example the label 'challenging behaviour' prevalent in the language of some educationalists, since the nature of the behaviours deemed inappropriate are seen in terms of a 'challenge' by one or more pupils against another pupil, group of pupils or staff. Quite frequently the term is applied to an individual pupil by an individual staff member; the latter then describing the former as challenging. To label a child as challenging is to point to the fact that the problem lies within the professional involved rather than the child concerned – if the professional had 'answers', the challenge presented would no longer be a challenge. However, it is more often used to imply that the child has some control over these behaviours (even if only a very little) and that control can be exercised by the child or young person concerned, or that such possibilities can be brought to his or her attention.

What, then, should we do about behaviour?

For the inexperienced teacher to read that not only is there not a single answer to the age-old issue of classroom misbehaviour but that there also remains a great deal of uncertainty about the determination of what constitutes such behaviour will not inspire much confidence in their ability to be in charge of children's learning. Truth to tell, there are many 'answers', all of which have merits. There has been a significant development for mainstream schools coming out of a range of reports and initiatives. These have ranged from curriculum initiatives such as the SEAL (2005) programme which sought to raise teachers' and children's awareness of the development of emotional intelligence and, along with it, an understanding of learning as a behaviour; through to interventions such as Nurture Groups (Cooper & Tiknaz, 2007) which sought to provide some children with periods out of the mainstream classroom so that particular social and emotional needs could be addressed. Increasingly, there has been an emphasis on children's overall well-being and its effect upon behaviour – first highlighted back in 2004. The *Every Child Matters* agenda (DCSF, 2010) highlighted the need for schools to widen their vision to include issues of 'well-being' as being a contributor in academic achievement.

While these are the 'latest' strategies to emerge within mainstream schools, they were preceded by a large number of others; many begun as local initiatives to be taken over by central government and then rolled out as nationally funded and supported strategies. All too often, the funding has proved to be short term, usually lasting two years or so before the initiative is overtaken by another. Visser (2002) refers to the tendency to 're-invent wheels' when exploring some of the initiatives which have been funded, with each generation of teachers 're-discovering' behaviour as being challenging. As Visser (2002) points out, teachers and the educational media repeat the following sentence or one very like it every seven to ten years: For the past 'A', a rising concern facing 'B' because of 'C' is a lack of 'D', where 'A' stands for a period of time, 'B' equals teachers or/and teaching assistants, 'C' any recent change in educational approaches generally and 'D' for one of the following: standards, behaviour, discipline, respect or order. The reaction to these concerns is usually a search for an implementation of a 'new' strategy. The core of the 'new' strategy can more often than not be found in previous provision made by earlier generations of teachers. Seldom do teachers, policy makers or administrators make use of previous research which indicates what systemic interventions produce changes in behaviour. More seldom still are questions raised as to the underlying principles which are key to the success of strategies and which might be useful as a litmus test for suggested 'new' strategies.

Systemic factors for successful interventions

There have been many reports on behaviour in schools. It almost seems that each generation of teachers and politicians need to investigate what they perceive to be a 'new' problem. The question they perhaps should be asked is: Is it a new problem, or an old one with features which arise within the culture pertaining to that generation? Reading many of these reports coupled with my experience of being involved in many different schemes devised for teachers to cope with behaviours they find problematic led me to consider what was common between them all. What factors do all these reports and schemes have in common when they 'work'?

The following draws upon a range of national and international reports which contain recommendations for improving behaviour in schools. The table (Figure 8.1) indicates the recommendations made and shows the degree of congruence that exists across these reports.

There is universal agreement on the need to have whole-school policies on behaviour. Daniels *et al.* (1998) found that a positive whole-school behaviour

Country	Source	Year	Whole-School Policies	Teaching and Learning	Teacher Education	Leadership	Respect of Students	Additional Support	Class Size	Parents	Multi-agency	Specialist Provision within Mainstream	Physical Environment
EIRE	Government Report	2006	√	√	√	√	√	√	√	√	√		
Scotland	The Educational Institute of Scotland	2006	√	√	√			√	√	√	√		
Scotland	Scottish Executive	2006	√	√	√	√			√	√	√		
Europe Wide	NFER & CIDRER	2005	√	√	√		√				√		
Europe Wide	Council of Europe	2005	√	√	√							√	√
England	Office of Standards in Education (Ofsted)	2007	√	√	√							√	√
England	Department for Child Schools and Families	2009	√	√	√	√	√	√	√	√	√	√	√
World Wide	The International Academy of Education	2002	√	√	√		√	√		√			
England	Department for Education and Science	1989	√	√	√	√	√	√		√	√	√	

FIGURE 8.1 Drawn from national and international reports.

policy is instrumental in providing a culture which fosters appropriate behaviours in schools. Whilst they indicated that it enabled a consistency of approach by staff towards inappropriate behaviour, they found that this consistency need not be total. Rather, they indicate that its implementation by key staff was the crucial aspect, alongside having the policy clearly accessible by all in the school – parents included. When starting in a new school as a teacher or teaching assistant, it would be more than wise to make sure that a full standing of the school's behaviour policy provided one with a context within which to plan for the strategies you will use in the classroom.

The second most common recommendation relates to the quality of teaching and learning in the school as a whole. It is not that a particular style of teaching is required, as outlined in Lewis and Norwich (2004), nor is a specialist teaching style required. Rather, it is that teaching of a high quality engenders in the learner the motivation to engage in the learning (Daniels et al., 1998). Though it might sound trite, it remains true that a learner engaged in a learning task will be displaying appropriate behaviour; on-task behaviour is not challenging!

Apparent in national reports such as Elton (1989), Ofsted (2005), Steer (2009), and Underwood (1955) is the need for a greater linkage between quality teaching and behaviour in both initial teacher training and in the provision of continuing professional development (CPD). Daniels *et al.* (1998) found that schools which had an emphasis upon CPD that links behaviour to learning were likely to experience fewer challenging behaviours. The lesson to be drawn here for the initial teacher is the value of engaging in further professional development which provides opportunity to examine behaviour for learning.

Attention to these aspects, however, can provide only a preventative framework within which successful interventions can flourish. This is not to downgrade their importance; rather, it is to point out that, as seen in Figure 8.1, their importance has been emphasised by numerous reports over a period of time, and yet there continues to be concern over the behaviour of pupils. There is a propensity for these reports to deliver quick, uncomplicated headline 'answers' to what are complex individual challenges. These headlines generally point to structures and systems needing change (Visser, 2002). What is required is greater emphasis upon the qualitative nature of those changes, the values that inform the individual's moral position and their emotional commitment to meeting the behavioural and learning needs of pupils. Visser (2002) first referred to these characteristics as eternal verities, and subsequent work has indicated that they are a useful way of ascertaining whether the strategies for classroom management you prefer are likely to meet both the behavioural and learning needs of the pupils in your class.

Verities

The term resonates with a personal quest for an underlying set of unifying principles within all approaches to meeting the educational needs of pupils with SEBD. Is there a set of principles that are seldom enunciated associated with good practice, which, to quote Whelan (1998), are the field's 'memory banks', subliminally passed on to each succeeding generation of teachers?

My quest has its origins in my early development as a teacher of pupils. I faced contradictions as I perceived them, between the various approaches put forward as ways of meeting these pupils' behavioural and learning needs. Some of the approaches seemed to me to be diametrically opposed to each other. In my role as a young teacher struggling to do what was right for the pupils in my charge, which should I choose? What could ensure that the approach chosen would work? And in my role as a provider of professional development for teachers and others working with 'challenging children', what approaches should I espouse? What advice could be given to examine the likely success of any given policy shift, 'new' initiative or change in provision?

As part of my professional development, I took a year off to gain a master's in education (MEd). The course provided me with the opportunity to visit a number of schools, among them one that espoused a behavioural approach and one that had a psychodynamic basis for its work. Both were perceived at that time as schools of good practice. I felt more comfortable in one setting than in the other, but it was evident that they were both successful in meeting the needs of pupils. Were there common underlying factors/principles/beliefs that accounted for this success? Are there eternal verities which are a part of all successful approaches? The DNA of approaches? Just as cells within the human body perform different functions but contain the same DNA, are there eternal verities to be found in all effective interventions to meet the needs of children and young people with SEBD?

What is an 'eternal verity'?

Verities are truths that are apparent in the web and weave in the methodologies which teacher use effectively in their classroom for learning and behaviour. They are eternal in as much as they are necessary to the proficiency of all approaches, regardless of the time frame in which the approaches are being developed and applied. They are the strongest links between different approaches and the achievement of successful outcomes. As such, they carry values and beliefs about the human condition and the quality of life to which we, and our pupils, are entitled. They are rarely made explicit, often emerging implicitly from literature, discussion and research. They are observable, but their quantification is seldom helpful and their measurement not linear. Having more or fewer of them is not so much the issue as their quality and presence within an approach. They sustain teachers and other professionals in times of stress, and good practice flows from them.

The list that follows is not presented as a definitive one. It is idiosyncratic. This list of eternal verities has drawn on three sources. The first is my experiences as a teacher in a variety of settings, from the classroom to researcher and provider of staff development programmes, and from parent to foster parent. The second is from my involvement with education in a number of research and consultancy projects. The third comes from a review of the literature, which describes the various understandings and perspectives of the emotional and behavioural difficulties which children encounter. Amongst these I have drawn particularly on the work of Ayers *et al.* (2000), Bowlby (1969, 1973) Cooper *et al.* (2009) and Cooper (2001), Elton (1989), Eric (1997), Greenhalgh (1994), Kauffman (2001), Laslett *et al.* (1998), Maslow (1943, 1954), Porter (2000), Steer (2005, 2009) and Whelan (1998). These writers offer the reader a comprehensive view of the variety of approaches to understanding behaviour and its relationship to learning, and thus provide a basis for seeking possible eternal verities. This list is offered as a litmus test: points which can be considered in relation to a particular classroom management strategy. It is suggested that interventions, strategies and approaches which support these verities will be successful. Where teachers blindly follow a given strategy or approach, often promulgated by a charismatic proponent of that strategy, without examining the extent to which it encapsulates these suggested verities, then I contend there is a much smaller chance of a successful meeting of children's learning and behavioural needs.

Eternal verities

- Behaviour can change: emotional needs can be met.
- Intervention is second to prevention.
- Instructional reactions.
- Transparency in communications.
- Empathy and equity.
- Boundaries and challenge.
- Building positive relationships.
- Humour.

Behaviour can change: emotional needs can be met

It may seem axiomatic that strategies and approaches are premised upon a belief that behaviour can change and emotional needs can be met. However, it is dangerous to assume that this is so (Visser 2014). Many of the approaches put forward wax and wane over time, now in fashion and then seem to disappear of the educational horizon. They seem to rely more upon the 'mood' of the time than on hard evidence from well-researched documentation. Reflection on this verity should also cover the question about the nature of the change being sought and the emotional need that the child's behaviour displays.

Effective teachers usually come from an understanding that behaviour is capable of change, whether it is viewed as learnt behaviour, or the result of internal intraphysic forces, or consequent upon a medical condition. and it is the actions and their consequences for him or her that are seen as the focus of the approach. There is an understanding that to be human is not to be at the mercy of instincts or genetic make-up. This is apparent even in the re-emerging medical understanding of aspects behaviour such as ADHD (Cooper, 2001). What, for example, is the teacher's view of the balance of effect on behaviour of nurture and nature? Nurture, the psycho-social development and the social context of the child or young person are always viewed as central to understanding. If human behaviour is the result purely of genetics, then what does that indicate about the possibility of a change in behaviour and how a given strategy will effect that?

This belief in the possibility of change provides teachers with the ability to continue to work with children when so often they reject the attempts to meet their needs. This quality, of going 'the extra half mile', is seen as being necessary in teachers (Cole *et al.*, 1998). As Rodway (1993) pointed out in his 1992 David Wills Lecture:

> However much a child may wound his own self-esteem … cannot change the esteem in which (the teachers) hold him (if the approach is to be successful).
> (p. 379)

Intervention is second to prevention

The history of nearly all approaches to children's misbehaviour shows that they have been derived from the identification of a 'challenge' presented by a group of children. The difficulties are identified before the approaches are developed. The interventions seek to meet the challenge presented by the identified difficulties. Publicising the success of the intervention inevitably leads to the identification of 'fault lines' within the child's environment, be that school, home or community. Prevention strategies become apparent. At some, usually early stage, aspects of the approach are highlighted as being able to contribute to the prevention of misbehaviour. All effective approaches underscore the proverb: 'Prevention is better than cure'.

Much of the literature on classroom management, for example, is derived from studies of the approaches that make for poor classroom management. Prevention in the form of ensuring that positive strategies are in place initially in teacher training has only recently been focused upon. Approaches which ensure that preventive strategies are at least as strongly represented as intervention strategies have more possibilities of achieving successful outcomes (Visser, 2000). What about the strategy chosen for managing children's behaviour and learning prevents the opportunity of misbehaviour to occur in the first instant?

Instructional reactions

Pupils with behaviours which teachers find difficult or challenging do not always understand the relationship between their behaviours and the reactions those behaviours cause. Few children set out with malice aforethought to be the disturbed and disturbing characters many of them become. When they do, it is to achieve some gratification or status that protects their self-esteem. Effective approaches recognise this and work to consistently portray to the child what the relationship is between cause and effect, and how they can achieve different reactions which meet their needs. Just telling pupils off or issuing sanctions for inappropriate behaviours has little effect except perhaps to persuade the child not to get caught next time. Teachers using strategies which give the child the reasons why the behaviour is inappropriate, together with alternative ways to react appropriately, achieve successful outcomes.

Transparency in communications

A consistent finding in the research mentioned previously is the degree to which clear, consistent, coherent communication is a factor in meeting the social and emotional needs of pupils (see for example Cole *et al.*, 1998; Daniels *et al.*, 1998). Teachers advocating a variety of approaches have always ensured that the adults coming into contact with a child have spoken from the 'same hymn sheet' and thus provided a consistency of approach. This consistency is best ensured when the school's behaviour policy is clearly set and agreed by both the staff and the children. This consistency also provides for a transparency in communications, where what is said is what is meant, and leads to a consistency of what takes place in any given situation. This in turn supports the development of a caring, learning and sharing school ethos in meeting the needs of pupils (Visser, Cole & Daniels, 2002).

Empathy and equity

Approaches to pupils' needs devoid of empathy seem to have had less effect than those that incorporate it. Proficient approaches encourage the development of a robust empathy with the children and young people. This is not as easy as some would make out. The case histories of most pupils with behaviours which teachers find difficult reveal significant family trauma, poverty in their range of positive experiences, a paucity of expectations, an absence of the emotional capacity to make and sustain relationships and, sadly all too often, physical, emotional and sexual abuse (Fortin & Bigras, 1997; Hayden, 2007). Though some teachers may have personal experience of one or more of these, few have experienced them in the depth and range experienced by some of the pupils they will come across.

Empathy, that ability to begin to see the world through the eyes of the child's experience, requires a degree of emotional commitment to the well-being of the child. Empathy provokes the question, which needs to be asked continuously when working with the child: 'Why do I think this child behaved in this way and what does that mean for the approach I use?' It provides the basis upon which the pupil can begin to feel valued and understood. Being empathic should not lead to excusing the behaviour; rather, it provides an understanding as to why the behaviour has occurred.

Boundaries and challenge

All approaches within the literature speak of the need for structure, particularly of the need to provide boundaries. They recognise that the lack of self-imposition or acknowledgement of boundaries has a correlation behaviour which can be challenging. This is hardly surprising given that it is the constant lack of being able to behave and display emotions within boundaries that most frequently triggers the identification of a pupil as difficult to control. The boundaries need to be set by the teachers, but they must have a flexibility which bends but never breaks (Cole *et al.*, 1998). In other words, approaches which have a rigid structure in meeting the needs of pupils are very unlikely to be effective. As Royer (2001) points out, the inflexible approach fails because it ends up identifying all difficulties as nails because the only tool in the teacher's kit is a hammer. Bentley (1997) saw this eternal verity as being very necessary if pupils with behaviours which teachers find difficult are to avoid being marginalised within schools and classrooms; the net result of which is that they fall behind academically and become even more difficult to manage.

With the boundaries should go high, achievable expectations of behaviour and educational achievement (Cole *et al.*, 1998; Daniels *et al.*, 1998; Ofsted, 1999a). The therapeutic effect of being set challenging achievable targets, even when initially a great deal of support is required, is noted by Wilson and Evans (1980) and others (Cooper, 1996; Greenhalgh, 1994; DCSF 2005). Since 1999, Ofsted (1999b) has reported low expectations in relation to pupils' achievements as a contributory cause in many schools 'causing concern' or with 'serious weaknesses'.

Building positive relationships

Bentley (1997) writes: 'social networks are powerful determinants of an individual's life chances'. He goes on to indicate that having access to a range of adults as role models is an indispensable resource for children and young people. Daniels (2001) and Ryan (2001) reinforce this with their view that the ability to develop genuine caring and learning relationships, and knowing where to go to make them, is an important skill for pupils to acquire if they are to be integrated members of their community. Children and young people with behavioural issues are not good at making and sustaining positive relationships; they constantly test out the adults they come across (Laslett, 1977). Porter (2000) indicates that, particularly for pupils with behavioural difficulties which teachers can find challenging, relationships need to provide emotional safety and protection, personal involvement and trust, and acceptance from others. Approaches which are successful emphasise the need to develop such relationships.

Humour

As Cole *et al.* (1998), Porter (2000) and Visser (2000) point out, having a sense of humour has been seen as a vital component in any approach. Humour is rarely mentioned in descriptions of strategies and approaches, and yet as one study (Cole *et al.*, 1998) found, it is consistently placed as one of the top three characteristics of the effective teachers working with pupils with behavioural difficulties. Fovet (2009) provides a useful insight into the mechanisms of humour, noting that it is a complex area of human communication rooted in subjective standards making investigation difficult. He notes from his study that the receptivity of students to humour is dependent upon 'genuine' positive relationships between students and staff. Children are often positive about learning when it is seen as fun, and that does not mean than it lacks rigour. Rather, it is that difficulties and challenges in learning can be overcome by engendering a sense of fun in doing so. Learning doesn't have to be painful!

The range of eternal verities

Teachers now work in an age where there has been an information explosion, and gone are some of the old certainties of testing the veracity of what we are told. The pattern, shape and accessibility of information is radically changing. If schools and teachers are to develop and adapt their abilities to meet the behavioural and learning needs of pupils, then having a set of eternal verities may provide a sound base upon which to test the information available – rather than relying just upon the latest social media quote or web site which purports to have the answer!

Are these the only eternal verities? Greenhalgh (1994) lists six characteristics he saw as important. Laslett (1977) gives 17 that he saw as pertaining to David Wills. Ofsted (1999a) indicates six features consistently associated with good practice, and

Whelan and Kauffman (1999) have three. All these accord with the eight listed earlier, differing in emphasis and range of terminology rather than content. There remains a lack of empirical quantitative evidence to support this qualitative consensus. Cooper et al. (2009), completing a meta-analysis of a wide range of reported research, point to a lack of replicable evidence to support approaches deemed to be good practice and delivering positive outcomes.

Review

Educationalists have long had the task of affecting the behaviour of young people in schools. The evidence base for the effectiveness of many of the approaches utilized is questionable (Dyson, 2001). Besides the need to halt the cycle of wheel reinvention, establishing a set of eternal verities may also provide a brake on the increasing categorization of pupils with behavioural difficulties. A recent analysis by Visser (2014) shows an ever-increasing listing of terms to describe children's behaviours. No amount of labelling will negate the need for teachers to use their independent and professional judgements in coming to a conclusion about a child's behaviour (Pirrie, 2001); rather, the verities may provide the basis upon which to make a judgement as to the effectiveness of the strategies he or she has used.

Practitioner-related take-away:

- There is no one successful one-size fits all approach to managing behaviour.

Practitioner reading:

Visser (2002). Eternal Verities: The strongest links. *Emotional and Behavioural Difficulties*, 7(2), pp. 68–84.

References

Ayers, H., Clarke, D., and Murray, A. (2000). *Perspectives on Behaviour: A Practical Guide to Effective interventions for Teachers*. London: David Fulton.
Bentley, T. (1997). Learning to belong. *Demos Collection*, 12, pp. 44–46.
Bowlby, J. (1969). *Attachment and Loss Vol. 1 Attachment*. New York: Basic Books.
Bowlby, J. (1973). *Attachment and Loss Vol. 2 Separation*. New York: Basic Books.
Buckley, S., and Maxwell, G. (2007). *Respectful Schools: Restorative Practices in Education*. Wellington, New Zealand: Office of the Children's Commissioner.
Cole, T., Visser, J., and Upton, G. (1998) *Effective Schooling for Pupils with Emotional and Behavioural Difficulties*. London: David Fulton.
Cooper, P. (1996). Giving it a name: The value of descriptive categories in educational approaches to emotional and behavioural difficulties. *Support for Learning*, 4, pp. 146–159.
Cooper, P. (2001). *We Can Work it Out: What Works in Educating Pupils with Social, Emotional and Behavioural Difficulties Outside Mainstream Classrooms*. Barkingside: Barnardo's.
Cooper, P., and Tiknaz, Y. (2007). *Nurture Groups in School and at Home*. London: Jessica Kingsley.

Cooper, P., Jacobs, B., and Martin, M. (2009). *Caring to Make a Difference: Educating Children and Young People with Social, Emotional and Behavioural Difficulties.* Dublin: National Council for Special Education.
Daniels, H., Visser, J., Cole, T., and de Reybekill, N. (1998). *Emotional and Behavioural Difficulties in Mainstream Schools. Research Report RR90.* London: DfEE.
DCSF. (2005). *Social and Emotional Aspects of Learning: Improving Behaviour, Improving Learning.* London: DCSF.
DCSF. (2010) *Every Child Matters.* London: DCSF. Retrieved January 1st 2010 from at www.dcsf.gov.uk/everychildmatters/about.
Dyson, A. (2001). Special need education as the way to equity: An alternative approach, *Support for Learning,* **16**(3), pp. 99–104.
Elton Report. (1989). *Discipline in Schools: Report of Committee of Enquiry Chaired by Lord Elton.* London: H.M.S.O.
ERIC. (1997) Common features of school wide behaviour management. *ERIC Research papers,* **1**(1).
Fortin, L., and Bigras, M. (1997). Risk factors exposing young children to problems. *Emotional and Behavioural Difficulties,* **2**(1), pp. 3–14.
Fovet, F. (2009). The use of humour in classroom interventions with students with social, emotional and behavioural difficulties. *Emotional and Behavioural Difficulties,* **14**(4), pp. 275–289.
Greenhalgh, P. (1994). *Emotional Growth and Learning.* London: Routledge.
Hayden, C. (2007). *Children in Trouble: The Role of Families, Schools and Communities.* Basingstoke: Palgrave/Macmillan.
Kauffman, J. (2001). *Characteristics of Emotional and Behavioural Disorders of Children and Youth* (7th Edition). New Jersey: Merrill Prentice Hall.
Laslett, R. (1977). *The Education of Maladjusted Children.* London: Crosby Lockwood Staples Publishing.
Laslett, R., Cooper, P., Maras, P., and Rimmer, A. (1998). *Changing Perceptions: Emotional and Behavioural Difficulties since 1945.* Maidstone: AWCEBD.
Lewis, A., and Norwich, B. (2004). *Special Teaching for Special Children.* London: McGraw-Hill Education.
Maslow, A.H. (1943). A theory of human motivation. *Psychological Review,* **50** pp. 370–396.
Maslow, A.H. (1954). *Motivation and Personality.* New York: Harper and Row.
Ofsted. (1999a). *Principals into Practice: Effective Education for Pupils with EBD.* London: Ofsted.
Ofsted. (1999b). *Lessons Learnt from Special Measures.* London: Ofsted.
Ofsted. (2005). *Managing Challenging Behaviour.* London: Ofsted.
Pirrie, A. (2001). Evidenced based practice in education: the best medicine. *British Journal of Educational Studies,* **49**(2), pp. 124–136.
Porter, L. (2000). *Behaviour in Schools: Theory and Practice for Teachers.* Buckingham: Open University Press.
Rodway, S. (1993). Children's rights: Children's needs. Is there a conflict? *Therapeutic Care,* **2**(2), pp. 375–391.
Royer, E. (2001). The education of students with EBD: One size does not fit all. In Visser, J., Daniels, H., and Cole, T. (Eds)., *International Perspectives on Inclusive Education: Emotional and Behavioural Difficulties in Mainstream Schools* (pp. 129–142). Amsterdam: JAI.
Ryan, K. (2001). *Strengthening the Safety Net: Home Schools Can Help Youth with Emotional and Behavioural Needs.* Burlington, VT: School Research, University of Vermont.
SEAL. (2005). *Social and Emotional Aspects of Learning. Improving Behaviour: Improving Learning.* London: DFES.

Steer, A. (2005). *Learning Behaviour: The Report of the Group on School Behaviour and Discipline.* Nottingham: DfES.

Steer, A. (2009). *The Steer Report: Learning Behaviour. Lessons Learnt.* London: DCSF.

Thomas, G., and Glenny, B. (2000). Emotional and behavioural difficulties; bogus needs in a false category. *Discourse: Studies in the Cultural Politics of Education*, **21**(2), pp. 283–298.

Underwood Report (1955). *Report of the Committee on Maladjusted Children.* London: H.M.S.O.

Visser, J. (2000). *Managing Behaviour in Classrooms.* London: David Fulton.

Visser, J. (2002). Eternal verities: The strongest links. *Emotional and Behavioural Difficulties*, 7(2), pp 68–84.

Visser, J. (2003). *A Study of Children and Young people who Present Challenging Behaviour.* London. Ofsted. Retrieved from www.ofsted.gov.uk/ofsted-home/Publications.

Visser, J. (2014). *Transforming Troubled Lives.* London, Routledge.

Visser, J., and Zenib, J. (2009). ADHD: a scientific fact or factual opinion? *A critique of the veracity of Attention Deficit Hyperactivity Disorder Emotional and Behavioural Difficulties*, 14(2), pp 127–140.

Whelan, R.J. (1998). *Emotional and Behavioural Disorders: A 25-year Focus.* Denver: Love Publishers.

Wilson, M., and Evans, K (1980). *Education for Disturbed Pupils. Schools Council Working Paper 65.* London: Methuen.

9

INTERNATIONAL PERSPECTIVES

Behaviour management in Finland

Erkko Sointu, Katariina Waltzer, Juuso Pursiainen, Aino Äikäs and Kristiina Lappalainen

This chapter brings (almost) to a close Part III of the book where wider perspectives have been considered. The chapter here, written by a team involved in teacher education, special education and teaching in Finland, offers an international perspective from a country famed for its high educational standards. One of my aims in including this chapter and asking the authors to write it is to help develop to an understanding of how behaviour management is influenced not only by personal views and beliefs, but also by the wider cultural context. As a result, this chapter links together some of the themes in Part I of the book (particularly Chapter 3) with those in Part II.

I have undertaken a number of collaborative research projects in Finland, and on my first visit to a school there, I was struck by the difference in expectations and norms; of children, behaviour, teachers and teaching. These were not simply a school-based difference but rather a cultural one. A number of approaches have been grafted onto the English system – particularly in primary schools such as the Danish concept of Forest Schools, pedagogical approaches in maths from Singapore amongst others. These have often had different outcomes in England from those in their home countries due to contextual and cultural differences. As a result, I am not suggesting directly transferring the ideas and approaches Erkko and his team discuss but rather comparing them with ideas in England and considering how and where our cultural and policy-related contexts are similar and different (this will be explored further in Chapter "*Final thoughts*"). The authors' discussions on how children are viewed and the beliefs that underpin practice with children in Finland is specifically pertinent and develops the focus of chapters, and of your activities, in Part II of this book.

The chapter following on from this will review some of the key themes and ideas discussed by the authors here and follow up on specific reflections and activities.

DOI: 10.4324/9781003035527-15

This chapter discusses the differences of the Finnish way of training teachers and working with children has on behaviour. This chapter aims to:

- Provide an overview of how education in Finland is guided by legislation and a national core curriculum
- Explain the educational support (e.g. for behaviour) model used in Finland that follows a three-tiered, Response to Intervention (RTI) type model
- Discuss how Finnish teachers acquire broad knowledge during their education concerning how to deal with issues concerning behavioural management
- Consider the evidence-based interventions and good practices that are used in schools to support pupils with behavioural problems
- Share how the open and flexible learning environments challenge teachers to find pedagogical solutions to support pupils with behavioural problems.
- Discuss the importance of supporting pupils' strengths by first assessing and identifying these strengths, and then concentrating on a strength-based approach to teaching
- Consider how methods to support behavioural management in schools require continuous research, testing, experimentation, implementation and learning

Introduction

Finnish schools and the Finnish school system have received significant international attention during the last two decades because of the success it has garnered in various international assessments (e.g. OECD, 2019). While different explanations for this success have been offered, the successful performance of Finnish pupils seems to be attributable to a network of interrelated factors related to comprehensive pedagogy, the pupils' own interests and leisure activities, the structure of the education system, teacher education, school practices and, in the end, Finnish culture (Välijärvi et al., 2002). In this chapter, we will outline behavioural management in Finland from multiple perspectives, aiming to provide readers with a more comprehensive understanding. The main purpose of this chapter is twofold. First, we present the Finnish education system from the various perspectives of:

- School culture
- School systems
- Teacher training and teachers
- Pedagogy and pedagogical support

Within our examinations of these viewpoints, we have integrated practical examples taken from actual teacher experiences. Second, we include a research component by presenting a strength-based assessment approach to behavioural management. A modern Finnish school and the work done there highlight the examples provided. The chapter ends with conclusions and critical viewpoints about Finnish education. From there, we will more thoroughly examine Finnish education systems.

Finnish school culture

One of the main targets of the Finnish education system is to offer equal educational opportunities for all pupils. Education in Finland is provided mainly through a so-called nearby school system for all pupils. In this system, pupils attend the school closest to them, as provided by the education provider (which is often the municipality). The concept of inclusive education is an undercurrent in the legislation of Finnish education, and it has been strengthened since the Basic Education Act (628/1998) and its Amendment (642/2010). The emphasis is on inclusiveness and the three-tiered response to intervention (RTI) type model. RTI framework according to Fuchs and Fuchs (2006) includes tiers of instruction which vary on their intensity. First, the pupils who benefit (have good response to) the intervention are identified with various strategies. Second, the pupils receive targeted instruction (intervention) which can be multitiered. The intervention may be universal (general support), targeted (intensified support) or intensive (special support). This framework for identifying, monitoring pupils at risk and focusing on the needed instruction, organization and the intensity of the support is similar to the Finnish support model. In Finland, this model is often referred to as a learning and schooling support model, implemented as one national model for supporting all pupils (Jahnukainen & Itkonen, 2016). According to Grosche and Volpe (2013), the RTI model has the potential to influence inclusion, especially in the context of behavioural support, by providing a strong implementation plan for inclusion practices; defining the roles, responsibilities, cooperation and collaboration of all educators; enabling the sharing of resources for the instruction and guidance of pupils with special needs; and avoiding early and unnecessary labelling of pupils with special needs, thus strengthening inclusiveness in schools. Moreover, the RTI model can be considered to assume a systematic approach; for example, the behavioural support needs of children and youth rely on data-driven decision-making (e.g. Salvia et al., 2013).

The Finnish National Core Curriculum for Basic Education (FNBE, 2016) guides municipalities and schools in educational arrangements and instructions (Pulkkinen et al., 2019). Every Finnish municipality is required to prepare municipality-level and school-level local curriculums for educational goals and arrangements of support services. The aim is to provide support services and equal opportunities for learning that include pupils with special educational needs. In practice, the Finnish education system consists of three phases:

- An initial, one-year, compulsory pre-primary education for all 6-year-old children
- A nine-year, compulsory basic education comprising primary education, grades 1–6 (taught by classroom teachers)
- Lower secondary education, grades 7–9 (taught by subject teachers)
- An upper secondary education, which starts at the age of sixteen and usually lasts for three years.

Upper secondary education is voluntary and is divided between vocational education and upper general education. Students can also pursue a double degree that includes both educations simultaneously (i.e. vocational upper general education), which takes four years. Upper secondary-level educations give students the ability to apply to higher education programs (e.g. polytechnic institutions and universities). Among Finnish children and youth, almost 100% of the age cohort finishes basic education, and 96% continue on to study at the secondary education level (Official Statistics of Finland, 2018a). The education itself – from pre-primary to doctoral degree – is free for pupils and students in Finland.

All pupils in the Finnish education system are also provided pedagogical support. The support system of basic education is divided into three tier levels, as followed by the RTI type model: general (tier 1), intensified (tier 2) and special support (tier 3) (FNBE, 2016). Three-tiered support focuses on educational and pedagogical preventative measures, with the aim of identifying problems early on and providing additional support in the pupil's own school and teaching group (FNBE, 2016; Hienonen et al., 2021).

The underlying concept of the Finnish support system is that support is available for all pupils, in a manner that is flexible based on individual need; thus, general and intensified support can be started when pedagogically warranted. According to Finnish legislation, no psychological or medical evaluations are needed (Basic Education Act, 2010; Thuneberg et al., 2014) for pupils to receive support services in Finnish pre-primary to upper secondary education. The decision to provide special support is made by school officials and is based on a written pedagogical statement made by the school's multi-professional team. Special education services should be determined based on educational needs, and general and intensified support should be provided as part of mainstream education in regular classes. While special support pupils attend regular schools either in regular or special classes, approximately 8.6% of pupils are placed in special schools (Official Statistics of Finland, 2018b). The shift from special education being a 'place' to embodying support services that are delivered as a part of pupils' everyday schooling has changed the educational culture in Finland into being more inclusive. Because the support system also includes multi-professional collaboration at all levels, pupils are entitled to receive support services from psychologists, social workers and heath care specialists during the time frame of the school day.

Schools, national core curriculum and transversal competence areas

In Finland, there are approximately 2,200 basic education schools provided by the municipalities that offer basic education for 564,000 pupils, and approximately 80 private schools, of which a few offer basic education (Official Statistics of Finland 2018a, 2018b). All of the schools that offer basic education are funded by the government; moreover, Finnish legislation disallows offering basic education in order

FIGURE 9.1 Rantakylä school general area for all pupils and teachers.
Source: Picture by Mari Hakanen.

to make a profit (Basic Education Act, 1998). In general, pupils commonly attend municipality-offered basic education schools; in certain cases, families choose to send their children to private schools, mainly for lingual, pedagogical or religious reasons (Figure 9.1).

> **EXAMPLE**
>
> Rantakylä School is one of the three teacher training units of the University of Eastern Finland (UEF). Even though the teacher training schools are part of UEF, these schools are part of the Joensuu municipality school network. Rantakylä School offers the whole basic education continuum – from primary education (grades 1–6), with 280 pupils, to lower secondary school (grades 7–9), with 130 pupils. There are approximately 40 teachers, 12 school assistants, school nurse and school social worker (i.e. curator). In addition, approximately 80 UEF teacher students participate in teacher practice periods three times a year.

The Finnish National Core Curriculum for Basic Education (FNBE, 2016) also guides behavioural management in Finnish schools. It recognises imparting skills related to good manners and its knowledge, and guiding behaviour as part of the schools' educational tasks. Jointly built rules, as well as taking other people and environments into account, are emphasised in the curricula. Appropriate, situation-sensitive behaviour and good manners are taught in various interactive situations of the school. The informal and ongoing assessment of behaviour is conducted as a part of the schoolwork, and pupils are given feedback to guide their behaviour. This work is closely tied to the objectives set by the local municipality and school-level curricula. The school community often sets its own educational goals, policies and rules for behaviour – guided by FNBE – and pupils are considered to be active members in their creation. Moreover, caregivers must have opportunities to define and participate in discussions about behavioural objectives and goals.

> **EXAMPLE**
>
> The national core curriculum (FNBE, 2016) guides the principles of both the UEF teacher training school and Rantakylä School. Curriculum quality and functionality are developed on a yearly basis by a school team that includes teachers from various grades. This team meets five to ten times a year. Even though the Rantakylä School and other teacher training schools are part of UEF, all the teacher training schools collaborate closely with the municipality of Joensuu schools, for example, in curriculum development, taking the municipality-level emphasis on curriculum into account.

Alongside its inclusion in the national core curriculum, behavioural management is also addressed via seven core outcome areas – called transversal competence (TC) areas – deemed important for one's growth as a citizen and as a part of society. The outcomes that are part of each subject taught in basic education are divided into the following areas:

- Thinking and learning to learn (TC1)
- Cultural competence, interaction and self-expression (TC2)
- Taking care of oneself and managing daily life (TC3)
- Multiliteracy (TC4)
- Information and communication technology (ICT) competence (TC5)
- Working life competence and entrepreneurship (TC6)
- Participation, involvement and building a sustainable future (TC7).

(FNBE, 2016)

The first, second and seventh competence areas are of particular importance when dealing with behavioural management.

> **EXAMPLE**
>
> FNBE (2016) transversal competence (TC) area development work is performed across multi-professional schema in Rantakylä School. It includes the principal of the school, TC teams and each individual teacher. Particularly, teachers develop and assess their work in light of TC areas as they plan their teaching strategies. Three TC areas are especially relevant to the behavioural management perspective. First, the *thinking and learning to learn* (TC1) area emphasises the ability of pupils to consider different information and behaviour from various perspectives. As such, pupils are guided to recognise their own and other pupils' behaviour in social situations, as well as the importance of understanding social situations and the viewpoints of different individuals. Second, while the *cultural competence, interaction and self-expression* (TC2) area can emphasise similar considerations as TC1, pupils in TC2 are taught to appreciate others and themselves. In addition to appreciating other pupils just as they are, pupils are guided to control their own behaviour, body, views, thinking and ideas in order to express themselves in appropriate ways. Recognising one's own emotions in terms of behaviour and behavioural management is an important facet of the learning experience. Even though this can be challenging for pupils with behavioural problems, examining their own behaviour can serve as an invaluable tool that may lead to more positive experiences in social situations. Pupils with behavioural problems practise emotional skills and behavioural management in social situations in small groups, and then do so in classroom and school social situations. The third important TC area for behavioural management – *participation, involvement and building a sustainable future* (TC7) – emphasises pupils' experiences in the context of the school community. In this regard, pupils are taught to take responsibility for their own behaviour as part of the community. For example, in small groups, daily and weekly behavioural objectives are used and monitored by pupils and teachers alike. These objectives are based on pupils' strengths and positive behaviour and, in some cases, includes reward systems. In these ways, pupils can practise assessing and developing their own behaviour in conjunction with the teacher and school assistant.

Having a sense of belonging positively influences pupils' development and their ties to the school community. It is of utmost importance that pupils feel this sense of belonging and that they have opportunities to influence mutual aspects of everyday school life, as such interrelationships create an atmosphere conducive to the positive development of self-concept and behaviour in social situations. Pupils in Rantakylä School have many ways to participate in their school community. For example, they can play an active role in influencing their own learning by participating in the school pupil council and pupil buddy programs. Of note, pupils with intensified and special needs support (with behavioural problems too) are active participants in these school community activities. In the following section, we will explain more thoroughly how learning environments can be seen in Finnish schools.

Learning environments

In addition to steering behaviour and TC areas, FNBE (2016) strongly emphasises diverse learning environments in Finnish schools. Newly developed learning environments and TC areas challenge the traditional views of behavioural management; in fact, in the last ten years, schools have been built using a new kind of architecture that favours open, flexible spaces. A flexible learning environment (Woodman, 2015) not only comprises a place where learning takes place, it also offers a flexibility that encompasses both the pedagogical and physical dimensions of the learning process. The physical features of a flexible learning environment are often movable walls and furniture, as well as a variety of multi-purpose areas. The versatility and flexibility of the spaces bring a pedagogical element to the learning environment, to which special attention must be paid. For example, noise and acoustic challenges are the biggest problems in open, flexible learning environments. Solutions can be found in pedagogical elements such as the appropriate planning of teaching, flexible grouping and co-teaching. However, a school's operating culture will not change in such new open spaces unless the staff is trained before the premises are commissioned (Kattilakoski, 2018). Vetoniemi and Kärnä (2019) also emphasise that the experiences of pupils with special needs – how they have participated in different environments –are essential aspects to consider (Figure 9.2).

FIGURE 9.2 An example of flexible learning environment of a grade cell.
Source: Picture by Mari Hakanen.

> **EXAMPLE**
>
> Rantakylä School is an example of an educational facility with open and flexible learning environments. The school staff was included in designing the school, which opened in January 2019. The learning environments of the school are divided into unified and open spaces, which are called 'cells'. There is a 1st–2nd grade cell, a 3rd–4th grade cell and a 5th–6th grade cell for the lower grades of the school, including approximately 80 pupils per cell. Each cell has its own small group space for pupils with special educational needs (e.g. behavioural problems), when necessary. The cells also have movable furniture that allows for the flexible division of groups of pupils during the school day. The cells employ four classroom teachers, a special classroom teacher, a special education teacher and a school assistant. They all work closely together to design and implement teaching and support. The higher grades of Rantakylä School follow a yearly grade structure, and pupils are taught by subject teachers.

It is not enough to adapt the physical learning environment so that everyone can participate: the social, local, technological and pedagogical views of the learning environment (e.g. Manninen *et al.*, 2007) must adapt to the needs of all pupils. We have to consider these dimensions as interaction (i.e. social view), as places of learning outside the school (i.e. local view), as the range of ICT on teaching and learning (i.e. technological view) and as environments that support optimal learning (i.e. pedagogical view). New types of flexible learning environments, as well as the creation of related pedagogy, present many opportunities in Finnish school development work nowadays, especially since these environments can promote the individual needs of each pupil.

> **EXAMPLE**
>
> The challenge of an open learning environment from the perspective of pupils with behavioural problems is, first, that many pupils are taught in the same space. The pedagogy in this type of learning environment must be designed to prevent excessive visual and auditory stimuli. For example, pupils with challenges of concentration benefit from minimising stimuli in the learning environment. Pupils may also be overburdened by social pressure from many other people. Some pupils prefer to work alone and in a quiet workspace rather than in an open learning environment with many others. Working in a large group

> requires self-direction, which is a challenge for pupils with difficulties in executive functions. In a small group space, the teacher may have more time to guide a pupil. In addition, the different types of project work that require social competence and division of labour, as well as the perception of different roles, can be challenging for a pupil with special educational needs or behaviour problems.
>
> However, in the Rantakylä School, teachers of small groups strive to integrate their pupils as much as possible into the large groups. When a pupil practises planned and supported schoolwork in an open and flexible learning environment, the pupil gains the ability to become more and more involved in the activities of the mainstream group. Some of the pupils taught in the small group setting receive significant support from social work specialists and health-care services in order to make their attendance possible. The behavioural problems of such pupils require a peaceful, small group, where instruction is carried out by the same familiar adults. Rantakylä School invests substantially in the application of teaching technology to support the processes of teaching and learning. Inclusiveness can be emphasised for pupils through a common e-learning platform and joint video conferencing, even if the pupil is in a physically different environment than the others.
>
> There are good ways of integrating pupils with behavioural problems into an open, flexible learning environment. First, the pupil from the small group listens to the five-minute-long instruction in the general group. The pupil is then placed in a group consisting of a few pupils to work collaboratively on a project. The teacher guides the group in dividing the workload, and the special education teacher instructs the pupil with behavioural problems to find a suitable quiet work space and guides them during the task. At the end of the lesson, the pupil with the behavioural problems visits the general group for five to ten minutes of final feedback and task assessment. It should be noted that a pupil's school condition may vary from day to day and from lesson to lesson, so it is not always appropriate to integrate a restless pupil into the general group; this is why the learning environments and the pedagogy must be flexible on a needs basis.

At the centre of the pedagogical dimension of the open, flexible learning environments are learner orientation, process-centricity and diverse teaching methods, guidance practices that support the pupil and the pupil's own activity and self-direction (see, e.g. Manninen et al., 2007). According to a study by Kariippanon et al. (2017), flexible learning environments have been perceived as increasing interaction and inclusion, and as supporting learner-centred pedagogy, pupil self-direction, collaboration and commitment to schoolwork. Flexible learning environments offer a variety of opportunities for diverse work in an appropriate space of sufficient size to meet the individual needs of each pupil.

> **EXAMPLE**
>
> The term 'learning-centred approach' is an umbrella term for different ways of organising teaching, learning activities and assessment. As a whole, the learning-centred approach also emphasises teachers' professional competences; facilitating learning is a demanding task. Moreover, educational institutions must consciously focus on how they weigh pupils' responsibilities and right to organise their own learning against the institutions' responsibility to teach, facilitate, assess and support learning.
>
> In Finland, the learning-centred approach also includes teacher autonomy. Teachers enjoy pedagogical autonomy in the classroom, are considered pedagogical experts, are entrusted with considerable independence in the classroom, have decision-making authority with regard to school policy and management, are deeply involved in drafting the local curricula and in development work and have responsibility for the choice of textbooks and teaching methods. Pupils profit from a national curriculum and highly qualified trained teachers, as well as research-based teaching.

Teacher training and teachers

In order to be appointed to a permanent teaching position, teachers must possess a master's degree. In Finland, teacher training for pre-primary, basic education and upper secondary education is organised in universities, and the training lasts approximately five years. Not only do Finnish student teachers, during the course of their education, gain competences that are critical to their future profession, they are also inculcated with a critical and reflective approach, and an ethical commitment to their work. According to Niemi and Jakku-Sihvonen (2011), student teachers have good skills in planning and in using various teaching methods, and they are aware of related responsibilities and teaching philosophies. In addition, in-service teachers are educated at universities in many ways. For example, additional and continuing education may concentrate on various themes, such as behavioural management, that vary in length. In addition, there is a strong research collaboration between schools and universities, and in-service teachers participate in various projects receiving continuing education (e.g. CICO Plus intervention; Karhu et al., 2020).

Teaching is a highly valued profession in Finland, even among its young people, and Finnish teachers are particularly respected and trusted by the society. Approximately one-quarter of applicants are granted the right to study. The five-year program of education leads, first, to a three-year Bachelor of Arts degree

(Education, 180 ECTS), and then to a two-year Master of Arts degree (Education, 120 ECTS); the whole degree is needed in order to have a permanent teaching position. Based on their degree emphasis, graduates are qualified to work in a variety of teaching roles, such as general class teachers, special education teachers, special education class teachers or subject teachers at basic education or secondary schools in Finland. (Subject teachers are required to have a master's degree in the subject they are teaching and to have completed a one-year programme of pedagogical studies.) Student teachers who are graduating develop extensive knowledge of education and teaching, as well as knowledge of special education and inclusive education. Content that addresses behavioural management for RTI model support are included in all teacher education programs, especially in special education teacher training. During the Teachers Pedagogical Studies, which last one to two years and to which all student teachers are entitled, contents addressing the themes of inclusive education, behavioural management and support are included. Student teachers are also introduced to and conduct research, specifically in the educational field, and they also participate in four teaching practices.

Research-based teaching and teacher education provide student teachers with the information and skills requisite for their future working lives. As an example of research-based teaching outcomes, student teachers are able to connect and integrate future work life skills and goals of comprehensive knowledge areas as part of teaching and supervising, as well as to plan integrative learning modules and to integrate local, societal and global phenomena into teaching and supervising. Also, they are able to facilitate the construction of a supportive environment for individual learning and well-being, as well as to evaluate and develop teaching and supervising based on research. Reflection and the development of one's own pedagogical expertise is also taught.

Finnish Teacher Training Schools provide practice for all student teachers during their studies. The teaching training programme that aims for a master's degree includes 22 ECTS of training for all student teachers. To work as a qualified teacher in Finland, everyone must first practise teaching with the guidance of professional teachers, who often have research-based backgrounds, i.e. doctoral degrees.

EXAMPLE

Teaching practices are implemented in university teacher training schools or other schools nominated for that purpose. Guided teaching practices – which are arranged during teacher education bachelor's and master's degrees – involve the giving of lessons, guidance discussions and familiarisation with tasks and responsibilities related to various issues arising in the everyday life in schools. The aim is for the student teachers to become independent and responsible, and to learn self-development, to become increasingly proficient

> in their own subject and to learn how to develop the work community in cooperation with other members of the teaching staff.
>
> The university sets certain goals for the training period. The role of the teacher supervising the teaching practice is to guide the trainee to achieve these goals in the school context. One of the key topics in the internships is supporting pupil behaviour, and in their university courses, student teachers are introduced to a variety of theoretical perspectives for achieving this support. In teaching practice, the student teacher becomes acquainted with and practises the application of various guidance methods that support pupils' behaviour. Moreover, the mentor teacher instructs the trainees in a mentoring process characterised by an ongoing developmental discussion on the provision of this support.

The collaboration between teacher training schools and the university is strong. The core idea is that trainees are given the opportunity to directly participate in research during the internship alongside their teaching work. During teaching training, for example, the trainee can participate in identifying the strengths of a pupil's behaviour through teacher questionnaires. In this way, the teaching trainee receives practical experience in how research can serve to support pupil behaviour. In addition, the teacher's practical expertise is highly valued in university training. For example, teachers from the field are regularly invited as experts to university courses related to behavioural management. Moreover, experts from the university often participate in different schools' in-service teacher training covering different topics, such as a strength-based approach, teaching and learning approaches and various ways to support behavioural management.

> **EXAMPLE**
>
> In addition to teacher training, research-based projects and interventions in between university and teacher training schools are an essential and natural part of collaboration. One example of this type of collaboration and schools' development work in which the student teachers participate is the TUVET/KTVA//#Bestschool project, which is funded by the Finnish National Agency for Education 2019–2020. In this project, one special education student teacher conducted educational design research in order to develop a mapping for multi-professional collaboration in school. Another special education student teacher conducted a study to investigate the perceptions of school staff

> about a pupil's well-being, psychiatric nurse work at the school and pupil support in school. Among these, one student teacher is finishing her master's thesis and concentrating on parents' and pupils' experiences with regard to well-being issues. Moreover, the project included a longitudinal (i.e. one-year-long), multi-informant (pupil, teacher, caregiver) research design investigating, for example, behavioural and emotional strengths and challenges of pupils, pupils' self-regulation and home-school collaboration. Student teachers' research projects are also conducted by means of these data. The aim of collaboration is to improve and develop teacher training schools' practices through research and collaboration, as well as to present the most recent research results for teachers, pupils and caregivers. In addition, researchers from the project have trained teachers and developed approaches for behavioural management in collaboration with the teacher.

Pedagogy and pedagogical support

Behavioural problems of pupils and classroom disruptions are a significant challenge for schools and educators. In Finnish schools, 1.1% of pupils received special support for behavioural problems (Official Statistics of Finland, 2011). However, it has been estimated that around 10–15% of pupils are at risk and require support for behavioural challenges (cf. Jahnukainen & Itkonen, 2016). Moreover, large-scale studies have identified that around 20% of pupils had been or are at risk for behavioural problems (e.g. Merikangas et al., 2010).

Pedagogy and support for behavioural management are constructed on a school-level curriculum steered by FNBE and the professional competences of teachers. The organisation of instruction and support is based on the strengths as well as the learning and development needs of each pupil and teaching group. Attention should be paid to the accessibility of learning and the prevention and early recognition of behavioural problems (FNBE, 2016). Recent knowledge of psycho-educational sciences highly emphasises the importance of viewing behavioural and cognitive processes as complementary – not separate – factors in learning and teaching (e.g. Liew, 2012; Sointu et al., 2017a).

School-wide behaviour methods have been implemented in the Finnish school context in order to prevent problem behaviour and create more positive support for pupils. One widely used, evidence-based, school-wide program is the KiVaSchool antibullying program. With an effectiveness that has been scientifically proven, KiVa offers a wide range of concrete tools and materials for schools to tackle bullying, emotion regulation and behavioural management (Garandeau et al., 2016). Some Finnish schools have implemented school-wide positive behaviour support (SWPBS) systems such as ProKoulu. The SWPBIS system is widely known internationally for providing positive behavioural management at multiple school levels (Horner et al., 2010). In Finnish schools, however, building SWPBS interventions and carrying out concomitant research on them is still needed (Karhu et al., 2020).

From the three-tiered support perspective, general support is the first response to a pupil's need for support. This usually means individual pedagogical solutions, guidance and support measures that seek to improve the situation at an early stage, as a part of daily school life (FNBE, 2016). General support requires the involvement of not only special teachers but of all teachers in order to take responsibility for pupils' behavioural management.

> **EXAMPLE**
>
> Special educators, classroom teachers or subject teachers and school assistants work closely together in Finnish schools. The classroom or subject teacher seeks to support the pupil's schooling first in the general group, providing them general support (tier 1). Support for the pupil's behaviour is always constructed according to the needs of the pupil and a written pedagogical assessment. There are different ways of supporting pupil behaviour in tier 1, such as educational discussions with the pupil, discussions with caregivers or modifying the learning environment (e.g. changing the pupil's seating, using hearing protection) and providing additional teaching support and co-teaching. Moreover, pupil support can take the form of a multi-informant behavioural assessment. For example, Rantakylä School is currently testing ways to use electronic assessment platforms in which all adults who teach and guide pupils can assess pupil behaviour.

A pupil who needs regular support, school attendance support or several support forms simultaneously should be provided with intensified support (tier 2) as the basis of a pedagogical assessment, in accordance with a learning plan devised specifically for the pupil (FNBE, 2016). The learning plan usually includes, first, the pupil's individual goals – e.g. the pupil's strengths associated with their behaviour. Second, it addresses pedagogical solutions related to the support provided for the pupil. The use of evidence-based interventions offers schools the possibility of developing their own inclusive education strategies (Guckert et al., 2016). Also, in Finland, there are promising results for using evidence-based interventions for pupils at risk of severe problem behaviours (Karhu et al., 2018, 2019). Check-in, check-out (CICO) support is one of the most studied interventions for pupils with mild problem behaviour (Hawken et al., 2014; Maggin et al., 2015), and its cultural adaptation has also been used and studied in the Finnish schooling system (Karhu et al., 2019) to support pupils' prosocial behaviour. Third, a learning plan includes collaboration and services – e.g. support provided by the multi-professional pupil welfare group. Finally, the ways of monitoring and assessing behaviour, as well as the evaluation of the support provided, are also included.

> **EXAMPLE**
>
> For tier 2 support, the teacher expresses their concerns to the school's pupil welfare group, in addition to the pupil and the caregiver(s), about the need for additional support. Pupil welfare groups are cross-sectoral, which means that in addition to teaching staff, the group includes representatives of school health care as well as psychologist and social worker services. The multi-professional pupil welfare team discusses the situation and makes the collective decision whether to transfer the pupil to intensified support. If intensified support is launched, a pedagogical assessment and individual learning plan are made for the pupil, with the involvement of teachers (classroom or subject teacher and special education teacher), caregiver(s) and pupil. The pupil's goals and strengths can be guided by formal assessment tools. Moreover, pedagogical solutions, such as the form of teaching and learning/support activities, are listed in the document. A learning plan for pupil behaviour can include support from a school assistant, remedial teaching and part-time special needs education, while also detailing how behaviour is to be monitored and assessed.

If intensified support is inadequate, the pupil may be transferred to special support (tier 3). The transfer requires a more extensive pedagogical statement made in collaboration with teachers and pupils' caregiver(s), and it often takes place on the basis of a discussion with the pupil welfare group. Individual educational plans should be drawn up for the pupils in special support, to include different types of pedagogical strategies and assessment of the learning environment, pupil welfare group support or other arrangements in order to provide support for the pupil.

> **EXAMPLE**
>
> In special support (tier 3) for pupil behaviour, similar means as in intensified support can be used. In addition, especially in special classes or special schools' interventions, aggression replacement training, or ART (Goldstein *et al.*, 1998), is commonly used. ART is a 10-week, 30-hour intervention administered to groups, consisting of social skills training and teaching pro-social behaviour to pupils who lack these competencies (Brännström *et al.*, 2016). For example, some teachers in Rantakylä School are trained ART facilitators and periodically use ART in their pedagogy and support methodologies. According to earlier international studies, ART seems to be a successful program; however, the effectiveness of ART in the Finnish context has not yet been studied.

One approach that has garnered significant attention in Finnish schools during the last decade is the so-called strength-based approach particularly from the behavioural and emotional strength-based perspective. Strength-based assessment has been defined as:

> The measurement of those emotional and behavio[u]ral skills, competencies, and characteristics that create a sense of personal accomplishment; contribute to satisfying relationships with family members, peers, and adults; enhance one's ability to deal with adversity and stress; and promote one's personal, social, and academic development.
>
> (Epstein, 2004, p. 4)

Strength-based research, as well as the strength-based approach, recognise that all pupils, even the most challenged ones and their families, have strengths, resources and competencies, and that their support can be built upon (Epstein, 2004). The strength-based approach has not only garnered attention in research and practice, but it has also received the attention of the National Core Curriculum (FNBE, 2016) and the Finnish National Current Care Guidelines for behavioural problems (Finnish Medical Society Duodecim, 2018), who highlight the importance of supporting pupils and their families' strengths.

In schools, strengths can be assessed in an informal or formal way. Teachers have always highlighted pupils and their families' strengths from the informal perspective. However, there are challenges in this type of assessment (e.g. reliability, fairness for all, multi-informant perspective). Moreover, a significant challenge is that in the official support documents (e.g. learning plans, individual education plans), the strength-based perspective is still vaguely reported (Heiskanen et al., 2019). Still, we want to remind the reader that recognising a pupil's strength informally is an important part of strength-based support.

Perhaps one of the most studied formal strength-based assessment tools in the Finnish context is the Behavioural and Emotional Rating Scale (BERS-2; Epstein, 2004), which is also translated into Finnish as KTVA (Sointu et al., 2018). BERS-2 recognises that measures of a pupil's strength derive from a multi-informant (teacher, pupil, caregiver) perspective, meaning that the wording of a statement is positioned relative to the informant's point of view. Teacher and caregiver assessment can be used from the first grade until upper secondary education, while pupil assessment is recommended for those in the fourth grade (i.e. 10 years of age) to upper secondary education (i.e. 18 years of age). BERS-2 can be used:

- To formally assess pupils' individual strengths for education and support
- To support strengths of pupils with support needs and behavioural problems
- To target goals for individual education plans of pupils and to document their strengths
- In caregiver, school and pupil collaboration

- In schools' multi-professional team collaboration
- In the work of other educational professionals (e.g. psychologists, curators)
- To support general skills and transversal competences of pupils for their learning and working in the future
- In the development and assessment of schools and municipality work and various programs (e.g. curriculum)
- In research

More information on BERS-2 is provided in the empirical part of this chapter's measures section.

EXAMPLE

Encouraging pupils with his or her strengths creates a positive dimension to all interactions with the pupil. This especially benefits the pupils who have challenges in behavioural management. Identifying the pupils' own strengths requires long-term practice and guidance, so that the pupil becomes aware of and internalises their own strengths. This also requires learning and ongoing practices from the teachers. The most effective way to identify pupils' strengths is when it is done systematically on a weekly basis and throughout the school year, possibly over several years. The pupil benefits the most if very concrete methods can be applied to support the identification of strengths. The identification of the pupil's own strengths is also supported by the participation of the pupil, their caregivers and the entire school community. Such identification is beneficial and effective when the protocol for supporting strengths is held in common and understood by all.

Teachers can support pupils' identification of strengths informally every day by using the strength-based approach to teaching. Lessons can be held with pupils to discuss their strengths and to identify their own or a classmate's strengths. From the identified strengths of the pupil, a concrete 'tree of strengths' can be built. In this way, a concrete reminder of one's own strengths is built for the pupil. Educators can guide pupils to identify their own strengths in different disciplines and, more broadly, in different areas of their lives. The support used to identify strengths and the strengths identified with the pupils can be reported in the pupil's learning plan or in the individual education plan. This is very important, so that all teachers who instruct the pupil during their basic education at school discover the pupil's individual strengths and can, in turn, use these strengths to support them. Moreover, in the Rantakylä School, BERS-2 has been used regularly during the 2019–2020 school year as a formal assessment tool for identifying pupils' strengths. This work has included pupils, teachers, student teachers, school assistants and caregivers.

Example of research on behavioural management

To investigate behavioural aspects and strength-based assessment, research was conducted with Finnish teachers, the main purpose of which was to investigate teacher-assessed behavioural challenges and strengths of pupils. Previous research has demonstrated that teachers are good informants for behavioural problems (e.g. Salbach-Andrae et al., 2009). However, there are many challenges to using assessment instruments of possible behavioural problems, such as the length of the assessment instrument (Sointu et al., 2017b). Thus, we used a short, 10-item screener for behavioural problems. Moreover, the sole use of problem-based assessments has faced extensive criticism (e.g. Sointu, 2014). Therefore, along with the Finnish education and support system ideology presented in this chapter, we used strength-based assessment approach in the study. The two research questions were:

- First, what is the reliability of a short, 10-item measure of Scales for Assessing Emotional Disturbance (SAED) screener (Epstein et al., 2020) for screening purposes of behavioural problems, and the strength-based measure (i.e. BERS-2) with a random sample of Finnish teachers?
- Second, are there differences between pupils' strengths identified as at risk for behavioural problems with the SAED screener and those not identified with a random sample of Finnish teachers?

We hypothesised that both measures possess adequate reliability, and that all pupils have strengths, but strengths may differ between those at risk and not at risk for behavioural problems. Our underlying assumption is that the strengths can be used in building up pedagogical support for the pupils and for behavioural management in schools. In total, 43 teachers assessed a random sample of 298 pupils from two Finnish basic education schools, from a region called Eastern Finland. Pupils were in grades 1 to 9 and between 6 and 15 years of age. The sample included 145 female and 150 male pupils. For three pupils, teachers did not want to identify pupil gender. From the pedagogical support perspective, 79.2% were identified as receiving universal support (tier 1), 12.8% as receiving intensified support (tier 2) and 8.1% as receiving special support (tier 3).

Data were collected as part of a KTVA/#Bestschool project in autumn 2019. An information letter and video describing the purpose of the project and what it required from the pupils was sent to all caregivers and teachers. Moreover, teachers were informed in teacher meetings at the schools. Participation for the teachers was voluntary, and caregivers had the opportunity to deny their child's inclusion in the study. Research followed Finnish National Board on Research Integrity (TENK, 2009) guidelines.

Data were collected with the Finnish versions of the BERS-2 (i.e. KTVA; Sointu et al., 2018) and the SAED screener (Epstein et al., 2020). BERS-2 is a multi-informant, strength-based assessment instrument for pupils' behavioural and emotional strengths. More particularly, pupils' strengths can be assessed from multi-informant perspectives (Sointu et al., 2014). In this study, we used the teacher perspective. The BERS-2 includes five subscales:

- Interpersonal Strengths (IS; e.g. 'listens to others')
- Family Involvement (FI; e.g. 'maintains positive family relationships')
- Intrapersonal Strengths (IaS; e.g. 'is self-confident')
- School Functioning (SF; e.g. 'pays attention in class') and
- Affective Strengths (AS; e.g. 'expresses affection for others').

These subscales can be combined to form the overall Strength Index (SI) score, which illustrates the emotional and behavioural strengths of pupils (Sointu et al., 2018). Teachers rate the pupil with a Likert-type scale (3 = if the statement is very much like the pupil; 2 = if the statement is like the pupil; 1 = if the statement is not much like the pupil; and 0 = if the statement is not at all like the pupil).

The SAED screener (Epstein et al., 2020) is a short, 10-item teacher rating scale developed to screen pupils at risk for behaviour problems. With the four-point Likert-type scale (0 = *not a problem*; 1 = *mild problem*; 2 = *considerable problem*; 3 = *severe problem*), teachers can assess pupil behaviour (e.g. 'fails to consider the consequences of own acts'; 'lacks skills needed to be friendly and sociable'). The 10 items of the SAED screener are summed for a total score (range = 1 to 30). Data were analysed with Cronbach's alpha (α) for reliability ($\alpha > 0.7$ for adequate reliability) and independent sample t-tests with bootstrap option to compare possible differences between pupils at risk and not at risk. Cohen (1988) d effect sizes serve to investigate the effect size of difference between two groups.

The results are presented in Table 9.1. Based on the results, all pupils, including those at risk for behavioural problems, had some strengths. However, when

TABLE 9.1 Reliability of BESR-2 and SAED screener, differences between at-risk and not-at-risk groups

	Whole sample (N = 298)	At risk (N = 62)		Not at risk (N = 236)		Bootstrapped t-tests			
	α	M	(SD)	M	(SD)	M difference	SE	p	d
IS	0.97	1.55	(0.52)	2.55	(0.44)	−1.00	0.07	0.00	2.19
FI	0.89	1.89	(0.50)	2.44	(0.43)	−0.55	0.06	0.00	1.24
IaS	0.92	1.71	(0.52)	2.47	(0.45)	−0.76	0.07	0.00	1.63
SF	0.93	1.49	(0.70)	2.40	(0.57)	−0.91	0.09	0.00	1.52
AS	0.90	1.59	(0.58)	2.38	(0.49)	−0.79	0.07	0.00	1.55
SI score	0.98	1.64	(0.44)	2.46	(0.40)	−0.82	0.06	0.00	2.01
SAED	0.88	10.08	(3.57)	1.33	(1.61)				

Note: IS = Interpersonal Strengths; FI = Family Involvement; IaS = Intrapersonal Strengths; SF = School Functioning; AS = Affective; SI score = Strengths Index Score; SAED = SAED screener score for behavioural problems; M = Mean; SD = Standard Deviation; t = t-test t value; p = significance; d = Cohen's d. Bootstrapping (1,000 samples) was used in t-tests.

the results were compared between at-risk and not-at-risk groups for behavioural problems, significant differences were found in all strength areas. The difference was biggest in Interpersonal and Strength Index score. The smallest difference was in Family Involvement. Cronbach's α indicate adequate reliability for all subscales.

While all pupils seem to have strengths, teachers in this random sample assessed the strengths significantly lower for the at-risk pupils than for those not at risk for behavioural problems. Strength-based assessment can be used to establish the foundation for various support purposes and for pedagogical documents. However, the notion that the difference between at-risk and not-at-risk pupils is of great magnitude should also be considered for pedagogical support purposes. Supporting the strengths of pupils at risk for behavioural problems requires continuous work, teacher training (including student and in-service teachers), teachers' competences and a sense of school community that seeks to support all of its pupils.

Clear implications can be built on the results of this study's data. Teachers can use the strength-based assessment for all pupils in general, and for pupils at risk for behavioural problems in particular. This type of data can be used to develop appropriate learning plans and individual education plans for support. As the strength-based approach aims to improve the personal knowledge of pupils, formal assessment can make this visible, and the aims of support for pupils can be strengthened via formal, strengths-based assessment methods. Moreover, strengths are highly useful for considering general competencies for learning, such as transversal competences (TC) in Finnish education. With the strength-based approach, teachers and schools can implement positive home-school collaboration and build more a positive atmosphere for the entire school community. Finally, the strength-based assessment approach has the unique potential to change the problems, pathologies and deficits of speech, or at least to put the strengths of speech on the same level as the problems in speech communicated to pupils, caregivers and among teachers.

Conclusions and critical viewpoint

The purpose of this chapter was to introduce the Finnish educational system and behavioural management from multiple perspectives. In addition, a research component was included. From the pedagogy and pedagogical support perspectives, we understand the complexity of support for pupils with behavioural problems. It is highly interconnected with learning or cognitive domains in education, and supporting behavioural problems also requires supporting learning. In seeking to provide pupils the support they need, preventative and early recognition efforts of behavioural problems are considered to be particularly effective. Behavioural management does not solely concern behaviour: it also involves learning, early screening and support.

The fact is that behavioural problems and classroom disruptions are significant challenges for schools and teachers. However, it must be noted that they are challenges also for the pupils themselves and for their caregivers. Supporting the positive development of pupils by employing strength-based approaches is essential to highlighting the positive aspects of pupils' lives. Strength-based approaches, as well as positive and strength-based practices, are ways to offer more holistic support for pupils. Unfortunately, the systematic use of evidence-based intervention programs for supporting behavioural problems is still quite minor (Guckert et al., 2016), and more research, particularly research-practice collaboration, is required. This is applicable to all levels of pedagogical support in the Finnish three-tiered support system.

In order to learn efficient and evidence-based methods in teacher training, student teachers need practice to recognise and assess pupils' strengths during their degree studies. In this way, these future educators can notice the strengths in pupils, especially in pupils at risk. Äikäs et al. (2020) express that the pre-service special education teachers who participated in their study and teaching practices during the years 2018–2020 perceived the assessment of pupils' strengths and the conducting of strength-based teaching to be both meaningful and powerful. In addition, teaching practice was experienced as an important opportunity to implement research-based methods and to bring new educational approaches to the school. Silvennoinen et al. (2020) noted that 73.8% of the pre-service special education teachers participating in their study ($N = 42$) concentrating on the outcomes of teaching practice stated that it is essential for future educators to understand the importance of the strength-based approach to learning and schooling support. In addition, the strength-based approach should be widely recognised in teacher training so that the whole school community could commit to the approach in the future. Although school and university training is approaching the aim of developing inclusive education for all, more intensive prevention and support programs are also needed.

Teachers and student teachers require in-depth training for behavioural management in school. Although this training is highly implemented in the special education student teacher programme, classroom teachers and subject teachers require it as well, particularly as one school serves all, and as inclusion is more and more present in Finnish schools. Additionally, in-service teachers' training often provides short-term exposure to the new perspective of behavioural management. Thus, innovative approaches for supporting in-service teachers are required. For example, university-driven learning management systems (LMS) that provide training via video tutorials, discussion platforms and distance training or face-to-face meetings could provide novel methods of training in behavioural management. Such considerations should also be considered and recognised from the employee's perspective when allocating time and resources in this regard. This is particularly important, as the understanding of new learning environments, approaches for learning and teaching and guiding documents for teaching (e.g. national core curriculums) are introduced for teachers. From a critical point of view, the possibility of learning the aforementioned aspects are not always clearly considered through the eyes of teaching practice. Thus, implementation may require a significant investment of time and effort for teachers, particularly considering the multiple aspects of behavioural management. Still, this is highly possible, as Finland, for example, has a good working collaboration between schools and universities.

In this chapter, we have introduced one Finnish school as an example. This university teacher training school is new and has been considered to be one of the most novel ways to arrange basic education nationally and internationally. Nevertheless, many schools follow more traditional learning environments and pedagogical approaches. However, there are also ways in which the mindset of people working in the schools has begun to change. For instance, the latest Finnish legislation and national core curriculum have set the foundation for one school for all and inclusiveness, and also for the new views for behavioural management in schools. The change of behavioural management from multiple perspectives also requires pedagogical leadership.

However, it is a fact that there are still 73 special education schools in Finland, with approximately 4,400 pupils (Official Statistics of Finland, 2018c). Moreover, there are also plenty of special classrooms within basic education schools. Some teachers find it challenging to support pupils with behavioural problems and rather propose pupils be transferred into a special education teacher's group for him/her to receive stronger support for his/her emotional and behavioural skills. Even though the official aim of special support is to help pupils to be able to participate in the general classroom with their peers, it is still common that pupils transferred to special education groups stay there throughout their basic education. Neither the teacher nor the pupil should be left alone with behavioural problems, but supporting the skills that are needed must be a shared concern of the whole-school community.

The structure of special education in Finland has changed during the past few years; however, this work also requires good examples from the new schools that have successfully implemented a one-school-for-all approach. In this case, Rantakylä School organises grades into two yearly cohort cells, utilises co-teaching, includes support from teaching assistants and offers a calmer location within the cell for pupils with special needs. The underlying ideology of Finnish three-tiered systems is that support can be provided early on a needs basis. However, the other side of the support milieu includes the idea that pupil support can be reduced and that pupils can return to mainstream education is of utmost important. With the practicalities of Rantakylä School, this is possible.

Behavioural management requires a continuous raising of pupils, considering the skills, competences and characteristics – particularly the strengths – of pupils, keeping the individuality of each pupil in mind. Moreover, it requires considering national and local curriculums, classroom practices, colleagues and specifically teacher professionalism. Behavioural management in schools is not the easiest task, but considering the message of this chapter and its multiple perspectives, as well as the high-quality information provided in this book, we are certain that it is very doable for all current educational professionals and for all teachers in the future.

References

Äikäs, A., Vellonen, V., Lappalainen, K., Atjonen, P. & Holopainen, L. (2020). Oppilaslähtöisen arvioinnin ja tuen edistäminen erityisopettajien opetusharjoittelussa [Promoting student-centred assessment and support in special education pre-service teachers' teaching practice]. In M. Takala, S. Lakkala, and A. Äikäs, *Mahdoton inkluusio? Tunnista haasteet ja mahdollisuudet* [*Impossible Inclusion? Recognise Challenges and Opportunities*] (pp. 109–138). Keuruu, Finland: PS-Kustannus.

Brännström, L., Kaunitz, C., Andershed, A. K., South, S., and Smedslund, G. (2016). Aggression replacement training (ART) for reducing antisocial behavior in adolescents and adults: A systematic review. *Aggression and Violent Behavior*, **27**, pp. 30–41.

Cohen, J. (1988). *Statistical Power Analysis for the Behavioral Sciences* (2nd ed.). Hillsdale, NJ: Erlbaum.

Epstein, M. H. (2004). *Behavioral and Emotional Rating Scale: A Strength-Based Approach to Assessment* (2nd ed.). Austin, TX: PRO-Ed.

Epstein, M. H., Cullinan, D., Pierce, C., Huscroft-D'Angelo, J., and Wery, J. (2020). *Scales for Assessing Emotional Disturbance* (3rd ed.). Austin, TX: PRO-Ed.

Finnish Medical Society Duodecim. (2018). *Behavioral Problems (Children and Youth): National Current Care Guidelines, Formed by the Finnish Medical Society Duodecim*. Finnish Child Psychiatry Association, Finnish Youth Psychiatry Association and Finnish Psychiatry Association Neuropsychiatry Division. www.kaypahoito.fi

Finnish National Board of Education [FNBE]. (2016). *National Core Curriculum for Basic Education*. Helsinki, Finland: FNBE.

Fuchs, D., and Fuchs, L.S. (2006). Introduction to response to intervention: What, why, and how valid is it? *Reading Research Quarterly*, **41**(1), pp. 93–99.

Garandeau, C. F., Vartio, A., Poskiparta, E., and Salmivalli, C. (2016). School bullies' intention to change behavior following teacher interventions: Effects of empathy arousal, condemning of bullying, and blaming of the perpetrator. *Prevention Science*, **17**(8), pp. 1034–1043.

Goldstein, A. P., Glick, B., and Gibbs, J. C. (1998). *Aggression Replacement Training: A Comprehensive Intervention for Aggressive Youth*. Champaign, IL: Rev. Research Press.

Grosche, M., and Volpe, R. J. (2013). Response-to-intervention (RTI) as a model to facilitate inclusion for students with learning and behavior problems. *European Journal of Special Needs Education*, **28**(3), pp. 254–269.

Guckert, M., Mastropieri, M., and Scruggs, T. (2016). Personalizing research: Special educators' awareness of evidence-based practice. *Exceptionality*, **24**(2), pp. 63–78.

Hawken, L. S., Bundock, K., Kladis, K., O'Keeffe, B., and Barrett, C. A. (2014). Systematic review of the check-in, check-out intervention for students at risk for emotional and behavioural disorders. *Education and Treatment of Children*, **37**(4), pp. 635–658.

Heiskanen, N., Saxlund, T., Rantala, A., and Vehkakoski, T. (2019). Lapsen vahvuudet esiopetusvuoden pedagogisissa asiakirjoissa [Child strengths in pedagogical documents]. *Oppimisen ja oppimisvaikeuksien erityislehti: NMI-bulletin*, **29**(1), pp. 26–42.

Hienonen, N., Hotulainen, R., and Jahnukainen, M. (2021). Outcomes of regular and special class placement for students with special educational needs – A quasi-experimental study. *Scandinavian Journal of Educational Research*, **65**(4), pp. 646–660. Advance online publication. doi:10.1080/00313831.2020.1739134

Horner, R. H., Sugai, G., and Anderson, C. M. (2010). Examining the evidence base for school-wide positive behavior support. *Focus on Exceptional Children*, **42**(8), pp. 1–14.

Jahnukainen, M., and Itkonen, T. (2016). Tiered intervention: History and trends in Finland and the United States. *European Journal of Special Needs Education*, **31**(1), pp. 140–150.

Karhu, A., Närhi, V., and Savolainen, H. (2018). Inclusion of pupils with ADHD symptoms in mainstream classes with PBS. *International Journal of Inclusive Education*, **22**(5), pp. 475–489.

Karhu, A., Närhi, V., and Savolainen, H. (2019). Check in-check out intervention for supporting pupils' behaviour: Effectiveness and feasibility in Finnish schools. *European Journal of Special Needs Education*, **34**(1), pp. 136–146.

Karhu, A., Paananen, M., Närhi, V., and Savolainen, H. (2020). Implementation of the inclusive CICO Plus intervention for pupils at risk of severe behaviour problems in SWPBS schools. *European Journal of Special Needs Education*. Advance online publication. doi:10.1080/08856257.2020.1809801

Kariippanon, K., Cliff, P., Lancaster, S., Okely, A., and Parrish, A.-M. (2017). Perceived interplay between flexible learning spaces and teaching, learning and student wellbeing. *Learning Environments Research*, **21**, pp. 301–320.

Kattilakoski, R. (2018). *Koulun toimintakulttuuri avautuvissa oppimistiloissa. Etnografinen tutkimus uuteen koulurakennukseen muuttamisesta* [A school's operating culture in open learning spaces – An ethnographic study on moving to a new school building] [*Academic dissertation, Jyväskylä Studies in Education, Psychology and Social Research 616*].

Liew, J. (2012). Effortful control, executive functions, and education: Bringing self-regulatory and social-emotional competencies to the table. *Child Development Perspectives*, **6**(2), pp. 105–111.

Maggin, D., Zurheide, J., Pickett, K., and Baillie, S. (2015). A systematic evidence review of the check-in/check-out program for reducing student challenging behaviours. *Journal of Positive Behaviour Interventions*, **17**(4), pp. 197–208.

Manninen, J., Burman, A., Koivunen, A., Kuittinen, E., Luukannel, S., Passi, S., and Särkkä, H. (2007). *Oppimista tukevat ympäristöt. Johdatus oppimisympäristöajatteluun [Environments that Support Learning: An Introduction to the Learning Environments Approach]*. Vammala, Finland: Finnish National Agency for Education.

Merikangas, K., He, J., Brody, D., Fisher, P., Bourdon, K., and Koretz, D. (2010). Prevalence and treatment of mental disorders among U.S. children in the 2001–2004 NHANES. *Pediatrics*, **125**(1), pp. 75–81.

Niemi, H., and Jakku-Sihvonen, R. (2011). Teacher education in Finland. In M. Valenþiþ Zuljan & J. Vogrinc (Eds.) *European Dimensions of Teacher Education: Similarities and Differences* (pp. 33–51). Ljubljana, Slovenia: Modern Language Association.

OECD. (2019). *PISA 2018 Results (Volume I): What Students Know and Can Do*. Paris, France: OECD Publishing.

Official Statistics of Finland. (2011). *Special Education, School Year 2009–2010*.

Official Statistics of Finland. (2018a). *Entrance to Education*. Statistics Finland. http://www.stat.fi/til/erop/2010/erop_2010_2011-06-09_tie_001_fi.html.

Official Statistics of Finland. (2018b). *Special Education*. Statistics Finland. http://www.stat.fi/til/erop/2018/erop_2018_2019-06-19_tie_001_en.html.

Official Statistics of Finland. (2018c). *Providers of Education and Educational Institutions*. Statistics Finland. http://www.stat.fi/til/kjarj/2017/kjarj_2017_2018-02-13_tie_001_en.html.

Pulkkinen, J., Räikkönen, E., Pirttimaa, R., and Jahnukainen, M. (2019). Principals' views on changes in the provision of support for learning and schooling in Finland after educational reform. *Journal of Educational Change*, **20**(1), pp. 137–163.

Salbach-Andrae, H., Lenz, K., and Lehmkuhl, U. (2009). Patterns of agreement among parent, teacher and youth ratings in a referred sample. *European Psychiatry*, **24**(5), pp. 345–351.

Salvia, J., Ysseldyke, J., and Bolt, S. (2013). *Assessment in special and inclusive education: International edition* (12th ed.). Belmont, CA: Wadsworth.

Silvennoinen, T., Äikäs, A., and Sointu E. (2020). Opetusharjoittelu erityisopettajaksi kasvun tukena [Teaching practice as a support for professional development as a teacher]. In O-P. Salo (Ed.) *Teoriaa ja työkaluja ohjatun harjoittelun kehittämiseen [Theory and Tools for Developing Guided Teaching Practice]* (pp. 111–123). Vassa, Finland: eNorssi Network.

Sointu, E. (2014). *Multi-Informant Assessment of Behavioral and Emotional Strengths* [Unpublished Doctoral Dissertation]. University of Eastern Finland. https://www.researchgate.net/publication/262672455_Multi-Informant_Assessment_of_Behavioral_and_Emotional_Strengths.

Sointu, E., Savolainen, H., Lambert, M., Lappalainen, K. and Epstein, M. (2014). Behavioral and emotional strength-based assessment of Finnish elementary students: Psychometrics of the BERS-2. *European Journal of Psychology of Education*, **29**(1), pp. 1–19.

Sointu, E., Savolainen, H., Lappalainen, K. and Lambert, M. (2017a). Longitudinal associations of student–teacher relationships and behavioral and emotional strengths on academic achievement. *Educational Psychology*, **37**(4), pp. 457–467.

Sointu, E., Lambert, M. Nordness, P., Geležinienė, R. and Epstein, M. (2017b). An initial study of the diagnostic utility of the emotional and behavioural screener in Lithuania. *European Journal of Special Needs Education*, **33**(1), pp. 73–85.

Sointu, E., Savolainen, H., Lappalainen, K., Kuorelahti, M., Hotulainen, R., Närhi, V., … Epstein, M. H. (2018). *Käyttäytymisen ja tunteiden vahvuuksien arviointiväline [Behavioral and Emotional Strength-Based Assessment Tool]*. PS-kustannus.

TENK. (2009). *Ethical Principles of Research in the Humanities and Social and Behavioural Sciences: Finnish National Board on Research Integrity (TENK) guidelines 2009*. https://tenk.fi/sites/tenk.fi/files/ethicalprinciples.pdf.

Thuneberg, H., Hautamäki, J., Ahtiainen, R., Lintuvuori, M., Vainikainen, M.-P., and Hilasvuori, T. (2014). Conceptual change in adopting the nationwide special education strategy in Finland. *Journal of Educational Change*, **15**, pp. 37–56.

Vetoniemi, J. and Kärnä, E. (2019). Being included: Experiences of social participation of pupils with special education needs in mainstream schools. *International Journal of Inclusive Education*. Advance online publication. doi:10.1080/13603116.2019.1603329.

Välijärvi, J., Linnakylä, P., Kupari, P., Reinikainen, P., and Arffman, I. (2002). *The Finnish Success in PISA—and Some Reasons behind It*. Jyväskylä, Finland: University of Jyväskylä.

Woodman, K. (2015). Re-placing flexibility: Flexibility in learning spaces and learning. In K. Fisher (Ed.), *The Translational Design of Schools: An Evidence-Based Approach to Aligning Pedagogy and Learning Environments* (pp. 51–79). Brill | Sense Publishers.

BEYOND STRATEGIES TO EMBEDDED ETHOS

Conclusion

The chapters in Part III began to think about the wider perspectives on working with children and how to support them in developing their own skills and managing their own behaviours. The section began by introducing the idea of using philosophy to develop children's understanding of the world and themselves. In Chapter 7, Aimee shared how working in this way with children impacted on their relationships with each other, as well as on their behaviour. She set out ideas in her chapter for using philosophical inquiry with children, and illustrated these examples with case studies from her own teaching experiences. Aimee also considered research in this area which demonstrated the wider benefits of philosophy on a range of children's academic, social and personal skills.

John introduced us in Chapter 8 to his concept of 'eternal verities', which he argued were truths that should underpin our practice with children whose behaviours challenge, but it could be suggested should also form the backbone of all of our work with children. His chapter drew together a range of themes that were discussed in previous chapters.

THINKING STOP 1

- Have you read anything in either of these chapters that has surprised you?
- Have you learnt anything new?
- Have you read anything that has made you reflect on the way in which you work with children in the classroom?
- Will anything change for you as a result of reading these chapters?

FIGURE C3.1 Sproson's (2004) 'behaviour suitcase'.

Returning to the idea of a 'behaviour suitcase' (Sproson, 2004), is there anything you have read in this section that you can add to your 'suitcase' of ideas to support children and their behaviour? If so, make a note of it in Figure C3.1. Review your previous 'suitcase':

- Is there a theme to the skills or ideas you are adding?
- What actions do you need to take to develop these further?

The final chapter in Part III considers not only a wider perspective, but an international one. Finland has a justifiably world-renowned record for its education system and can often be seen at the top of a number of international league tables. For example, they regularly score higher than the PISA averages, and 67% of Finnish students in the study stated that they had a growth mindset (OECD, 2018). Finnish education is also famed for having no standardised testing, performance management or external accountability for teachers and children begin school later than their UK counterparts (World Economic Forum, 2018). Teachers also enjoy greater autonomy over their curricula, have no external inspections, spend some of the least time across OECD countries teaching, as well as spend relatively little time on administration and extracurricular work (Paronen and Lappi, 2018).

I have been privileged enough to visit the Rantakylä School in Finland – featured in Chapter 9 – as part of a research project, and although the highlights in the previous paragraph give some idea of the differences between the Finnish and English systems, they do not highlight the cultural differences between the countries and their education systems that underpin these differences. In Chapter 9 some of these are discussed and shared which gives an indication of the contextual factors behind the 'headlines' of Finnish education that many of us are familiar with.

Over the years, English systems have imported some aspects of international practices that have been 'proven' to work, or to be effective in some way within those contexts. Simple examples are the concept of forest schools from Denmark and the 'mastery' approach in maths from Shanghai. However, without looking at the wider cultural contexts of these countries, the interventions in the English system are not always supported or embedded in the same way and, as a result, are sometimes not as 'effective' as in their original countries. In the Finnish culture, teaching is a very attractive career; all teacher trainees have master's qualifications, all levels of education are free and only 2% of the school system is privatised. As a result, this cannot be directly compared to the English system. However, Erkko, Katariina, Juuso, Aino and Kristiina raise a lot of interesting points that are transferable and relatable to the English context(s) in their fascinating chapter. They consider the holistic elements that shape the way behaviour is managed in schools and include discussions centred on:

- School culture
- School systems
- Teacher training and teachers
- Pedagogy and pedagogical support

THINKING STOP 2

Pause to consider the English equivalents for the areas the Finns outline:

- What would define these aspects from your own experience?
- What impact do you think these differences make?
- To staff?
- To children?

The chapter outlines some aspects which mark their school culture as particularly Finnish. These include a focus on equity and equality, with almost all children attending their local schools and very few independent or specialist schools. As a result, the education system has not been marketised in the way it has in England. With no formal exams for children (until the end of their education) and no external inspections, the Finnish schools do not experience the same issues as English schools in relation to parental choice and perceptions of 'good' or 'bad' schools linked to inspection results. This means schools in Finland have greater autonomy to trial strategies based on research without being concerned about a dip in result triggering an inspection, as many English schools are.

Another significant difference, although there are some parallels here with the English system, are the three levels of support available for all children. What marks this system as significantly different from the one operating in many English schools is the concept that this support is available to all pupils. Funding and provision in the current English system can mitigate against this philosophical position and mean that additional support is perceived not so much as a right for all children, but as an add-on. The multi-disciplinary teams that support children in Finnish schools are harder for many English schools to access and often require a significant paper trail – an issue which is not required to the same level in Finnish schools.

In England, the curriculum is mandated for all schools (although academies have some autonomy) from central government, whereas in Finland this is done regionally, which allows for greater personalisation and more context-relevant curricula for children. Social and behavioural skills also form a fundamental part of the Finnish curricula, where children are encouraged to develop a sense of belonging to a school community through forming positive relationships with staff and peers. This sense of belonging is also developed through negotiating rules and expectations in the classroom, a focus on being taught what positive behaviour and manners look like and the opportunity to shape what and how they learn. All children – including those receiving support at any level – are expected to be actively involved in shaping the life of the school and taking a role in making decisions which affect them and their education. Although some aspects of this formed the Personal, Social, Health and Citizenship Education (PSHCE) curriculum in England, it is now non-statutory and, like many non-core subjects, has been squeezed out of a lot of primary schools in favour of a focus on maths and English to meet external targets. This narrowing of the English curriculum is now so problematic that a new inspection framework has been drawn up by Ofsted to ensure that the full range of subjects are being taught in school (Ofsted, 2019), although there are some arguments that it is, in fact, the pressure of external results and their ability to trigger an Ofsted inspection that has led to the narrowing in the first place. Berliner (2011) argues that the focus on testing in England results in children not having the opportunity to learn the skills that are most useful:

> Curriculum narrowing reduces many students' chances of being thought talented in school and results in a restriction in the creative and enjoyable activities engaged in by teachers and students.
>
> (p. 287)

This is in sharp contrast to the autonomy described in Finnish schools. In Finland instead, 'transversal competencies' form outcomes for the taught curriculum and are viewed as 'important for one's growth as a citizen and as a part of society'. This is indicative of the wider aim for education in Finnish schools which is not seen in many English schools due, perhaps in part, to the culture of external metrics.

Collaboration appears to be a key driver in many of the aspects identified by Erkko and his colleagues – active collaboration with children, with other professionals and with other teachers. One example of this openness and collaboration is through the spaces in which learning happens. As suggested in the chapter, new Finnish schools are often designed to be open-plan, with flexible use of spaces encouraged. The photographs (Figures 9.1 and 9.2) show this, and from visiting the school described in this chapter, the open spaces in the school certainly appeared to encourage a different relationship between staff and children who seemed much more used to working together flexibly. This is significantly different from what has been described as the 'egg-box' (McGregor, 2003) culture of teaching in traditional (English) schools, where the teacher closes the door and is alone and isolated in the classroom with children. Much research highlights the importance of relationships to support well-being – for staff and pupils. Open-plan spaces (without the concern of inspections and so on) could be a significant way to develop positive relationships, supportively observe others' practice, magpie strategies and have a source of help and support for behaviours that challenge.

> ### THINKING STOP 3
>
> Open-plan schools have fallen out of favour in England, despite being prevalent during the 1960s and 1970s. Although now not common in schools, many foundation stage units and classrooms still run very well in this way. Pause and think for a moment:
>
> - What might be the advantages of working in this way?
> - What might need to change to draw on these advantages?
> - What could the disadvantages be of working this way?
> - How many of the disadvantages are linked to current English expectations?
>
> Refer back to Chapter 9:
>
> - What specific benefits to this way of working do they highlight?
> - How many of these benefits do our current classroom set-ups facilitate?
> - Does your school or setting do anything additional or innovative to develop these skills/processes?

Associated with the previous points are the way that teachers are trained in Finland. As noted in Chapter 9, teacher training is competitive, well-respected and a master's-degree qualification where students are engaged in substantial research to develop their theoretical as well practical skills in teaching. Once students qualify in Finland, there is a large emphasis on working collaboratively with other teachers in the school or municipality to collectively develop practice in ways which benefit them, their setting, and their context. This expectation of working with others and developing practice collaboratively may meet many of the functions of mentoring that form part of the extending provision for newly qualified teachers in England. However, due to the range of schools (academy, free-school, independent and so on) there are usually very limited opportunities for staff to work with other teachers, and rarely in an ongoing manner. Due to funding issues, many teachers in England also now have reduced access to external courses for professional development. This can result in possibilities for developing practice, gaining supportive feedback and working in collaboration with peers to be much more limited for English teachers than for those in Finland. When considered in relation to behaviour and developing skills and support in working with children whose behaviours challenge, having a team of peers to work with, to gain support from and in turn to support, could be very advantageous.

As the chapters in this book have detailed, there are a multitude of different approaches to support children with their behaviour and to develop our 'suitcase' of skills as teachers. Many of these would benefit from teams of staff from different contexts working together to trial the ideas and feedback to develop a community that could support each other as experts in their areas. This has been developed in some form in England with the proposed introduction of 'behaviour hubs' (DfE, 2020). However, these are schools which have been selected by government advisors and are working largely with behaviourist strategies in line with DfE policy, as opposed to developing a broad complement of skills, strategies and interventions that are individual, group, age or context specific. As discussed throughout this book, the overwhelming majority of mainstream English schools use a behaviourist system of rewards and sanctions to manage behaviour. This child-deficit model, although it has advantages, has also been widely critiqued. As Erkko and his colleagues note, strength-based rather than deficit approaches have gained prevalence in Finnish schools. Like the sociological models (discussed in Chapter 5), this view starts from the belief that all children have a range of strengths than can be developed and supported. Interestingly, the authors note that behaviours can be challenging for the teacher but also for the child and their parents/carers. Much research in Finland has developed strength-based strategies to support children and a range of interventions which focus not on managing behaviour as a discrete and dislocated issue but on making clear links between behaviour and learning.

To conclude, it might be interesting to turn back now to the second thinking stop.

- Have any of your views or ideas changed?
- What might you like to do as a result of reading this book?

Remember too, no matter how much you read or how many interventions you use and try on for size, 'good teaching cannot be reduced to technique; good teaching comes from the identity and integrity of the teacher' (Palmer, 1998).

References

Berliner, D. (2011). Rational responses to high stakes testing: The case of curriculum narrowing and the harm that follows. *Cambridge Journal of Education*, **41**(3), pp. 287–302.

Department for Education. (2020). *Behaviour Hubs*. London: DfE. https://www.gov.uk/guidance/behaviour-hubs

McGregor, J. (2003). Making spaces: Teacher workplace topologies. *Pedagogy, Culture and Society*, **11**(3), pp. 353–377.

Ofsted. (2019). *School Inspection Handbook*. London: Ofsted.

Organisation for the Economic Co-operation and Development. (2018). *The Programme for International Student Assessment (PISA). In County Note - Finland*. Paris: OECD.

Palmer, P. (1998). *The Courage to Teach: Exploring the Inner Landscape of a Teacher's Life*. San Fransisco: Jossey-Bass.

Paronen, P., and Lappi, O. (2018). *Finnish Teachers and Principals in Figures*. https://www.oph.fi/download/189802_finnish_teachers_and_principals_in_figures.pdf

Sproson, B. (2004). Some do and don't: Teacher effectiveness in managing behaviour. In Wearmouth, J., Glynn, T., Richmond, R., and Berryman, M. (Eds.), *Inclusion and Behaviour Management in Schools: Issues and Challenges* (pp. 311–321). London: David Fulton Publishers.

World Economic Forum. (2018). *10 Reasons Why Finland's Education System is the Best in the World*. https://www.weforum.org/agenda/2018/09/10-reasons-why-finlands-education-system-is-the-best-in-the-world

FINAL THOUGHTS

The aim of this book has been to provide time and space to consider practice and theory alongside each other. I hope that you have been able to reflect on the breadth of practice you already utilise to support children, and also to consider how it is informed by language, policy and a range of theory and research. A key element in developing and understanding practice is the chance to stop and reflect; ironically, this is also probably the most challenging thing to be able to do in the pressured school day, week, term or year! As we have discussed, research has suggested that teachers often do not make automatic links between their own behaviours and those of their classes (Derrington, 2008), yet there is significant anecdotal and research evidence that shows the importance of reflection. Jennings and Greenberg (2009, cited in Postholm, 2013) underline the advantages of seeing the teachers as part of the 'interactive process' of managing or supporting behaviour. Postholm (2013) highlights the importance of not only 'acquiring new knowledge' – for example, by reading this book – but also having the time and space to think about what has been learnt;

> When teachers acquire knowledge about classroom management, this does not mean that they can apply this in a technical or mechanical manner. The teacher must be mindfully present in his or her own classroom context and use theory as a thinking tool in classroom management.
>
> (p. 399)

To this end I have highlighted at the end of each chapter possible whole-school and individual teacher actions. I am sure you have noted that many of these centre around opportunities to think and talk as a staff.

This book is not in any way intended to be a 'you should ...' tome, but rather an opportunity to revisit, review and refresh your personal practice and perhaps make clearer links to the theory and research that underpin it. Research by Eversten and Weinstein (2006, cited in Postholm, 2013) used the term 'warm demanders' which mirrors Rogers's (2015) suggestion that good teachers are 'respectfully confident'. Teachers who are 'warm demanders' are typically 'warm, attentive, caring and supportive' in their relationships with children, but also provide a balance between 'supporting, challenging and demanding effort' (Postholm, 2013, p. 389). I hope it is clear throughout this book how the ideas and approaches suggested can help provide this balance between support and challenge whilst also embedding and developing relationships with all children in your care.

> **THINKING STOP 1**
>
> To conclude, reflect for one last time:
>
> - Have you read anything in this book that has surprised you?
> - Have you learnt anything new?
> - Have you read anything in this book that has made you reflect on the way in which you work with children in the classroom?
> - Will anything change for you as a result of reading this book?
> - What existing good practice of your own have you highlighted?

To ensure the 'new perspectives' in this book actually become 'new' in your thinking and practice, it would be beneficial – not just to reflect on what you have learnt and what changes might have happened in your thinking – but how this might 'live' and become part of your practice day-to-day and as a result 'new' to the children in your care – now and in the future. The book has necessarily asked you to reflect and think up to this point, but now I am asking you to act!

> **ACTIVITY STOP 1**
>
> What might you DO to develop the new perspectives you have read about to become new parts of your own practice? Add to the list, amending the suggestions as you go, to plan how what you have read can become part of what you do.

Short-term actions (for example):

- Talk to the children in your care to see which of the approaches they would like to try first.
- Trial the approaches that fit within the boundaries of your setting. For example, you could plan a series of philosophy4children sessions.
- Follow up on the reading suggested in the chapters and the appendix.
- Meet with your school's SENDCO/behaviour/well-being lead and see if you can shadow their work.

Medium-term actions (for example):

- Enrol in specific CPD courses. For example, this might be exploring further the impact of trauma-informed practice, or even be a recognised qualification such as the NASENCO course.
- Plan a staff meeting/INSET/Twilight to feedback on what you have learnt and share ideas with colleagues.
- Set up a lesson-study group within your school, trust or area to investigate the informal impacts of some of the 'new approaches' you have implemented
- Join, or even set up a BrewEd type of event (ticketed discussion events – usually held in pubs – by educators, for educators).
- Write a practitioner-focused blog and submit for publication.

Long-term actions (for example):

- Enrol in further formal education (this could be a postgraduate qualification, a master's or even a doctorate).
- Work with researchers (if you wish) to plan an action research project investigating the impact on teachers and pupils of some of these 'new approaches'.
- If you are in a senior leader/management role, initiate a review of the behaviour and/or well-being policy.

References

Derrington, C. (2008). *Behaviour in Primary Schools Final Report*. London: DfES.
Postholm, M. (2013). Classroom management: What does research tell us? *European Educational Research Journal*, **12**(3), pp. 389–402.
Rogers, B. (2015). *Classroom Behaviour: A Practical Guide to Effective Teaching, Behaviour Management and Colleague Support* (4th Ed). London: SAGE Publications.

INDEX

Note: Page numbers in italic indicate figures.

achievement/attainment: and off-rolling 58–59; and well-being 9–11, *11*, 22–23, *24*
ADHD 40, 95, 164, 169
affective questions and statements 115–116
affirmation, behaviour and affect 116
Ajmal, Y. 131–133, 135–136
Armstrong, D. 44, 48, 90, 108
assertive discipline 46, 81, 83
assessment: strengths-based approaches, Finland 192–197
Atkinson, M. 22, 25–27, *28*
Augustine, C. *et al.* 112, *113*, 120
authoritarian vs restorative approach *111*
autonomy: children 108, 121–122, 128, 138, 140; teachers 63–64, 76, 186

Ball, S. 53; *et al.* 53
Bateman, J. 125, 129–130, 134
behaviour: and classrooms 162–163; 'good behaviour' and 'misbehaviour' 163–164; management strategies 164–165; review 173; systemic factors for successful interventions 165–167
Behavioural and Emotional Rating Scale (BERS-2) 192–195
behaviourism 46, 61–62, 81–82, *99*–100; possible strengths and limitations 82–85; vs restorative practices 107, 110
'behaviours that challenge' 17, 28, 37–38
'behaviours that concern' 41
'behaviour suitcase' 4, 72, 143–144, 203

behaviour, well-being and mental health 17–18; building blocks 25–30; foundations 18–25; review 30–32
belonging, sense of 61, 182–183, 205
biological theories 79, 95–98
biopsychosocial model 96–98, *99*
Blow, M. 19, 22–23
boundaries and challenge 171
'bounded autonomy' 76
Brown, E. *et al.* 137
Brown, R. 27
Buckley, S. 162
bullying, restorative approaches to 119–120

Cassidy, C. 151, 157; and Christie, D. 150, 154; *et al.* 151; Heron, G. and 151, 157; and Mohr-Lone, J. 149, 151
Chafouleas, S. 96
'challenging behaviour' 17, 40–41, 164
Chan, J. *et al.* 35–36, 41
check-in, check-out (CICO) support, Finland 190
Child and Adolescent Mental Health Services (CAHMS) 22
child-centred approach 89–90
child-deficit model 78, 95
Children's Act (1989) 38–39
Children's Society, 'Good Childhood' reports 19
circle time activities 90–93
Clarke, E., own experiences 6–8

cognitive-behavioural theories 85–86, 99–100; possible strengths and limitations 86–88
Cole, T. 65; Daniels, H. and 37–38; *et al.* 169, 171–172
collaboration: teachers 105–107; university and teacher training schools, Finland 188–189, 197–198
Commissioner for Children, New Zealand 162
community-based restorative practices 107–108, 120
community of inquiry, *see* philosophical inquiry as tool for well-being
'compliment game' 136–137
consistency in school policies 27, 60, 67, 170
continuing professional development (CPD) 167–168
'continuum of tolerance' effect 44
control: language of 46–47; social control window 109–110, 128
Cooper, P. 37–38, 58, 96, 169; *et al.* 173; and Jacobs, B. 40, 78, 81–83, 85, 88–89, 93, 96–97, 100, 105–106; and Tiknaz, Y. 164–165; and Upton, G. 92–93
counselling-based approaches 126
Covid-19 pandemic 24
Cowburn, A. 19, 22–23
cross-country comparisons 19, 40, *166*, 176; PISA 54, 203
Cubeddu, D. 127–128

Daniels, H.: and Cole, T. 37–38; *et al.* 165–167
Datnow, A. 55; and Stringfield, S. 53, 55
Derrington, C. 11, 209
De Shazer, S. 124–125
'developmental disorders' 97
DfE 9, 18, 22, 25, 27, 45, 54, 56–60, 86, 119–120; and DoH 17–18, 39
DfES/DES 38–39, 45, 54, 60, 62, 126
Diagnostic and Statistical Manual of Mental Disorders (DSM) 40
differences among children 77–78
Diller, L. 40
disadvantage/vulnerability: empathy and equity 171; and off-rolling 57–59; and zero tolerance policies 25
'Discipline in Schools', *see* Elton Report (1989)
Dodge, R. *et al.* 21

Eaton, A. 18, 20, 38
Education Acts (1944 and 1981) 38

Education and Health Care Plan (EHCP) 39
Education Endowment Foundation (EEF) 81–82, 86
Elton Report (1989) 38–39, 54, 60
embedded ethos 202–207
'emotional and behavioural difficulties' (EBD) 38–39
'emotional and behavioural disorders' 40
emotional needs and behaviour change 169
empathy and equity 171
'engagement, explanation and expectation' 118
'episodic' interventions 54–55
Epstein, M. H. 192; *et al.* 194–195
eternal verities 161, 167–168, 202; definition of 168–172; range of 172–173
Evanovich, L. *et al.* 118
exclusions 57–58; off-rolling 58–59; and restorative practices 112
'expert', child as 125–126, 129

Fernie, L. 127–128
Finland 110, 176–177, 203; and English schools 204–207; learning environments 183–186, 206; pedagogy and pedagogical support 189–193; research on behaviour management 194–196; school culture 178–179, 204; schools, national core curriculum and transversal competence areas 179–183, 205–207; summary, conclusions and critical viewpoint 196–198; teacher training 180–181, 186–189, 197–198
Finney, D. 29
funding 40, 165, 205

Garner, P. 86–87; and Gains, C. 36, 40
Glazzard, J. 90; and Bostwick, R. 18, 22, 26
'good behaviour' and 'misbehaviour' 163–164
Goodman, J. 54, 63, 89
Gott, J. 20, 22–23
government policies: language of 45–48; *see also* DfE; DfES/DES
Graham, B. *et al.* 58, 67, 101
Gray, P. *et al.* 11, 24, 44

'Handicapped Pupils and Health Service Regulations' (1945) 38
Hansberry, B. 106, 108–110, 113, 115–119
Heron, G. 151, 157
historical development of terminology 37–41

Hornby, G. 22, 25–27, *28*
House of Commons Education Select Committee 57–58
House of Commons Health and Education Committees 9, 19
humanistic approaches 89–90, *99–100*; possible strengths and limitations 90–92
humour 172

inclusive education, Finland 178
individuals vs systems focus 28–29, 39, 42
Ingram, R. 126, 128–129
instructional reactions 170
internalised behaviour 128
intervention and prevention 169–170

Kavale, K. *et al.* 44
Kohn, A. 61, 91, 100

labelling 36–38, 163–164
Lam, C. 126, 138
language 17–18, 20–21, 35; building blocks 45–48; English as an additional language 138; foundations 35–45; influence on actions and interventions 43–45, 48–49; review 48–49
learning and behaviour relationship 46, 62, *63*, 91, 110
'learning-centred approach', Finland 186
'learning difficulties' 38
learning environments, Finland 183–186, 206
learning plan, Finland 190–191
Levin, B. 53–54
Loxley, A. 52–53, 55–56
Lund, R. 60, 63

Macleod, G. 42, 78
Maguire, M. *et al.* 24, 55, 57–58, 83
marketisation of schooling 54
Maslow, A. 89
Maxwell, G. 162
McCluskey, G. 1, 106–107, 111; *et al.* 106–109, 111, 113, 120
McLaughlin, M. 54–55
medical and biopsychosocial models 95–98, *99*
mental health: definitional challenges 20–21; statistics 18; *see also* behaviour, well-being and mental health
meta-cognitive awareness 85–86
Milner, J. 125, 129–130, 134
miracle question 130–132
multi-agency/multidisciplinary working 94, 98

National Curriculum: Finland (FNBE) 178–183, 189–190, 192; UK 54, 57, 205
nature and nurture 97, 169
Norwich, B. 18, 20, 38
NSPCC: solution focused toolkit 132–133, *134–135*

O'Brien, T. 56; and Guiney, D. 36, 77–78, 90
off-rolling 58–59
Ofsted 56, 60, 171–173, 205; inspection 54
open-plan learning environments 183–186, 206
Overstreet, S. 96

'pastoral support'/'pastoral interventions' 27–28
Payne, R. 61–62, 81, 91, 110
Personal, Social, Health and Citizenship Education (PSHCE) 205
philosophical inquiry as tool for well-being 147–148, 202; building blocks 152–156; experiences of behaviour and strengthening well-being 156–157; foundations 148–152; review 157–160
PISA 54, 203
Porter, L. 82, 86–87, 89–90, 93–94, 127, 172
positive relationships 26, 91, 113–114, 172
power relations/teacher power *100*; restorative practice 108–110, 120; solution focused working 128, 137
praise 84; 'compliment game' 136–137
prevention and intervention 169–170
Primary National Strategy–Behaviour and Attendance 126
proactive and reactive school policies 57
psychological theories 78, 81–88
punishment vs restorative practices 108
pupil consultation process 60
pupil resilience 60–61
pupil self-esteem(s) 27, 60–61, 90, 169–170
pupil welfare teams, Finland 191

Rantaylä School, Finland 180–185, 190–191, 193, 198, 203
Ratner, H. 125, 127–128, 131–133, 135–137
reactive school policies 63; proactive and 57
record-keeping 117
response to intervention (RTI) model, Finland 178–179, 187
restorative conferences 112, 117–118, 120
Restorative Justice 4 Schools 118
Restorative Justice Council 119–120

restorative practice 105; building blocks 113–119; foundations 105–114; possible advantages and disadvantages 119–121; review 121–122; and solution focused approaches 128, 138
rewards and sanctions 62–63, 83–84; *see also* behaviourism
Rigoni, D. 83
Rodway, S. 169
Roffey, S. 19, 23, 25–26, 76, 113
Rowe, J. 58–59
Rowling, J. K. 148

Scales for Assessing Emotional Disturbance (SAED) screener 194–196
scaling 132–137
school culture, Finland 178–179, 204
school policies 52; building blocks 60–65; consistency in 27, 60, 67, 170; foundations 52–60; and language of government policies 45–48; review 65–67
schools, impacts and role of 19–22
'school to prison pipeline' 25, 59
school-wide positive behaviour support (SWPBS), Finland 189–190
self-esteem(s) 27, 60–61, 90, 169–170
SEND 18–19; new Code of Practice 17–18, 39; pupil exclusion 58
senior leadership team (SLT) 27, 63, 139
sense of belonging 61, 182–183, 205
Siddiqui, N. *et al.* 150, 153
Simm, J. 126, 128–129
social and emotional aspects of learning (SEAL) 86–87
social control window 109–110, 128
'social, emotional mental health' (SEMH) 39
sociocultural theories 79, 88–95
solution focused working 124; building blocks 128–129; foundations 124–128; miracle question 130–132; possible advantages and disadvantages 137–138; review 139–140; scaling 132–137
special education needs 38–39; and disability, *see* SEND; Finland 179, 182–184, 187–189, 197–198
Spratt, J. *et al.* 21–22, 26, 28, 47
Sproson, B. 4, 65, 72, 143–144
storyboards/vignettes 10, *11*, 29–30, 42–43, 64–65; behaviourist approach 84–85; biopsychosocial approach 98; humanist approach 92; restorative practice 119; solution focused approach 138–139; systemic approach 95

strengths-based approaches, Finland 192–197
systemic approaches 92–94, *99–100*; possible strengths and limitations 94–95
systems: factors for successful interventions 165–167; vs individuals focus 28–29, 39, 42; tensions and dilemmas between 77
systems theory 79, 89

tariff related policies 57–58
teacher power, *see* power relations/teacher power
teacher training: Finland 180–181, 186–189, 197–198; *see also* continuing professional development (CPD); training
teacher–pupil relationships: positive 26, 91, 113–114, 172; reciprocity of well-being 24–25, 32; trust 25, 59
teachers: actions 31, 49; autonomy 63, 76, 186; collaboration 105–107; language of control 46–47; off-rolling policy 58–59; 'pastoral support'/'pastoral interventions' 27–28; role 22; and school behaviour policies 56–57; views on causes of behaviours that challenge 42; *see also* whole-school approach, and individual teacher actions
terminology, *see* language
theories of behaviour and classroom practice 75; building blocks 80–99; foundations 76–80; review 99–102
therapeutic approach, introduction of 38
Thomas, G. 52–53, 55–56
training: restorative practices 111–112, 120–121; solution focused approaches 140; *see also* continuing professional development (CPD); teacher training
transparency in communications 170
transversal competence (TC) areas, Finland 181–182, 205
trauma-informed approaches 96–97

university and teacher training schools collaboration, Finland 188–189, 197–198

vignettes, *see* storyboards/vignettes
violence 162
Visser, J. 60, 96, 108, 165, 167, 169–170; *et al.* 170; own experiences 162–163, 167–168; and Stokes, S. 54
vulnerability, *see* disadvantage/vulnerability

Wachtel, T. 112, 114–115
Wagner, P. 46, 57, 60, 63
Walford, G. 83
Warnock Report 38–39

Watkins, C. 46, 57, 60, 63
Weare 20, 23, 25–26
Wearmouth, J. 95; *et al.* 36–37, 44, 54–55, 57, 76, 78, 83–84, 91–93, 95–96, 106–107, 113–114, 120
well-being 18; and achievement/attainment 9–10, *11*, 22–23, *24*; definitional challenges 20–21; *see also* behaviour, well-being and mental health; philosophical inquiry as tool for well-being
whole-school approach 27, 46, 165–166; Finland 189–190; and individual teacher actions 31, 48–49, 66, 101, 121–122, 139–140, 159, 209; and teacher autonomy 63–64, 66; *see also* school policies; systemic approaches
World Health Organization (WHO): definition of 'child friendly school' 20, 61; 'emotional and behavioural disorders' 40

Yuen, M. 126, 138
Yusuf, D. 125, 127–128, 137

zero-tolerance policies 25, 44, 58–60, 82–83

Printed in Great Britain
by Amazon